B KIRSCHNER S.
KIRSCHNER, ANN.
SALA'S GIFT :MY
 MOTHER'S HOLOCAUST STO
2007/03/03

WITHDRAWN

P9-DWE-920

*f*P

Sala's Europe
1939–1945

FINLAND

Rattvik

SWEDEN

ESTONIA

LATVIA

LITHUANIA

HOLLAND

○ Bergen-Belsen

○ Berlin

INITIAL
GERMAN INVASION
(SEPTEMBER 1939)

○
Warsaw

BELGIUM

GERMANY

Neusalz ○

POLAND

GENERAL
GOVERNMENT

FRANCE

Schatzlar
Geppersdorf ○

UPPER
SILESIA

Bendsburg
○ Sosnowitz
Auschwitz Krakow

Prague ○

Nuremberg
○
Ansbach

CZECHOSLOVAKIA

Vienna ○

SWITZERLAND

AUSTRIA

HUNGARY

RUMANIA

Sala's Gift

My Mother's Holocaust Story

Ann Kirschner

Alameda Free Library
1550 Oak Street
Alameda, CA 94501

New York   London   Toronto   Sydney

FREE PRESS
A Division of Simon & Schuster, Inc.
1230 Avenue of the Americas
New York, NY 10020

Copyright © 2006 by Ann Kirschner

All rights reserved, including the right of reproduction in whole or in part in any form.

FREE PRESS and colophon are trademarks of Simon & Schuster, Inc.

For information about special discounts for bulk purchases,
please contact Simon & Schuster Special Sales:
1-800-456-6798 or business@simonandschuster.com

DESIGNED BY ERICH HOBBING

The map "Sala's Europe 1939–1945" from the exhibition "Letters to Sala" is used
courtesy of the New York Public Library. All remaining illustrations
are from the author's private collection unless otherwise noted.

Manufactured in the United States of America
1 3 5 7 9 10 8 6 4 2

Library of Congress Cataloging-in-Publication Data
Kirschner, Ann.
Sala's gift: my mother's Holocaust story / Ann Kirschner.
p. cm.
Includes bibliographical references and index.
1. Kirschner, Sala Garncarz, 1924–. 2. Jews—Poland—Sosnowiec (Województwo Slaskie)—
Biography. 3. Kirschner, Sala Garncarz, 1924– —Correspondence.
4. Kirschner, Sala Garncarz, 1924– —Family. 5. Garncarz family.
6. World War, 1939–1945—Conscript labor—Poland. 7. Holocaust, Jewish
(1939–1945)—Poland. 8. Sosnowiec (Województwo Slaskie, Poland)—Biography. I. Title.
DS135.P63 K55753   2006
940.53'18092[B]—dc22   2006043743

ISBN-13: 978-0-7432-8938-2
ISBN-10: 0-7432-8938-2

To my mother

CONTENTS

Do you know why I write so much? Because as long as you read, we are together.

Raizel Garncarz,
April 24, 1941

I have the pictures of our dear father and dear mother, together with all the mail I received from home, starting from the first minute that I left for camp. All along, I watched it and guarded it like the eyes in my head, since it was my greatest treasure.

Sala Garncarz,
October 10, 1945

Sala's Gift

Before She Was My Mother

My mother had a secret.

I knew that Sala Garncarz was born in Poland, the youngest of eleven children, and that she had survived a Nazi camp. I knew the names of my grandparents. I had one living aunt, but I didn't know anything about the rest of our once large family, not even their names.

In rare moments of retrospection, my mother would tell us about her arrival in the United States as the war bride of a handsome American soldier, ready to build a new life. I liked hearing her tale, especially since my brothers and I had starring roles. But even as a child, I was unconvinced. My mother was substituting a happy ending for an untold story. So fast, so complete a transformation from Sala, the survivor, to Sala, the happy American housewife and mother, seemed impossible. It was as if she had been snatched by extraterrestrials in 1939, and set down in New York in 1946.

Where did the old Sala go? What happened in the camp? Why didn't she have a number tattooed on her arm?

I had no one to ask. I never broached the subject with my brothers or my father. My mother's silence seemed to swallow up questions before they could be spoken aloud. When someone else—a new friend, a careless relative—wandered into the forbidden territory of Sala's years during the war, she turned her face away as if she had been slapped. Not all survivors refused to speak, I knew, and not all children were eager to listen. I had friends whose parents wouldn't *stop* talking about the past. Enough already, my friends would say, we're tired of playing Anne Frank.

I studied the faces in the old black-and-white photographs that stood like silent sentinels on her dresser. My favorite was a striking portrait of young Sala in profile, gazing intently at an older woman: "My friend Ala Gertner," my mother told me. She offered no details. Where did they meet? What happened to Ala Gertner? Sala, with her thick, glossy hair pulled back from her face and cascading down her back, her sharp cheekbones catching the light, looked like an irresistible ingénue from my favorite old movies with Katherine Hepburn, Claudette Colbert, Moira Shearer, Irene Dunne. Ala was not nearly as pretty, but there was something bold and sophisticated in the tilt of her hat and something hypnotic in the way her eyes locked with my mother's.

Of course, despite her best efforts, Sala could never build an impermeable wall between our present and her past. The fog seeped in. During the televised trials of Adolf Eichmann in 1961, she sat and watched for hours, chain smoking, stony and silent. She read every Holocaust book, watched every Holocaust movie, observed every Holocaust anniversary, but silently, privately, as if I wasn't watching.

I thought she might yield when I became a mother. Let's give it a try, I decided, when my children were old enough to ask questions. My daughter was preparing a school project on family history and wanted to interview both of her grandparents. The setting was auspicious: we sat comfortably in my parents' living room, the dishes washed and put away, the sofa cushions straightened, the toys back in the closet. My father was entirely cooperative, his memories of New York in the '30s charming and evocative. When it was Sala's turn, she began to fidget, to squirm, unable to find a comfortable position. She threw out a few innocuous anecdotes, about the rag doll that was her only toy, about her circle of friends, their school uniforms. I had heard these all before. But then her discomfort became acute; her always troublesome arthritis and back pain interrupted her, she had to stand up, she had to walk around, and the tentative, sputtering flow of memory dribbled to a halt. She kept her secrets.

All that ended in 1991 on a day that would change her forever in my eyes, a day that was to change my life as well.

Sala was about to be admitted into the hospital and she was spending her last weekend with my family. New symptoms had become acute while she was traveling in Israel. Suddenly, the hills of Jerusalem were too steep for her to climb. She returned to New York and learned that she needed triple-bypass surgery.

She was sixty-seven years old, miserable in her first week of giving up smoking, and her hands looked empty without her usual cigarette. I could tell that she was getting ready to say goodbye. It was a beautiful summer day, we had just finished lunch, and I was sitting alone. She came outside to join me. In her hands, I saw a red cardboard box that had once contained my old "Spill and Spell" game.

She held it out to me and said, "You should have this."

Her jewelry, I thought.

Instead, I found within the box a small, worn brown leather portfolio about the size of a paperback book. Within the portfolio were hundreds of letters, postcards, and scraps of papers, some written in barely legible, tiny, cramped handwriting, others in beautiful italic script, some dashed off in blunt pencil scrawls on scraps of ragged paper, all neatly tucked away. "These are my letters from camp," she said. She spread them before me. Postcards and letters and photographs covered the table, the smell of old paper escaping into the summer air.

"What do you want to know?" my mother said.

And so I began to ask.

Questions spilled out randomly. Where had she been? Who had written the letters? How had she managed to save them? Where were these people now? My mother answered as best she could, her voice wound tightly around names and places long unspoken.

She was soon tired. Together, we returned the letters to the box that had held them for so long—but now the box was mine.

My mother's letters didn't just fill in a blank spot on the map of her past. They brought her to life—my mother as a young girl—and they also led our family out of the shadows, the grandparents, aunts, uncles, and cousins who were killed during the war.

The letters were written by more than eighty different people. They told the story of a family, a city, and an elaborate system of slavery organized by government and embraced by businesses. Only the first few postcards were written in Polish; the rest of the correspondence was in German, with a sprinkling in Czech and Yiddish. Some markings seemed obvious, like the "Z" stamp that indicated review by a censor (*zensiert* in German), but others took more study to yield their secrets. There were dozens of charming hand-drawn birthday cards, some with poems and quaint printed illustrations of flowers and children. I commissioned English translations. I was impatient; the arrival of each translation was as thrilling as if the letters had been written yesterday, and to me. I found letters from Ala Gertner, whose writing proved to be as distinctive as her photograph. There were love letters that had been smuggled to my mother by a suitor named Harry, whose existence had been entirely unknown to me. My Aunt Rose, still living in Brooklyn, became a different person. The faded photographs on my mother's dresser began to come alive.

My mother and I read the letters together. She needed the English versions almost as much as I did; at the end of the war, she had spoken and written German fluently, and had also added a smattering of Russian, and a bit of Czech to her two native languages, Polish and Yiddish. But she put away those languages in 1946. Her command of Polish and German had been extinguished to the point where she read only with great difficulty, her rusty translation skills clogged by emotions. As she pronounced the strange syllables in her familiar voice, it seemed like an odd trick of impersonation.

We talked and talked. She tolerated my questions and my tape recorder, offering up revelation after revelation as if the prohibition against sharing her memories had never existed. She was telling these stories for the first time and I was an eager listener.

What I had always imagined as my mother's relatively brief ordeal as a prisoner in one Nazi camp turned out to be almost five years in seven different labor camps.* She was one of about fifty thousand slaves, young and healthy Jewish men and women from western Poland. They were the valuable property of Organization Schmelt, an SS division that was set up soon after the Nazi invasion of Poland.

Hundreds of labor camps were created in the early years of the war, usually attached to construction projects or factories that belonged to German businesses. Conditions varied, but in Sala's camps, they wore whatever clothes they had brought from home. Unlike the prisoners of Auschwitz, these men and women were not tattooed with numbers. These Jews were meant to survive, at least to finish the day's work. They had been torn from their loved ones, they were hungry, they worked impossible hours under unimaginable conditions, they slept in overcrowded wooden barracks without heat or ventilation, and they lived in constant terror—but the Nazis delivered their mail. Letters and packages were allowed, even encouraged, as if they were not prisoners but first-time campers away from home and the Nazis were eager to reassure anxious parents that all was well. By the summer of 1943, however, all the regular mail stopped.

Organization Schmelt is a minor footnote in history. Relatively little has been written about the partnership between Nazi bureaucrats, Jewish leaders, and German businessmen that spirited away tens of thousands of people from the Eastern Upper Silesian region of Poland. Few books even mention Albrecht Schmelt, the chief architect who lent his thick slap of a name to a rapidly expanding slave trade that made him a rich man. The very existence of labor camps where Jews received mail is hardly known, and their locations are all but forgotten—except by those who were imprisoned there.

*There is a complete list of Sala's seven labor camps on p. 263.

This is not surprising: to write about these places, which were constructed on the outer circles of hell, not its very core, might have appeared to compromise the agonizing reality of Auschwitz. In the Schmelt camps, there were no gas chambers, no crematoria, and no legions of spectral *Musselmen,* the walking dead who were common in Auschwitz, where the average survival time was three months.

Because the conditions in the death camps were so much worse, a certain competitiveness sometimes creeps in, even among survivors. "Oh, your mother was in the *labor* camps," one survivor told me, waving her arms dismissively, just enough for me to glimpse the number tattooed on her forearm. I had been showing her some of the letters. "I was in Auschwitz," she declared. "We could *never* have had such letters in Auschwitz." She had remained at home in Hungary until the summer of 1944, and most of her family had survived. How long was she in Auschwitz, I asked. "Four days," she said, her tone flat.

Four days in Auschwitz . . . five years in seven different labor camps. My mother lost her parents, sisters, brothers, nieces, nephews, cousins: at least forty members of her extended family. I do not want to compare. Some threshold of suffering defies measurement.

I prefer the raucous laughter that I heard on this subject from Sala and her friends. "My father was so rich, he sent me to camp for two years!" boasted Gucia, pounding the table and laughing over her coffee. "Ha!" Sala snorted in derision. *"My* father was much richer than your father—he sent me to camp for five whole years!"

Sala's courage and daring were matched with the instincts of an archivist. For five years, she kept everything hidden from camp guards, risking severe punishment. By creating a documentary record of her ordeal, she was participating in a time-honored tradition of chronicling communal disasters, as ancient as the Bible. In ghettos and concentration camps throughout Europe, people were writing and preserving firsthand testimonies and other documents. Contests were held to encourage individual chronicles and diaries. "Brothers, write down everything you see and hear," the historian Simon Dubnow urged as he was leaving the ghetto at Riga. "Keep a record of it all!" In milk cans buried in the Warsaw ghetto, in containers deposited within the wretched earth of Auschwitz itself, archives were carefully hidden. In contrast to the many eyewitness testimonies taken after the war, these primary sources are not subject to the vagaries of memory. In most cases, they quickly outlived their creators.

Sala's letters are drops of time, spontaneous outpourings rendered with the shapelessness of real life, their emotions raw and unfiltered. They never touch on world events. Since it is impossible not to read them without thinking about their context, I have filled in some essential background in telling my mother's story. The forward march of the German army, the entry of the United States into the war, Italian collaboration and treachery, the battle for the Pacific—none are mentioned by the correspondents, if indeed they were known to them at all. They had only limited insight into what was happening to them. It was a world of shadowy rumor and tentative prayer. Instead of focusing on external events, these private papers create an emotional history of the war, a complex fugue of fear, loneliness, and despair, always returning to the dominant theme of hope for tomorrow.

"Do you know why I write so much? Because as long as you read, we are together," her sister Raizel wrote. Their connection was alive in a piece of paper. Once the letters were in Sala's possession, she had to preserve them. Sala's letters *were* the individuals she loved, the friends and family who loved her. So she hid the letters during lineups, handed them to trusted friends, threw them under a building, even buried them under the ground. The preservation of these written words—for which she could have easily been killed—was directly and inextricably linked to saving her own life. I began to understand her logic: the risks she undertook to preserve the letters were nothing compared to the ultimate danger she would face without them, because she would have lost her motivation to live.

I heard many poignant stories from survivors about letters from home. My mother's friend Sara fell gravely ill with typhus after liberation, and entrusted her letters to someone she hardly knew, someone who promised to keep the papers safe while she was hospitalized. The doctors told Sara that in her delirium, she kept jumping up to search frantically under the bed for her letters. When she recovered, the person was gone, and so were her letters. Danke, a woman in her late seventies, looked like a young girl again, her eyes brimming with tears, as she told me about the old suitcase that was stolen by Russian soldiers after liberation. The suitcase held her letters from her mother and father, and the poetry she had written during the war. "What did they think I had there?" she wailed. Zusi, who lost her letters during a brutal camp inspection, could not believe the sight of her own handwriting on a 1944 birthday card to my mother: "How could your mother have done this?" she said in amazement. "How could you have these? See how smart, how brave your mother was!"

Ten years after the first discovery, in response to a heated family debate about whether we should keep the original letters or entrust them to a library, my father declared that he too had a box of letters: his wartime correspondence with his friends and family when he was serving in the Army. "And it is bigger than Bubbe's," he boasted.

The box was indeed bigger. It included my father's energetic and optimistic reports to his brothers and sister, letters to his Army buddies, even the mischievous telegram that he sent to my grandmother about his wedding plans. As I set about the task of cataloging these new documents, I found another fifty-six letters that had been written to my mother during the war. Twelve of them were from Ala Gertner.

There was also a singular treasure: my mother's diary from October 1940. Until then, I knew her young self only as she had been portrayed in the letters of her friends and family, and by her recollections. But now Sala stepped to center stage, recording the first few weeks of her five-year journey. I saw her at sixteen, staring at the strange scene through her luminous grey eyes, assessing her future with a sharp awareness of her need for something that she could hardly define.

Years afterward, I asked my mother what she expected that day when she gave me the letters. "Nothing in particular," she said. "I didn't want you to find them later. I wanted you to have the letters from me with my blessing. This way, I can tell you what I want, that whatever you do with them is OK, and this was my reason for giving them to you."

I take some comfort in knowing that I am not the first child to pursue the hidden truth behind a parent's painful memories; not the first who felt compelled to learn how the long shadow of the past shaped my own identity and beliefs. It has been a journey of self-discovery for both of us, although I am holding the pencil. The letters have taught us about mothers and daughters, about the power of friendship and laughter, and the persistence of life and love amid the most extraordinary circumstances.

Here, then, is my mother's story.

CHAPTER ONE

In Place of Her Sister

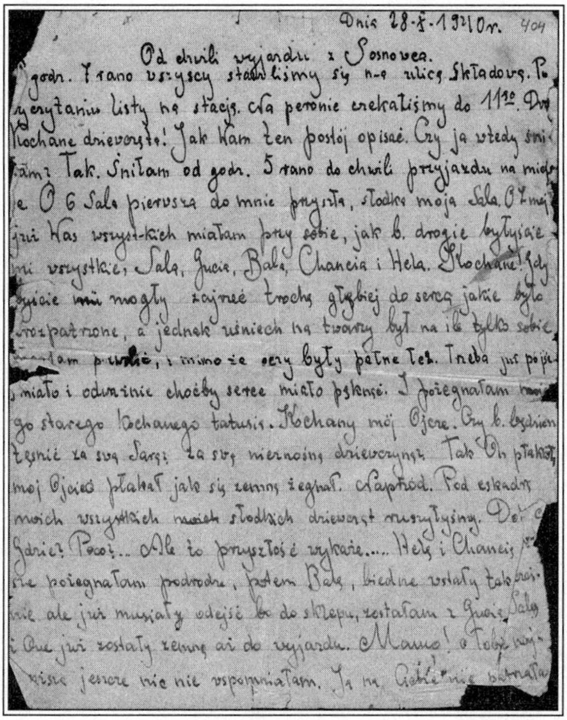
Dnia 28-V-1940 r. 404
Od chwili wyjazdu z Sosnowca.
godz. 7 rano wszyscy stawiliśmy się na ulicę Składową. Po
wyczytaniu listy na stację. Na peronie czekaliśmy do 11tej. Dro
Kochane dziewczęta! Jak Wam ten postój opisać. Czy ja wtedy śni
łam? Tak. Śniłam od godz. 5 rano do chwili przyjazdu na miej
e. O 6 Sala pierwsza do mnie przyszła, słodka moja Sala. O tymj
już Was wszystkich miałam przy sobie, jak b. drogie byłyście
mi wszystkie, Sala, Gucia, Bala, Chancia i Hela. Kochane! Gdy
byście mi mogły zajrzeć trochę głębiej do serca jakie było
rozpatrzone, a jednak uśmiech na twarzy był na ile tylko sobie
...łam p..., i mimo że oczy były pełne łez. Trzeba już pójść
miało i odważnie choćby serce miało pęknąć. I pożegnałam
go starego kochanego tatusia. Kochany mój Ojcze. Czy b. będzie
tęsknić za swą Sarą za swą wierną dziewczyną. Tak On płakał,
mój Ojciec płakał jak się ze mną żegnał. Naprzód. Pod eskortą
moich wszystkich moich słodkich dziewcząt musiałyśmy. Do
Gdzie? Po co?... Ale to przyszłość wykaże..... Helę i Chancię
się pożegnałam podrodze, potem Balę, biedne stały tak
nie ale już musiały odejść do sklepu, zostałam z Gucią, Salą
i One już zostały ze mną aż do wyjazdu. Mamo! o Tobie wyj
wiście jeszcze nic nie wspominałam. Ja na ... nie ...

Her sister read the letter, translating from Polish into Yiddish for the benefit of their parents:

By order of the Jewish Council of the Elders, Raizel Garncarz will report on October 28, 1940, for six weeks of work at a labor camp . . .

Sala spoke as soon as Raizel finished: she would go in her sister's place.

Neither sister knew anything about a "labor camp." Nor did their parents. But since the calamity of the Nazi invasion of Poland the previous fall, the Garncarz family had been bracing for the next blow. Now it had arrived in the form of this short and official-looking document, vague on details, but stamped with the mark of the Council of Jewish Elders. The Council had recently been created by the Nazis. The first young men selected for labor camps by the Council had left the city a few weeks ago. No one had heard from them yet.

The family needed money. Raizel's name was on the list because her parents could not afford the "head tax" set by the Council; if you paid the tax, you were relieved of the obligation to send a family member. Only the poorest Jews would be going to the camps. The letter said that these so-called volunteers would be paid. No one else from the family would be required to leave.

Sala was the youngest of the eleven children of Josef and Chana Garncarz. Three died of natural causes before adulthood, and a fourth was killed during his stint in the Polish army, a victim of an attack by his fellow soldiers. Two older daughters and one son lived nearby with their own families. Another son had recently fled to Russia. Sala and her unmarried sisters, Blima and Raizel, still lived at home.

13

Already struggling before the war, the Garncarz family was caught in an escalating cycle of poverty and danger. The father had become a virtual prisoner of the apartment since the invasion last year, when hacking off beards and beating elderly Jews became a Nazi sport. Some religious Jews had already shaved their beards and trimmed their side curls; Josef would not. He was no longer able to walk safely in the streets, no longer able to pray in the synagogue or to meet his students for Hebrew lessons.

Anyone who had ever met Raizel would know that her selection must be some kind of random, bureaucratic mistake. Raizel was pious and scholarly, always buried in a book, the least likely choice for anything involving labor. If the Germans were looking for someone strong, someone who adapted quickly to new, uncertain circumstances, they had found exactly the opposite. Childlike in her tiny frame, her eyes magnified by thick glasses, Raizel looked perpetually startled. Eighteen years old, she was already an astute judge of character, but few people knew it. She stayed close to home, preferring the company of her sisters, and filling the pages of her notebooks with essays and poetry. Frail and sensitive, she shrank visibly from contact with new places and people, nor were strangers particularly drawn to her—except children. Children loved her, never noticing her odd mannerisms and reveling in the intense delight she took in their comings and goings. It was easy to dismiss her as eccentric. But Raizel's demeanor disguised a powerful character and intellect: she was the best educated of the sisters, soaking up knowledge wherever she could, and for her single-minded devotion to prayer and Jewish studies she was known and respected throughout the closely knit community.

Until the Nazis came, the two sisters attended Polish public school, walking together in their navy blue uniforms with white cuffs and collar, always crisp and clean. In the afternoon, they continued to the nearby *Bais Yaakov* school, where classes on Jewish studies were taught in Yiddish, the vernacular of their community. They were the first girls in the family to receive any formal education, secular or religious.

The *Bais Yaakov* schools had been created in 1918 by a revolutionary educator named Sarah Schenirer. Her concept of religious curriculum for Jewish girls was controversial, but it had spread rapidly to some 250 schools and nearly 40,000 students all over Eastern and Central Europe, taught by women who had graduated from a new seminary in Krakow, founded in 1925 by Schenirer. These smart young teachers projected an elevated sense of purpose. Their intellectual energy delighted and inspired Raizel and Sala. Everything about the teachers seemed special, even their clothes, stylish yet modest, and as unmarried women, they were allowed to keep their hair natural, not yet covered with a wig.

Sarah Schenirer herself was idolized by the girls. She personally visited every school, and when she died in 1935, thousands of her students mourned her passing as their spiritual mother. In the diary that Sala kept faithfully, she recorded events such as the visit of Sarah Schenirer to their school, and confided her grief over the death of the visionary who overcame the objections of old-fashioned religious leaders resistant to newfangled notions about educating girls. Her father, too, had been wary, but he acknowledged the changing times, and permitted his daughters to attend.

The sisters justified his confidence. Both were good students, but Raizel was a dedicated scholar who dreamed of being a teacher. She was gratified at first when her Polish teachers recommended that she pursue advanced studies at the *gymnasium,* but she was repelled by its more secular curriculum and atmosphere. She would never compromise her religious principles.

The Nazi invasion ended all thoughts of more education. The Jewish schools were closed down. The interesting young teachers dispersed to their homes. The doors of the Polish school were shut to Jewish students. Undeterred, Raizel continued to learn independently, and she began to tutor younger girls at home, offering Hebrew lessons and religious instruction in the style of the *Bais Yaakov* school.

It was no surprise when Raizel proved to be an excellent teacher, gently coaxing young students to follow her into more demanding and rigorous studies. Raizel had less patience for her sister, however. Sala squirmed under Raizel's strict discipline and dreaded the hyper-critical eye that never missed an academic mistake or overlooked a religious impropriety. She meant no disrespect by using a comb on the Sabbath, or rolling up her long sleeves on a hot summer day, exposing a few inches of forbidden skin above the wrists. But she was horrified when Raizel threatened to tell their father. Shocking her sister was one thing, but she adored her father, who never raised his voice to her, and was indulgent of his youngest daughter. She could not bear to disappoint him.

Raizel was brilliant and strong-minded—but also uncompromising and inflexible. Whatever the requirements of this thing called a labor camp, Raizel would never adapt. It was even more unthinkable for the next oldest sister, Blima, to leave home. Blima was the emotional core of the family; even the parents depended on her gentle ways to soothe the rough edges of their grinding poverty. Blima was young and attractive. She wanted to leave Poland and join a cousin who was living in Palestine, but when her father disapproved, she accepted his decision. She always put the family's needs first, encouraging her sisters to rely on her rather than on their mother, who was careworn and tired after twenty years of childbearing. Sala had been a sickly, colicky baby, and it was Blima who carried the crying child out of the house to give some rest to her mother. As Sala grew into a strong and high-spirited young woman, Blima overlooked her sister's teenage exuberance and served as Sala's advocate.

At sixteen, Sala found life painfully predictable. Looking around the low-ceilinged room that she shared with as many as six family members, she could hardly believe that things could get worse. By day, the room was a crowded and noisy workshop, with Blima on her machine for embroidering linens, and their father and Raizel taking turns at the table with their students. The room had a few pieces of furniture: a worn, wooden table, which served as desk, workbench, and dining table; a rickety armoire that held clothes and linens. A small, low door led to a storage space and the communal clotheslines for the building. Neighbors filed through the apartment to reach their clothes, not always asking for permission. In winter, the clothes would freeze into thin sheets of ice that smacked Sala painfully in the face if she ran by carelessly. The storage space also held the family's straw mattresses and the chamber pot for the evening hours when it was too dark to walk down three flights of stairs to the privy in the courtyard. She shuddered to think of the filthy outhouse, where she walked on tiptoes and prayed that the neighborhood boys were not watching through the holes she knew they had drilled in the thin walls. At night, the family put the sewing machines away and dragged out the mattresses and covered them with cloth; she and her mother shared one, her sisters on the second and their father alone on the third. Once in a while, visiting relatives slept on another mattress in the storage space.

Her only escape beckoned through a small slanted window that led to the roof. When there were no neighbors in sight, she would climb through, a drop of butter rubbed on her face to catch the sun. It was worth risking even the sheer drop to the courtyard below and a scolding from Raizel for a few golden moments of privacy.

This was the only home that she had ever known. Soon after the death of his first wife in childbirth, her father had taken his young sister-in-law Chana as his second wife, according to Jewish custom. Together, Josef and Chana raised the baby girl and the ten children who followed. From the small town of Wolbrom, the family moved a short distance away to the larger city of Sosnowiec, where Josef hoped to find more students.

Chana struggled to find food for the family—always cooking something from nothing, their father said ruefully. Blima was already a talented cook and baker, her mother's confidante and helper. Their family meals were spare but nourishing, and any special ingredients were saved for the Sabbath meal and festivals. Everyone's favorite dish was goose, a special treat in the winter months, when the bird was fattest. The preparations took all day, and her mother used every bit of the bird: the meat for dinner, the bones for soup, and the feathers for a down pillow or a cozy blanket. The fat was rendered and put away in the coldest part of the storage space, the *schmaltz* that she saved from the winter until the spring, when it would be used for Passover preparations.

On bad days when the cupboards were empty, Chana burned some paper instead of food and pretended that there was something in the stove. It was important to avoid the appearance of needing charity. "People will see the chimney smoking and think that we're cooking some food," Josef instructed her.

In the winter, Chana's knitting needles were in constant motion, producing wool scarves, mittens, and stockings to keep her girls warm. When Sala closed her eyes, that was how she saw her mother: dressed in the black dress that she always wore, her brow furrowed beneath the wig that had been fashioned from Sala's own long braids, her mother's hands busily knitting, knitting, knitting.

She was frustrated by Chana's ceaseless activity. She disliked housework herself and dreamed of making money to release her mother from the daily grind of cooking and cleaning. Even as a child, she was full of plans. Her friends still laughed about last summer's scheme to sell homemade ice cream. They helped her to churn a hand-cranked contraption that she borrowed from a neighbor, but when they tried to sell the meager output, they were chased off the streets by a policeman.

To the relief of her parents, Sala had a practical streak as well. She apprenticed herself at the age of eight to her sisters and brothers. Her first ambition was to earn enough money for a new coat. Her sisters and brothers ran small businesses at home and taught her to operate their most complicated machines: she was soon helping them to embroider linens, assemble sweaters, and attach leather uppers to shoe soles. By the time she was sixteen, she was an excellent seamstress.

Friday was the busiest day, the preparation for the Sabbath when work would cease, and prayer and family would smooth over the stresses of the week. She loved the weekly activities, even the chores that she usually preferred to avoid. Her mother and her sisters prepared something special for the evening meal, perhaps a piece of carp for *gefilte* fish, reserving the head of the fish for Sala's father. Water came from a pump in the courtyard. Sala needed several breathless trips up and down the stairs before she had enough water to fill the large pot that her mother used for boiling the fish. Since no work was permitted on the Sabbath, they prepared Saturday's meal in advance, assembling a special stew, a *cholent,* with potatoes, barley, and sometimes a piece of meat. A sweet and savory pudding made from leftover bread simmered within the stew. Her mother removed the pot from the coal stove and covered it with brown paper, then tied it around several times with string. Sala wrote their name on the paper and carefully carried the large pot around the corner to Shimon the baker, who inserted it on a long paddle into the recesses of his giant oven, together with dozens of other pots from neighbors, each tied and identified, ready to be served hot for the next afternoon's meal.

Everything had to be finished before sundown on Friday. The single room, always clean, was now immaculate. Sala's last chore was to clean the floors. She scrubbed every inch of the old wooden planks, spread sawdust over them and protected them with burlap, then removed the rough cloths and swept the floor clean again at the last possible minute. Her mother washed Sala's hair and braided it into two long plaits. Finally, her mother changed into her other clothes, the stiff black dress that she wore only on the Sabbath.

It was time for her mother to light the tall candles in her brass candlesticks. When her father returned from synagogue, wearing his black long coat tied around with a sash, he would gather them to the table and lead the songs that welcomed the start of the Sabbath.

In the morning, she walked to the synagogue with her father, carrying his prayer shawl, and then returned home for her own prayers, supervised closely by Raizel, who reprimanded her if she asked questions in Polish, since their father had asked them to speak only in Yiddish on the Sabbath. Before lunch, Sala returned to the baker to retrieve the cooked stew. Once she took the wrong pot, and hid behind her mother when the rabbi's wife charged up the stairs in search of her *cholent.* She heard their voices with relief; the exchange was made with good humor on both sides.

The rest of the Sabbath was spent with her friends. She was their leader, the fastest runner, and the most daring. It was their habit to spend the day moving around to different apartments. Since her family's one room was already overcrowded, the girls would meet her outside when the weather was fair, jumping rope or playing hide-and-seek around a dilapidated wooden wagon in the courtyard. No one knew why the old wagon was there, but it was their favorite landmark for a noisy game of tag, at least until angry neighbors would yell out the window or pour water over the girls, who were helpless with laughter.

They saw each other during the week as well. Blowing in like a storm after school, still dressed in their uniforms and full of high spirits, they usually gathered at the large and welcoming apartment of the Rabinowicz family. Sala was well liked by her friend's older brothers, handsome and well-educated boys with a gallant air about them, who needed no encouragement to be nice to their sister's prettiest and most vivacious friend. She was also a favorite with their younger sister, Frymka, who clamored for a game of cards and had to be chased from the room when the older girls needed some private conversation.

When the Polish army paraded through Sosnowiec, she disregarded her mother's entreaty to stay home and convinced her friends that they could get an excellent view of the parade by climbing up to a small balcony on the second floor. The balcony collapsed, injuring several people. She and the other girls escaped unharmed; no one ever knew how dearly they almost paid for her curiosity.

The games began to change even though Sala was still a tomboy. Romance was already in the air. She steered her friends to the streets where the teenagers of Sosnowiec gathered for an afternoon promenade. Boys walked on one side, girls on the other, their exchanges limited to an energetic nod of the head or a stiffly formal greeting. Sala was beginning to attract attention, with her finely sculpted features and womanly figure, her thick dark hair no longer held captive in the two long braids of her childhood. Her natural poise and style belied her family circumstances. Although marriage still seemed far off, she had already preempted any possibility of an arranged match, the usual rite of passage for the young women of their community. Her mother lamented the scarcity of learned young men who would take a bride without a dowry, especially in these uncertain times, but when the matchmaker came to call, Sala took off through the window and sulked on the roof. She would not be like her mother, who had been required by Jewish law to marry her brother-in-law. Nor would she be like Blima, who was already meeting suitable young men in a designated public place, everything arranged by the matchmaker. Blima never suspected that her sister and her friends were spying on her as she walked and talked with a prospective suitor. Imagine having everyone know exactly where, and with whom, you were courting! Sala would find her own husband.

Caught in the strange and unprecedented circumstances of 1940, Sala was searching for adventure and freedom. Even the unknown world of a Nazi labor camp seemed like an acceptable alternative.

She was resolute in her decision to take Raizel's place. Her wages would help the family, her sisters would be left in peace with her parents, and she would get the opportunity for change that she sought so desperately.

Her parents weighed their alternatives. It was only for six weeks, or so the letter said. There was a certain restlessness about their youngest child, they recognized. Unlike her sisters, who flourished within the narrow orbit of their religious community, Sala chafed against her limitations as the youngest daughter of a poor Hebrew schoolteacher and his tired, worried wife. What about her future? Would she outgrow this rebelliousness and settle into her place as a traditional wife and mother? She was struggling against their way of life. The poverty that the rest of the family disregarded as merely inconvenient, she found mean and confining.

Josef Garncarz thought that these matters were settled a few months before, when he refused to allow her to go to Russia with Hersh Leib, the last unmarried son. Hersh Leib had been attending secret political meetings, risking the wrath of his father as well as the Nazis. Like other religious Jews in Sosnowiec, Rabbi Garncarz rejected any radical influences, regardless of whether the ideological source was secular, Communist, or Zionist. Now his son declared that he was a Communist, and was threatening to run away and take his sister with him. Even worse, Hersh Leib warned his father that they should all be leaving Poland.

Sala cared nothing for her brother's politics, nor was she frightened by his tales of future catastrophes; she saw only the alluring prospect of change. Together, she and Hersh Leib campaigned for her freedom.

Josef Garncarz was unconvinced. People were running away, it was true, but to where? They had no resources and few connections outside of Sosnowiec. They had no passports, and it was far from certain that Hersh Leib would even be able to smuggle himself into Russia, let alone with his teenage sister. The Garncarz family had always lived in Poland, the center of Jewish intellectual, cultural, and religious life for nearly one thousand years. They lived in relative peace with their Polish neighbors. Although the 28,000 Jews of Sosnowiec formed a smaller minority among the general population of 130,000 than in cities such as Warsaw or Lodz, they were a thriving community. Sosnowiec had Jewish banks, business associations, hospitals, orphanages, and schools. There was an equally large Jewish community in the nearby city of Bedzin. Of their seven surviving children, all but one lived in Sosnowiec. Blima had abandoned her plan to leave for Palestine and would be the next to marry and raise a family within the community. It was better for Sala to stay and hope for the best.

Hersh Leib left without her. They received one postcard from him postmarked from Russia, and then, silence.

Hersh Leib's departure and the grim reality of the occupation had not changed her parents' outlook. But now the Council's letter had arrived.

Suddenly, the very air seemed charged with uncertainty. The risks were considerable wherever they turned. If they did not comply, they could be arrested or lose their ration cards. If Sala stayed at home, she would face other threats. The policeman who chased a teenager for selling ice cream was now more likely to be wearing an SS uniform and carrying a gun. A young girl could no longer walk proudly by her father's side. She was courting danger every night, racing along the rooftops of the buildings and dodging Nazi snipers to be first in line at the bakery in the morning. Her daring escapades thrilled her friends but terrified her parents.

The decision was made: she was determined to go and they would not stop her. Someone had to show up at the train station—and they agreed that Sala was the best choice.

One year earlier, on the night of September 3, 1939, the sounds of heavy artillery had been heard just outside Sosnowiec for the first time.

Only a day's march from the German border, Sosnowiec was the gateway to the strategically important region of Eastern Upper Silesia, the center of Poland's coal mining industry. On September 4, the Germans had entered the city from all directions, on motorcycles, from the train station, riding in tanks and armed vehicles, walking the streets, rifles turned toward the buildings. SS troops followed closely behind the German soldiers, arresting people indiscriminately, shooting others on the spot. Dozens of shops were plundered. Hundreds of Jews were forced to assemble in the marketplace and watch the Great Synagogue, and two other smaller synagogues, burn to the ground.

The Germans had long coveted the coal- and iron-rich land around Sosnowiec and considered it rightfully theirs, one more insult by the League of Nations in 1920 when it designated the area of Eastern Upper Silesia, also known as Zaglembie, as Polish territory. The Germans immediately annexed this region and a few other selected areas into the greater Reich. One large section of Poland became a separate Nazi administrative district known as the General Government. The rest of Poland, and over one million Jews, fell under Russian occupation, in accordance with the secret alliance between Hitler and Stalin.*

The invasion of Poland had been swift and successful, but along with the territory had come a large and unwelcome civilian population. There were simply too many Jews. Although Hitler would eventually require their elimination, the Nazi government was not fully prepared to deal with the immediate reality of removing or killing two million people. In Germany and Austria, the number of Jews had been gradually reduced as they fled to other countries during the six years of Nazi brutality and repression that led up to the start of the war. But now the borders were closed.

The Nazi government considered the alternatives. Since any final solution would require mass evacuations, they commenced a program to consolidate the population. Soldiers systematically emptied the smaller Polish towns and *shtetls* into urban areas, where railroad connections would facilitate the deportations to come. In the General Government region, the Jews were herded into enclosed ghettos.

The annexed region around Sosnowiec, however, merited a second look. Its abundant natural resources and manufacturing facilities would keep the German war economy strong. The availability of such a large skilled labor force in close proximity to Germany could have practical and economic benefits. The Polish Jews were not rich: before the war, the eight hundred thousand Jews of Austria and Germany owned more property than the more than three million Jews of Poland. But as slaves, they were highly valuable.

Nazi industrialists and army experts successfully made the case for a different approach here. While the rest of the Polish Jews lived in guarded ghettos, the Nazis would make an exception within the annexed region. These Jews would be concentrated within the cities, but not forced into ghettos—at least, not for the time being.

In the spring of 1941, the five thousand Jews of Oswiecim were

---

*The Russian occupation of Poland was a result of the secret nonaggression treaty between Hitler and Stalin, also known as the Ribbentrop-Molotov Pact, signed in Moscow on August 23, 1939.

given a few hours notice before they were evicted. Oswiecim had been chosen as the site of a major Nazi labor camp and industrial complex. A small town within the annexed region, it met the most important criteria: good rail connections and close proximity to densely populated areas that would supply slave labor for the enormous factories already under construction. But first, the Jewish local residents had to be forced to relocate to the nearby city of Sosnowiec. Since Jews were banned from the railways, horse-drawn wagons were used to transport the sick, aged, and small children of Oswiecim, while everyone else walked in a caravan that stretched for miles.

Overnight, new maps appeared. The familiar Polish designations had been Germanized. The postmark for Eastern Upper Silesia became Ostoberschleisen. Sosnowiec was renamed Sosnowitz. Bedzin became Bendsburg. Sala's own Kollataja Street became Oderbergerstrasse. Oswiecim would be known henceforth as Auschwitz.

As the Nazis continued to debate the fate of the Polish Jews, the delays opened up unexpected opportunities for wealth and power. Albrecht Schmelt was a Nazi officer and former police chief. Moses Merin was an obscure Jewish politician. They were soon to become informal partners who would play a major role in the lives of 130,000 Jews, including Sala and her family.

Schmelt was a World War I veteran who joined the Nazis in 1930 and rose quickly through the ranks. Average in stature, he was described in his Nazi party application as "ostisch" or "eastern" in appearance, but neither his swarthy and undistinguished figure nor his lack of formal education stood in the way of his career. In rapid succession, Schmelt became the local representative to the Prussian parliament and government deputy, then a member of the Reichstag. He was named regional police president in 1934, and joined the SS in 1939, rising quickly to the post of SS *Oberführer.*

Because of his familiarity with the local political and social conditions in the annexed region, Schmelt was handpicked by SS head Heinrich Himmler to be "Special Representative of the *Reichsführer*

SS for the Employment of Foreign Labor in Upper Silesia." After his official appointment in October 1940, Schmelt took up his post aggressively, setting up headquarters in Sosnowiec and formulating a plan for the creation of the labor camp system that would become known as Organization Schmelt.

Schmelt's first camps were dedicated to the major construction projects undertaken by his patron Himmler. Chief among these was "the Führer's Road." Hitler himself broke ground for a modern highway, declaring that the Autobahn would symbolize his empire: modern Germany's answer to the Acropolis or the Great Wall of China. The war gave urgency to the completion of the highway, which would transport trucks, tanks, and troops. Initially, only Germans were permitted the privilege of being construction workers, but as more and more of them were conscripted as soldiers, or found better jobs, other sources of labor were essential. To keep the project on schedule, Schmelt requisitioned thousands of strong young Jewish men, and also brought women to work in the office, kitchen, and laundry.

The German town of Geppersdorf was chosen as one of the first labor camp sites. In addition to its strategic location along the highway's route, it was close to large Jewish populations in Sosnowiec and Bedzin. Geppersdorf also had sentimental associations for Schmelt himself, whose family settled there in the mid-eighteenth century.

After Schmelt's first attempts at large-scale labor deployment proved slow and cumbersome, he sought an ally within the Jewish community. Moses Merin was thirty-seven years old, small and intense, a Zionist and minor political figure with a questionable reputation as a divorced man and a gambler, an ambitious hustler who was always looking for a loan or a favor. He impressed the Nazis early in the occupation when he volunteered to negotiate the release of influential Jews who had been kidnapped and imprisoned. Although Merin spoke no German, he successfully raised a large ransom from the frightened families, mediating skillfully between the Jews and the Germans through his trusted assistant, Mrs. Fani Czarna, who spoke German fluently. The Nazis rewarded his initiative by appointing him as the head of the new Jewish Council, known as the Judenrat, which they substituted for the autonomous Jewish community organizations that existed before the war. Similar Councils were created throughout Nazi-occupied Poland.

In Sosnowiec, Merin put a Jewish face on Nazi policies and actions. One of his first duties was to conduct an accurate census of the Jewish population, segmented by sex, age, and occupation. Signs appeared on the walls of the city and in the stores, written in German, Polish, and Yiddish, requiring all Jews to register immediately with the Council and threatening anyone who failed to comply with the loss of ration cards and prosecution. The Nazis warned the Council leaders that they would be held personally responsible for the results of the census under the threat of being deported. The result was a comprehensive list of eligible workers for Organization Schmelt.

Merin proved to be an impressive administrator, as autocratic and efficient as his Nazi patrons. The census was completed ahead of schedule. Still unknown to many of the Sosnowiec Jews, and mistrusted by his former colleagues, Merin rapidly consolidated his power. Soon, nothing of importance happened in the Jewish community without his knowledge.

Once the census was completed, Merin and his staff matched the lists to Schmelt's labor requirements. Families that paid the Council's head tax were exempted. To the rest, Merin promised "mountains of gold" and the safety of their families. Merin's staff counted heads, not specific names. Soon, they had enough volunteers to fulfill Schmelt's quota. Most of them were from the poorest families of Sosnowiec.

In his zeal to comply with Schmelt's orders, Merin deported the first workers to Germany at least four weeks too early. They reached their destination at night, only to discover that little more than a sign marked the camp; there was no water or equipment, and the wooden buildings that would serve as barracks were still under construction. Merin did not dare to recall the transport, which might discourage other volunteers. The men slept in the open for weeks.

27

A handful of women were on the short list that Merin gave to Schmelt for the deportation of October 28, 1940, including Raizel Garncarz. But it was Sala who was bound for the camp.

The date set in the letter for her departure was three days away. Each person was allowed to bring a small suitcase and some money. Sala borrowed an old leather briefcase, which would hold her few belongings. She had no money to bring. At home, her mother cried all the time, and the three days seemed endless.

She escaped from the weight of her mother's grief by spending time with her friends. She was the only one who was leaving. Her parents had accepted the order from the Council, had never considered an outright refusal to comply or the possibility of borrowing money for the required tax. Should they have tested the resolve of the Council? The risk of arrest or losing their food ration cards was too terrible to contemplate.

She had made her decision and wanted only to look ahead.

She spent her last night with her friends. They planned a festive occasion and pooled their resources for a parting gift: a warm and colorful wool hat, scarf, and mittens, plus some spending money. It will be bitter cold in Germany, they said, and we want you to remember us when you are wearing this.

It was almost time for the evening curfew. They would meet again in the early morning and walk together to the train station.

They embraced. She was surrounded by her best friends and basked in their admiration. They shared her belief in a future without limits.

On October 28, 1940, Sala rose early. She removed a few blank pages from her diary and folded them within the clothes she had already packed, locking the rest of the small paperbound journal and her favorite blouse in the one drawer that belonged to her. She had designed and sewn the blouse by hand, delighting in the bright coral color, but decided that it was too delicate. Instead, she took a sturdy navy blue shirt that her brother Hersh Leib had left behind.

The sleepers on the other mattresses stirred, then came to life. The room filled with activity, as her sisters and her mother dressed quickly to accompany her to the station. Her mother wore her everyday black dress, and adjusted her wig neatly on her head. Her father could not risk leaving the apartment. He called her to him and held his youngest daughter close to his heart. As he wept, he blessed her and prayed for her protection.

Unexpectedly, it was Raizel who forced a joke: "Remember me, I'm the ugly one, but I'll be the one to write to you."

CHAPTER TWO

One Clean Jew

Sala stood with her mother in the waiting area of the train station. She had traveled by train once before. On that joyous day, the station rang with the vibrant laughter and high spirits of her classmates as they gathered for a class trip to Krakow.

Today, the cavernous space echoed her unease as she joined a jostling crowd of young men holding small suitcases and packages, stamping their feet and breathing on their fingers to keep warm in the early October frost. She saw only a few other women in the crowd. SS guards were shouting and pushing the men into lines that led to tables where officials sat with large charts and lists. The trains were waiting in the distance. Her friends had risen early to accompany her to the station, but they had stepped aside, and she was alone with her mother. Arguments were breaking out, as some of the bolder men argued with the officials to make an exception, put them on a later transport, or keep them together with a friend. A burly Jewish policeman advanced toward the loudest of the men, who turned and melted into the crowd.

It was her turn. She stepped up and identified herself to the official. In her best Polish, she began to explain that she had already been to Skladowa Street to register for the transport. She was here in place of Raizel Garncarz, her sister. He stopped her recitation and pointed toward a long line that was forming next to the train under a handwritten sign: Geppersdorf.

Returning to her mother's side, Sala drew a protective arm around her mother. She could feel her trembling and beginning to cry.

A few yards away, a woman watched the mother and daughter. With a few long strides, she stood before them, straight and tall, a jaunty felt hat pulled low over one eye, matching her warm woolen coat. She drew close to the older woman and offered her assistance, speaking in a brisk, well-educated Polish accent. "She's my baby," Chana Garncarz sobbed in Yiddish. "I don't know where she is going." The woman's eyes rested on Sala for a long moment. "My name is Ala Gertner. I will be with her. I will take care of her. Please, don't worry," she said, her voice soft and soothing. Chana's tears slowed; reluctantly, her grip relaxed. Ala gently disentangled the mother and daughter. The tall stranger offered her arm to Sala and they walked together toward the train, looking back to see her mother standing alone, a solitary figure in black.

Her education began on the train. It was only a few hours' travel between home and the camp, but the train stopped often, and at each station it took on more cars filled with young men and women. She huddled with Ala, exchanging confidences and family histories with her new companion. Ala's attempts to speak Yiddish made her laugh. She began to imitate Ala's refined Polish accent, marveling at the good luck that brought them together at the train station.

How different Ala was from the other women on the train—and from anyone else she had ever known. Although they had lived just a few miles apart, Ala might well have been born on another continent, instead of the neighboring city of Bedzin. Although smaller than Sosnowiec, Bedzin had a proportionally larger Jewish population, and boasted one of the few Jewish deputy mayors in all of Poland, as well as an influential and affluent community of Jewish industrialists, merchants, and professionals. Ala's parents showered their three children with the gifts of education, culture, and travel. She was well-read in German and Polish, and was contemplating several career options before the war derailed all plans.

For the Gertner family, being Jewish was an afterthought, involving little more than a generous annual donation to the synagogue and a perfunctory visit for New Year services. Proud, assimilated, thoroughly Polish, the Gertner family was one terminus for nine centuries of Jewish life in Poland, and the Garncarz family was another.

Sala hardly knew how to behave in the company of someone like Ala. Until today, religion had governed every aspect of her daily life, where she lived, how she dressed, what she ate, where she worked. At home, they would have never met, never been friends. But their sudden intimacy, sealed in Ala's spontaneous promise to her mother, augured well for the six weeks they expected to be together.

Sala began to write in her journal as the train left the station.

Monday, October 28, 1940

From the time of departure from Sosnowiec

At 7:00 o'clock A.M., we all arrived at Skladowa Street. After our names were checked, we went to the railroad station where we waited until 11:00 A.M. Dear beloved girls!

How can I describe this waiting period? Was I dreaming? Yes, I had been dreaming, from 5:00 o'clock in the morning until we arrived at the designated location. At 6:00 o'clock, it was Sala [Rabinowicz] who first arrived, my sweet friend. By 7:00 o'clock, I had you all with me: all my dear ones: Sala [Rabinowicz], Gucia, Bela, Chancia, and Hela.

My dearests! If you could have looked deep in my heart, you would have seen how desperate I was; still I tried to keep a smile on my face as best I could, though my eyes were filled with tears. One must go on bravely and courageously, even if the heart is breaking.

I said goodbye to my beloved old father. Dear father, will you miss your Sala very much? Me, the intolerable girl? My father cried . . . yes, he did cry when we were saying goodbye. Onward. Accompanied by all my sweet girlfriends, we started out. Where to? Why? Only the future will tell . . .

Mother dearest, I have not mentioned you until now. I was not looking at you, though I was consumed by you. You were pleading with me, you were begging me, almost yelling at me—yet, I want to do what I want to do. Now it's so hard to say goodbye; what can I say to you, what to wish you?

I said nothing. I did not wish you anything, did not ask you for anything. Still, I could not stop looking at you Mother, because I felt something inside of me tearing, hurting. One more kiss, one more hug, and my mother does not want to let go of me. Let it end already, it is torture. Then I say goodbye to my sisters.

I step into the lineup, and looking around me, I see Sala [Rabinowicz] and Gucia, my faithful friends, standing at a distance since they are not allowed to be near. Except for my mother and sisters, here everybody and everything are strangers to me.

With whom are you leaving me, and to whom are you sending me?

Dear girls!!! I am accustomed to you more than to my sisters, and now I have to leave you and must go into the unknown world. Will I ever see all of you again? Sala, does it seem possible that I will not be in your house tomorrow to play cards with [your little sister] Frymka? And [your brother], can you believe that he won't see me again tomorrow? I wonder if he will remember me, or talk about me. But what right do I have to demand it?

We are starting to move. Goodbye everybody; remember me, only please do not pity me, because nobody forced me to do this. I got what I wanted. God help me!!!

I am together now with Miss Ala. There are about fourteen women, and we shall try to enable our brothers to live in a way where they will not feel the change that has taken place in their lives.

Her first working days at Geppersdorf passed in a blur of activity, as she and the other women had to organize the housekeeping and food preparation for hundreds of laborers and the German staff.

There was much to learn, and she met more strangers in the first day than she had ever encountered before.

The days quickly settled into a pattern. The men were marched out every morning to the nearby construction sites. The women remained at the camp, randomly assigned to cleaning duties and the kitchen, except for Ala, who worked as a typist and translator, preparing letters and official documents in the small office that served as the headquarters for the camp administration, the "Bureau."

Tuesday, October 29, 1940
I woke up early as I slept very little. I look around; so it seems I spent one night in my "new home." I am shivering from cold and my head feels terribly heavy. One by one, the girls look around, taking their time to get up. Get up! Lots of work is waiting for us. A stove is being set up; [one of the girls] makes the stovetop very hot, and now my soul is uplifted. Somehow, things will turn out all right.

Miss Ala also cheers us up, she is such a terrific and courageous girl. Even though she came from a wealthy home, she is able to adjust to present circumstances without fighting them; what's more, she is able to give us hope. Our dinner consisted of barley soup, which was less than tasty. Well, that too shall pass. In the evening, we were assigned bunks. Wonderful. There is a lower level and an upper level. I can imagine how it will feel to sleep on the upper level. Miss Ala and I reserved one such accommodation. We will be sharing the bunk with one other girl who is very lively, and like all girls, she likes to flirt. In addition, there are four other girls in the room.

Tonight, I slept with Miss Ala; what a delight. I love her. This afternoon, as they were giving out food coupons in our room, an old Jew came by feeling weak and hungry. He warmed himself by the stove. We felt pity for him and asked him where he is from; he poured his bitter heart out telling us about himself. He is from Sosnowiec, has a wife

and children, and all of them are in our community. He
was supposed to be allowed to stay home . . . but one
person insisted that he must go. So even here an act of
maliciousness was carried out—against whom? Against
an old, sick Jew. Oh, be cursed, you who did it, and the
others who are like you.

After that, we cried for half an hour, Ala hugging me,
about him and our own fate. We have to get hold of ourselves.

At the table, I spoke a bit with our young German office
clerk, who seems pleasant. I found out from him that he
knows my brother [Moshe David]. I like to hear him talk,
because I like the German language a lot, and besides, he is
a pleasant fellow. After we straightened up the beds, we
cleaned up, and I helped to wash the dishes. I peeled potatoes.
One more thing—I mended gloves for a soldier, for which I
had to accept [a small payment], even though I objected . . .

Ala kept the promise she made at the train station. They slept
together in a recently constructed wooden barracks, Ala by her side
in the narrow bunk, as her mother had been on their straw mattress
at home. She was grateful for the words of encouragement and
advice that Ala whispered into the chilly night air.

More and more men arrived at the camp. Among the newcomers,
she discovered a handful of relatives and friends from home, including
her cousin Rozia's fiancé, Leib, and Rozia's younger brother, Abram.

Wednesday, October 30, 1940
We slept quite well last night. After a bit of cleaning and
shaking out the blankets, we ate breakfast. One of the girls
had brought with her some Lithuanian cheese, which she
shared with us. We also had bread and butter—an excellent
breakfast. For dinner, we had cabbage soup, quite tasty too.
I found out quite by chance that Leib, the boyfriend of my
cousin Rozia from Olkusz, is here, among the men.

I looked for him and found him. When I spoke to him in the evening, he told me sadly that he is imagining Rozia to be crying now. He is such a sweet man, strongly built, but his face betrays his young age. He really does love my cousin. Yes, Rozia, you can be proud of him. Everybody likes him; I shall try as hard as I can to help him since he is my future cousin . . .

Also this evening, Ala and I gave him a postcard to send home, which we hope will get there. You must understand that we are not allowed to let anybody hear from us, while everyone at home is going crazy with worry, thinking that we have disappeared.

I washed his socks and I dried his shoes; the poor fellow has a cold, still he went to work. He was told that he might be excused tomorrow and I would be glad if he is excused.

I have much to worry about today. Leib was let go by our boss on Thursday, but it now appears that it's a bad situation. The authorities came to check on the workers, and discovered that nine of them stayed home. It was a scandal, and all of them were put in a separate room and then they were sent to work.

And so, before bedtime, the entire camp was ordered to assemble. [The boss] requested, in a hoarse voice, that we do not make it more difficult for him to carry on his already difficult duties.

Men are absolutely forbidden to be in the women's section of the camp. There will be punishment for not obeying orders. Also we are forbidden to contact them. For us, it's not too bad, but for the men, that is difficult. Well, maybe it's better this way.

Sala's diary recorded her daily duties for the week. As she reached her first Friday evening away from home, loneliness struck.

Friday, November 1, 1940

The day was uneventful except that we were assigned to another room, an unpleasant change for me, since the four of us were hoping to stay together in our little room. Well, after all, this is not for us to decide. We will have to get used to the faces of still more new strangers. I also worry about where I will sleep since, while I was away dressing, bunks were set up and no space was left for me to be with my beloved Ala. I had to agree to take the bunk under Ala, but so far, I have not slept in it, because Ala always finds a spot for poor me next to her. She always takes me in.

Now the traditional Friday evening approaches, time for the family to be together, and for closeness to uplift the soul. That day finds me now far away from home. I suddenly realize where I am, and I know that whether this is Friday or not, I will not eat with all of you at the same table, and I will not hear my beloved father say kiddush.* No, I cannot be with you because I am in a barracks in a camp!

Something moves me, but there is nobody here who is close to me. I have to hope that Ala will be back from the office soon. Yet my thoughts are with you; could you feel my nearness to you? And so I walked around like a lunatic for I had nobody to share my sorrow, nobody to console me as I cried my eyes out, finding it hard to breathe; it was stifling. Never before did I miss you so much, beloved parents, and my dear girlfriends! Today I was not with you when prayers were said. I did not hear [your brothers] say the prayers. Oh, my dearest ones! Did you remember me just then? I will find out when we are together again.

Ala just arrived; I feel relieved. Would you believe that I could not tell her all that I was feeling? I prefer to write things down, since I don't know how to talk about such

*Blessing over wine that begins the Sabbath dinner.

matters. Still, her presence is good for me for it helped me to fall asleep here in Geppersdorf, while my thoughts were with you.

Although she could not yet confide completely in Ala, she took comfort in the older woman's presence and sought her approval. She was proud of her special status as Ala's chosen companion, especially since Ala's strong personality and intellect had also won the admiration of the other girls. She worried, however, that her inexperience would eventually alienate her important new friend.

Saturday

I woke up thinking that I was drunk. Do you know why? Because just a week ago today, I was actually drunk after drinking beer on Friday. You drank to my health and a wish for me to remain home, but I am one stubborn girl, am I not? I have to admit that I was a bit tipsy, but it won't happen again. Today we work only until 12 o'clock.

Something new happened. As I was sitting on my bunk writing, the SA man* came in. He said, "Get your coat, we are going to the movies." I was amazed and I took it for a joke. But, an order is an order, so I put on my coat and beret and together with [two others], we all went out. He took us to [the office] and we helped him to do some dusting. They were very nice to us there, and they gave us some beer. It warmed us since it's quite cold. Then we went back to our place and brought back cigarettes for our boys.

Sunday

Today is our holiday. From early morning, there is much activity, and no wonder. One wants to outdo the other. I

---

*The SA (*Sturmabteilung* or Storm Troopers) was the Nazi paramilitary organization that eventually lost most of its influence to the SS. In the early years of the war, they were assigned as guards in the Schmelt camps.

personally do not feel joyful, even though this is supposed to be our holiday. [Another girl] and I started cleaning: we made all the beds, washed the floor. Unfortunately, even today Ala has no free time because there is work to be done in the office.

In the afternoon: my conscience bothers me because while Ala was working in the office I did something foolish. Music was playing, so I danced with [one of the girls]. When she invited [a boy], I quickly stopped, and soon everybody gathered near my door. Suddenly, Ala appeared, entering the room in her steady, manly way, and everybody moved over. I am so proud that everyone respects her and pays attention to her but now I feel guilty because I hurt her. Might I lose her because of it? It would be a terrible blow to me. We go to sleep and when I am near her, I feel good again and blissful. Our conversation resumed on the same subject we so often talk about. I told her about my doubts, my desire to see and experience everything, and I related a lot about myself so that she could understand and forgive my behavior today, which was caused by my youth and inexperience. I think she understood and she forgave me. She is so sweet, and so strong . . . It is so wonderful to be with my Aluchna, so wonderful.

As one of the youngest girls in the camp, and Ala's protégé, Sala became the pet of the elite "Geppersdorfers." The group was headed by Kronenberg, a dapper fellow from Sosnowiec who had been designated by the Germans as the Judenalteste, the Jewish Elder at the camp. Several inmates were transferred to other camps in the growing network of labor camps, and she feared that she would be separated from Ala. Kronenberg helped to keep them together. However, Leib was transferred to another camp, which deprived her of the special sweetness of their conversations about his love for her cousin.

Monday

The SA man came in the evening and seeing a German-Polish grammar book on the table started reading the Polish part. It made me laugh. Later that evening, I went for a walk with Leib, and he told me more about himself and Rozia. We shook hands to seal our friendship. This boy suffered so much because he had to fight with his parents about Rozia, and just as they were ready to give him permission to marry, this new misfortune struck all of us. Oh, what wonderful dreams he has for the future! Rozia, Rozia, you should know that even at night, he keeps repeating your name; he has no better subject for conversation than you. You, Rozia, should be so happy.

At night in the bunk, Ala read to me the letter she wrote home, in which she mentioned me. That made me very glad.

The world is moaning, life is terrible, and there is much to lament. Is it any surprise that I am seeing people's misfortune, their sufferings and the injustices done to them? The world is complaining, and there is a void around us. Now the winds are blowing hard; what are you bringing us—your madman? Will it be fair weather or foul weather? Will there be quiet or turmoil?

Time to start working. Ala left for the office, while the wind picked up speed and became more mournful. A hubbub arose as everyone started running toward the square and onto the roofs to tie things down. Panic broke out and everybody got scared, some girls started crying. We have some sick ones who need to be consoled.

Six more women are to leave. Will I be among them? Ala comes running to me. "Listen, one of the office girls will have to leave as well, so if it's me, you will come with me." The truth is that I agreed without even giving it a thought. Well, it became apparent that they have no intention of sending Ala away, and Kronenberg did not want to put me on the list.

Little Keiti, the poor girl, cried and did not want to leave; still, in the end, she had to. I felt sorry for her, the poor child. But that was not the end of this matter. Next day, 60 more men had to leave, among them Leib. I felt very sad. He will probably have no one to talk to about Rozia. At the last moment, he was designated a "group officer" and he departed. The following days were very unpleasant, still, they were sweetened by the fact that I remained with Ala.

Friday

Oh, it's Friday again. What a horrible day for me here. Again, my thoughts turn to home, and again, I am overwhelmed by despair. Dear God, will Fridays always worry me so much when I am away from home?

It's quiet now. All the girls are in bed . . .

Transports were arriving continually, bringing new laborers and taking away those who had already fallen sick. Merin sent his representative, Mrs. Fani Czarna, to report on the conditions at the camp. Black-haired, black-eyed Mrs. Czarna was twenty-five years old, and was nearly as well known as Merin himself. The visit of a Jewish Council representative to the camp was the first link to home. Sala hoped that a few words from Mrs. Czarna would reassure her family.

The SA man pointed to me and said, this girl is clean, and he seemed to be almost glad about that. Fani Czarna looked at me and asked for my home address, so I asked her to tell them the best news about me. When she said goodbye, she shook my hand. They left.

In the afternoon, a small blow: 120 workers are being sent out. Everyone is fearful that someone among relatives or friends will be sent away.

Just look at us, tired and exhausted,
And how our hearts are bleeding.
Where are our aged parents,
Whose life is being poisoned?
So let it all be enough
For You to take off our burden,
Let us hope and be certain
That soon our parents and family will be one with us
That is the essence of our hope.

The worst deprivation of Geppersdorf was being away from home. The cold, crowded barracks with its rough floors, hard and narrow bunks, the meager rations, and the crude latrine were shocking to some of the girls. But she could hardly suffer from the loss of luxuries that she never had. She ached instead for the different riches of Kollataja Street: beloved parents and sisters, her friends, her freedom.

No letters or packages had yet arrived; perhaps it was too soon for any mail to reach the camp. She had brought a few postcards from home, and had written one at the first opportunity, following instructions to write only in German. The cards were then brought to the Bureau office to be stamped, hole-punched, and presumably censored. She longed for the sight of Raizel's familiar handwriting, and news of home.

Conditions in the men's camp were much harsher than for the women. The day began with the early morning roll call. The men stood in line, sometimes for hours, while the supervisors organized work crews for Moll & Mathies, the German company that was under contract to build this section of the highway. Accompanied by armed guards and German shepherd dogs, the men were marched to the construction site. Some men prepared the road surface by lifting rocks and clearing debris, some dug up the clay soil and loaded it on wagons. Other men worked on railway extensions and upgrades. The strongest among them would heft the steel beams for the rest to go under and move to the designated spot, like a group of pallbearers.

The din of clanging iron was accompanied by the constant barking of the guard dogs and their German masters, who stood ready with thick clubs that landed on the heads and shoulders of the laborers if the pace lagged. On rainy days, the men stood for hours in water up to their ankles or higher, and shoveled the heavy mud. Their shoes and clothes were soon in tatters.

Digging all day in the freezing earth or the oozing mud, pulling heavy iron supports with their bare hands, just a cup of tepid brown water in their stomach, cold and watery turnip soup and an occasional slice of bread at night—no wonder so many of them looked too weak to stand unsupported at the nightly roll call. The sick were taken away and never returned.

In addition to Kronenberg, the Jewish Elder, the elite group of prisoners included Dr. Wolf Leitner, a handsome physician; Chaim Kaufman, a tall and quiet tailor who served as the camp shoemaker; Bernhard Holtz, a brilliant young university student; and Hokilo Dattner, an athletic jack-of-all-trades who had found favor by demonstrating a knack for carpentry—and for his undefeated record in the boxing matches that were arranged by the guards.

As more camps were created and workers were transferred, Kronenberg intervened to keep Sala at Geppersdorf. He gave her a photograph of him, sitting on a park bench before the war, inscribed on the back to "my little housekeeper." He was one of her protectors, but not the only one. Chaim Kaufman also kept a close watch on her. Shy but persistent, he hoped that someday she would be more than a friend, and in the meantime, he tended to her shoes—no small advantage in the world of the camp, where a pair of shoes was irreplaceable. Hokilo shepherded her around the camp like an older brother, making sure that the roughest of the Geppersdorf men, German or Jew, knew that she was under his care. He sighed theatrically about his hopeless crush on her, and satirized the swirl of competition for her affections. How could he compete with Herr Kronenberg's guardianship or the cigarettes supplied by the dashing Dr. Leitner or the shoe repair skills of Chaim Kaufman?

She needed these watchful and affectionate eyes: when Nazi doctors visited Geppersdorf in search of young women for surgical experiments, it was Ala and Dr. Leitner who hid her from the makeshift operating room. Not all the women in the camp were as lucky.

The Bureau announced that the camp needed a seamstress for the German officers. She volunteered, not sorry to say goodbye to the turnips and potatoes. Her lithe figure was soon a fixture around the officers' quarters and the Bureau, hauling bundles of clothes to mend and launder. As the SA guard had predicted, the Nazis accepted her as "one clean Jew." Fearing contamination from the other laborers, however, they forbad any work on Jewish clothes. It was true that she made an extra effort to avoid the filth of the camp, sometimes waiting until the middle of the night to wash at the one faucet available to the women. Since her arrival, she had been hoarding a sliver of soap. But it was also her "good appearance," her light eyes and high cheekbones, that won her their approval.

One evening as she was leaving the Bureau with a basket of laundry, she was stopped by the head of the camp Lagerführer Ackerman. Considered a rising star among the Schmelt officials, he had just returned to Geppersdorf from his honeymoon. Tales of his brutality to the men were widespread. In retaliation for an escape attempt, he recently conducted a roll call that lasted most of a cold night. The men were ordered to splash themselves with freezing water and to stand in line as guards struck them arbitrarily with rubber hoses. Ackerman then forced the men to march in a circle in their wet, thin clothes and sing for an hour in the frosty air before they were allowed to return to their barracks.

Now Ackerman was pointing his whip at her, ordering her back to the Bureau to pick up the laundry from his wedding trip. While the idea of working for him personally was terrifying, his order could not be questioned. She followed the directions of Ackerman's aide to pick up a large trunk filled with dirty clothes and carry it, nearly staggering with the weight, to a small room that was restricted to officers. She had hardly a moment to react before the door was slammed and locked from the outside.

For three days and three nights, she worked on the mountain of laundry until each article of clothing was expertly cleaned, mended, ironed, and folded. Rations were left for her at irregular intervals and the dirty plates quickly removed, lest they touch the laundry in any way. She was taken at random intervals to the latrines behind the women's barracks and then back again to the airless and solitary room, the door slammed and locked. Repulsed by the personal service she was performing, she could not resist some delight in touching the sumptuous trousseau of Ackerman's bride: pure linen sheets trimmed in lace and elaborately monogrammed, handmade lingerie of silk and satin that flowed over her hands like a captive waterfall.

When Ackerman's aide reappeared, Sala was dozing lightly next to the trunk of clothes, now in perfect order. He tapped her on the shoulder and ordered her to leave.

The first distribution of mail took place about two weeks after Sala's arrival. Each postcard or envelope had been hole-punched and placed in a special binder. It was one of Kronenberg's few happy responsibilities as Jewish Elder to act as the mailman. For Sala, the sight of Raizel's handwriting released a jolt of pure joy. Neither Blima nor her parents could write in Polish or German; still, she imagined that she could hear all their different voices, asking questions, sending messages, as if they could reach through the scrap of paper and pull her to their heart.

> Sosnowiec
> November 4, 1940

Dear Sister,

We were very happy to get your postcard, as you can well imagine. But Sala, don't think that we stopped worrying just because we received your postcard—nothing of the kind, because you write so little about yourself. Write in more detail. How is the food? What do you eat, when, and do you like the food? Do you cook? Write as often as possible! How are the sleeping arrangements? You write that you have separate beds, do you have covers? Do you have heating? We are anxious to know everything. Dear Sala, we certainly want to know everything about you, but one forgets the right thing to ask, so please fill in whatever is missing.

Sala! We did not send a package as yet, because there was no time. We will try to send it, maybe tomorrow, as soon as we find out how . . .

All is well with us . . . when Mother received your postcard, she was the happiest person in the world. May your words only prove to be the truth. As of now, our brother-in-law David remains at home. We don't know if he will leave. Laya Dina and the children are in good health. You should have seen how Salusia kissed the postcard from Aunt Sala.

Raizel

So now even the postman knew where she was. The card was addressed clearly to Sala Garncarz at RAB Lager (the Reichsautobahn camp) in Geppersdorf. Judging from Raizel's dates and the post-marks, the first mail was exchanged with surprising rapidity. It had taken less than one week for Sala's first letter to reach Sosnowiec, where it was delivered to the Council's post office and then to her family's building.

It was a delight, and a surprise, that Raizel had written in Polish. Sala scrutinized every word. Was the tone forced in its bright cheer-iness? The postcard overflowed with writing that spread to every margin, sometimes upside down, on an angle, extra phrases spilling over into every corner, all in a neat and compact hand to conserve space.

She pictured the scene at home when her first letter arrived. Her sister would read her words aloud once, twice, and perhaps a third time, translating with some difficulty from Sala's labored German to Yiddish. Work on the sewing machines would cease temporarily. There would be her mother, crying with relief that her baby had arrived safely and had finally been allowed to write, if only in an unfamiliar language. Her father would be listening carefully, stroking his beard and pondering the dark and unforeseen circumstances that had swallowed up his youngest child. Salusia, his grandchild, would be sitting on her grandfather's lap, asking question after question about Aunt Sala.

Raizel's allusion to Laya Dina and her family brought a special pang. The most enterprising of the sisters, Laya Dina had a sweater-making business, for which she had purchased an expensive, commercial-quality Singer knitting machine made in America. She paid on a monthly installment plan. Sala loved to watch her manipulate the complicated machine, and she hoped that one day she would be allowed to work at her sister's side.

Laya Dina had a beautiful singing voice, and on Friday nights her voice reverberated throughout the building. Everyone loved to hear her sing, but poor Laya Dina, the neighbors clucked: a voice like an angel, and a good businesswoman too, but no beauty; one side of her face was covered with a strawberry mark. Despite the dire predictions, Laya Dina had married well, and had two beautiful children, Salusia and Moniek. With the help of her husband, David Krzesiwo, she expanded her profitable business. The Krzesiwo family lived on an adjacent side of the same courtyard, the more prosperous part of Kollataja Street where the apartments were larger, and had indoor plumbing and a small balcony. Laya Dina visited her parents and sisters every day, and her children were especially fond of their Aunt Sala. David Krzesiwo had already received one summons to a labor camp from the Council, but had managed to evade it after extended negotiations. He continued to brave the risks of being on the street to deliver the knits that he and Laya Dina made for their customers.

Sala kissed the letter and tucked it away within her small briefcase, together with her diary and her other possessions, relics of home hidden under the bunk.

Now that the postal connection had been established, her friends and family began to send letters regularly. But for how long?

Her friend Regina was the next to write.

Sosnowiec
November 11, 1940

Dear Sala,

Finally, a letter from you. I keep reading it and starting it
again and again, because it is hard to believe that you are so
far away from us. You described your life quite artistically:
you are a romantic and maybe that is what took you so far
away from us. You draw a beautiful panorama as you
describe that little red house in which you would like to
live with . . . ! ! But don't worry: you know the saying that
there is a time for everything (I should only believe it).
Sorry, but he should be reminded of Mickiewicz:* "how
much one should appreciate you, only the one who lost
you will know" (though I doubt he thinks otherwise, even
for a minute). Apparently, you were meant for something
better. I hear you left behind quite a few broken hearts.

Enough about strangers, now about me. I am foolish, I
envy you, I am strangely distracted and trying not to break
down. There is nothing new here, thank God all is well. I
am glad that you found a kindred soul, I understand what
[Ala] means to you. I bid you farewell a hundred times, and
wish you much happiness on your new path of life. From
the bottom of my heart I wish to see you happy because
you deserve it. Have hope! Be strong and remember that
man must travel through life on all kinds of roads. Best
regards for your Ala. I wish I could be together with you.

Regina

Regina's sister Chana added in a postscript that Sala's letter had
traveled almost two weeks before it reached them. Worried about the
length of her letter, Chana appealed to the invisible censors that
"they should only take such a heavy letter."

*A quote from Adam Mickiewicz (1798–1855), Polish romantic poet and author,
one of the most popular nineteenth-century Polish patriotic poets.

Still writing in Polish, Raizel was finding it hard to understand the nuances of her sister's letter. *"You write,"* Raizel marvels, *"but it doesn't really seem to be you, in German."* Raizel was disappointed at the trickle of mail from her sister.

> Sosnowiec
> November 11, 1940
>
> Dear sister Sala,
>   What happened, why didn't you write us more than once? We are almost sick thinking about what happened to you, wondering if you are well and whether you are working . . . Also, why don't you write to your girlfriends? They all walk around like chickens without heads. We find it hard to believe that you, who promised to write, are silent.
>   Everything here is as always. Remember that there is one God.
>
> Raizel

As the family correspondent, Raizel was also charged with special greetings to Ala. In her most formal language and handwriting, Raizel addressed her in German:

> Sosnowiec
> November 16, 1940
>
> Dear Sala,
>   Please ask Ala to read the following on behalf of our parents and all of us:
>
> Dear unknown Miss Ala,
>   You are probably surprised why some total strangers are writing to you. We are very obliged to you and grateful for your thorough care and protection of our sister and daughter and we tell you that you are an additional

member of our family. We send you the kindest regards and thank you. Be well and happy together.

Raizel

Ala's proximity to the German command at the Bureau brought its own privileges: more mobility around the camp, extra food from the officers' table, and soon, she was authorized to move to a private room outside the communal woman's barracks. She negotiated for another bunk and invited Sala to share the tiny paradise of privacy.

But Ala's patronage did not deter Raizel from exercising her prerogative as elder sister. She used her letters to assure her sister about the well-being of their large extended family, but also struck a serious chord. It was her duty to remind her sister of her responsibilities to her family, to her friends, and to God.

Sosnowiec
November 26, 1940

Dear Sala,

Yes, we did receive your letter and how much joy it gave us! I received the letter in the community office and I cried and cried, hardly comprehending my own tears.

Now, dear Sala, we received the greetings you sent through friends. But Mr. Merin and Mrs. Fani Czarna did not give us your regards. We were very upset at how they behaved, since you wrote that we should receive greetings through them.

Dear Sala, you told us that you don't have stockings. Unfortunately, we cannot help you in this regard. Blima, excuse the expression, goes about entirely without stockings. Just imagine! Since you left, she hasn't been working. You are probably getting the picture now. We are very distressed, but what can we do? However, we figured that the community office might send you some, if you just write to them. We have to send soap to you by any means possible. Right now, butter is unavailable and sugar only once in a while, and then only if you have the money.

Dear Sala, you can't imagine how happy we were to read that you have a special room and that you can be together with your "Alinka." Dearest Sala, how happy we are that you have a supervisor like your dear Ala: we have no words to express our appreciation for her. If you will permit us and you won't be ashamed of us, I will write her a long letter.

Dear Sala, if you possibly can, take the opportunity to learn typing, it cannot hurt. If I should have a chance, I will try to learn typing here, too. You are probably getting tired already of reading my letter, which isn't as interesting as yours, which are always more interesting and composed stylistically very well.

Something else, Sala: you write that you are a different person. Really, we would like to see you as a different person and you know for yourself in which respect.

Now, enough already! What else could I write you? As you know, everything here is as always. Thank God, we are all healthy and if we only could earn a little money and had no trouble, if Blima, too, might have some work, then we might even be able to help you a little. We all hope that God will not forsake us, one must not lose faith.

Raizel

When a few weeks went by without mail from Geppersdorf, Raizel grew frightened. In case some of her Polish letters had been discarded by the censors, she switched permanently to German.

Whatever the reason for the delay, her plea for more letters cut Sala sharply.

Sosnowiec
January 6, 1941

Dearest Sala!

Our ordeals are beyond words. How can you neglect us by not writing us for such a long time? One would have thought you would try, but no! Remember, there is a God and write, otherwise we'll go out of our minds. For days on end we have been worrying about what may have happened to you. Are you, God forbid, sick? No matter what, write us as soon as possible, for we are already crazy and sleepless from worrying.

Sala! I have to warn you again, Sala, in the name of our dear parents, particularly our dear mother, who cries all night . . .

Again, remember that there is a God. Write soon.

Raizel

Sala had already run through the supply of stamps and post-cards that she had brought with her and had received more from Kronenberg. But if she had a thousand pages, she could never write enough. Raizel was quick to reproach her, as if sending mail from a forced labor camp was a simple matter of putting pen to paper and flagging down the postman, as it used to be at home, instead of subject to a thousand dangers: censors at the camp and more censors at the Sosnowiec post office, the whim of a capricious camp official who might confiscate a precious postcard just to torment her, or a change in the regulations that would reduce the monthly quota for mail. Even if the mail reached Sosnowiec, it might be lost in the Council office, or destroyed by a careless postman.

She pleaded for some understanding, but Raizel was intractable. *"If you don't write, everything is lost,"* she warned. There were simply no limits to how hard they both must work to ease the suffering of their aged parents and to remain true to their faith.

Raizel had guessed correctly: Sala was mailing as many letters as she could, usually one letter every two weeks, but not all of them were addressed home. She had chosen to divert some of that precious quota to her friends. They too clamored for her attention, but it was not for their sake that she tolerated Raizel's nearly unbearable reminders of her parents' pathetic state. It was for her own sanity: she longed for the lightness of these exchanges with her friends, the occasional injection of gossip and trivia, their delightful irrelevancies. She needed to write to them. It was the antidote to her correspondence with Raizel, which invariably delivered a jab or two, and left behind a residue of guilt.

Her closest friends—the ones who had brought her to the train station in October—stayed close to Sala's family, knowing that their presence offered some comfort to her parents.

> Sosnowiec
> January 20, 1941
>
> Dear Sala,
>   We read the postcard you sent to your parents. Why don't you write a special note to us? Didn't you get our letter? What is new with you, what do you do? Write everything. There is nothing new with us, time goes quickly, just as usual. Only we miss you, we would very much like to see you and to know what you look like today. We'd be happy to get you the photo you asked for, and told your parents about it. All of us had pictures taken, but when you will come home and see us, you will have a lot to laugh about, because one looks worse than the other.
>   (Chana cannot write in German, and I write the regards for her.)
> Sala [Rabinowicz], Gucia, Bela, Chana

"Write everything," they demanded, but it was beyond her ability to explain. Her writing was constricted first by her limited vocabulary, then by the necessity to employ codes to evade the censor. To improve her chances of getting a letter through, she tried to minimize her complaints about the food, the filth, and the constant fear of being called to the Bureau for punishment, sometimes because she had been insubordinate to a guard.

She no longer bothered to inquire each day about going home. The increased camp population and Nazi staff were signs that the

Geppersdorf camp was becoming more permanent. As Raizel had noted, Merin and his representative, Fani Czarna, had refused to meet with family members, had not passed along Sala's regards, and had not bothered to reassure her family that she was well or that she would soon be home. But Raizel believed that Sala would return, at least temporarily: *"How can this be settled, who could you write to, in order for you to get a vacation?"*

When the letters stopped for an entire month, Raizel became frantic, and tried writing to Ala instead.

> Sosnowiec
> January 12, 1941
>
> Esteemed Ms. Ala,
>
> To begin with, please don't take offense at my taking the liberty to bother you. However, knowing that you are a friend of our dear sister and daughter, Sala Garncarz, we turn to you, asking a big favor, which perhaps will not be so big for you.
>
> We haven't heard [from Sala] for the past four weeks and are at our wits' end. Maybe you could tell us something about her. There is no point in writing to her directly because we already sent many letters, but received no answer. We are going out of our minds. Oh, our dear parents! If only you knew the bitterness with which they spend their days and nights. Please write us. Don't refuse us the great favor of letting us know what happened to her. I even went to see your brother, to see if he knows something about my sister, but all without success. My only hope is news from you. If only Sala could see our dear parents, how heartbroken and dejected they are.
>
> But enough. Please accept my apologies. Warmest regards from us . . .
>
> Raizel

There was no longer a consistent pattern to how long the mail took, or any assurance that a letter would ever reach its destination. Despite the "Z" mark, however, there was no evidence that each letter had been read carefully. Judging from the fact that the censors did not black out particular words or phrases, it was likely that they did not bother to omit specific references, but simply discarded the whole letter if anything seemed objectionable. Sala could not control the flow of mail, but resolved nonetheless to be more circumspect in her writing, to hint rather than explain, and to do a better job of covering up her fatigue and frustration.

Her days were filled with endless piles of laundry and mending. When an officer demanded that she improve on the already perfect hand stitches with which she had repaired his swastika band, she responded by throwing the cloth on the ground and stepping on it, right in front of him. He dragged her immediately to the Bureau. She escaped with a lecture rather than a beating, and returned unrepentant.

Acknowledging with a smile that she was young, fearless, and stupid, she shrugged off Ala's warnings. She did not care about the Nazis. If they did not beat her today, they would tomorrow. If it was meant for her to survive, she would, and if it was not, well, she was ready for that, too.

She had volunteered for a six-week stay, had sought this change eagerly, only to discover a perversion of freedom. How little any of them at home could understand this strange place, where everything was upside down. She could not live by the old rules, and surely Raizel would understand the pressures she was under. Even Raizel might deliver her lectures with a lighter hand, if she spent just one day at the camp, where a good day was one of hunger and fatigue. And the worst day? That could be tomorrow.

The deadline for her return was long past. She had filled up all the diary pages she had torn from her journal at home. The person who wrote those pages seemed to be another creature. In their hiding place beneath her bunk, her stack of letters was growing.

CHAPTER THREE

Sarenka

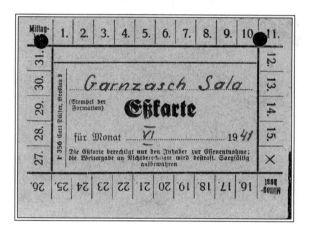

The Garncarz family gathered on Friday nights, grateful to be together and to have withstood whatever threat had surfaced during the week. Raizel reserved a few quiet hours of the Sabbath to pore over her sister's words again, puzzling over each nuance, considering new interpretations. On one letter, Sala had forgotten to sign her name. *"Why?"* Raizel inquired in her next letter. *"Oh, that this may mean something good!"*

Sala's friends brought their letters when they visited, but Raizel suspected that they received a different picture of life at the camp than she did. She frowned at the thought of the dangerous influences that her sister might encounter. There was a wealth of goodness in Sala, but she was young and vulnerable. Would she be strong enough to resist the pressure to compromise, to abandon the religious practices of their home? Raizel must remind her sister to uphold the highest standards. Sala must be prepared to make any sacrifices and remain faithful to God. She, Raizel, would demand no less of herself, even in these perilous times.

It was time to write. Salusia, her young niece, was eager to sit with Raizel as she composed her letter. *"The child doesn't stop pestering me. She wants to write something and doesn't let me finish. Well, she wants to please you. She says that she would love to [show you] something that she learned to write. I think you will like it very much."* Salusia added a sample of her best penmanship on the letter for Aunt Sala. Her innocent delight awoke Raizel's affectionate nature, which was always ready to celebrate the accomplishments of a child.

When Salusia was not beside her, Raizel found it harder to stave off the fear that had become her constant companion. Work and food were scarce. Even paper was too precious to burn in the stove, so if there was nothing to cook, her mother abandoned any pretense for the neighbors. Conditions were no better for the other members of the Garncarz family: Moshe David, who lived nearby with his wife and two children; or the eldest sibling, Miriam Chaya, who was also struggling to feed her family of four in the nearby town of Wolbrom. The war was a great equalizer: rich or poor, most families depended on the goods and services that were provided through the Sosnowiec Council. For those who could not afford to buy even those meager rations, communal kitchens served up to seven thousand meals every day.

Moses Merin's effective leadership had been rewarded by his Nazi patrons, who named him chief of all the Jewish Council of Elders in Eastern Upper Silesia. His sphere of influence now extended to the entire region, which gave him control over more than one hundred thirty thousand Jews in forty-five cities and towns. He reported regularly to Schmelt in Sosnowiec and to SS Obersturmführer Hans Dreier, chief of Jewish Affairs for the Gestapo, in the nearby regional center of Katowice. Dreier and Schmelt set the policies, and relied on Merin to implement their plans.

From a building formerly occupied by the chief rabbi of Sosnowiec, Merin and his central staff of 260 people coordinated a complex web of administrative agencies including labor, social welfare, finance, law, housing, education, statistics, and health: a complete shadow government. Hundreds of additional Council staff worked at satellite offices in Bedzin and other locations. Merin's organization was led by well-educated professionals in their early thirties; some were from Zionist organizations, as Merin himself had been; others had no religious or political affiliation. They were loyal to Merin and shared his belief that productivity through labor was the only possible strategy for survival. The Council staff regulated the food supply, enforced an evening curfew, and managed the mail service through a special Jewish post office. Merin created a large police force of Jewish men to patrol the streets and maintain order. The Council distributed signs for mandatory display in the windows of the few remaining Jewish businesses: "For Jews Only." In February 1940, all Jews were ordered to wear a white armband on the left arm, six inches wide, with a blue Star of David. They were not forced into a ghetto, but they were forbidden to walk on the main city streets.

The Council's large operating budget was funded by taxes and fines paid by Jews, and from payments received from Organization Schmelt. From a warehouse filled with confiscated luxury items, Merin and his staff dispensed a treasure trove of bribes—jewelry, coffee, tea, cameras, radios, suitcases, furs, and alcohol.

As Schmelt and his supporters had predicted, the heavily industrialized region around Sosnowiec was bustling with economic activity from eager German entrepreneurs. Huge construction projects were proceeding on schedule, and armament and textile factories were operating at peak capacity, fueled by the ready access to slave labor. By relying on Merin's larger staff, Schmelt had kept his own bureaucracy to a minimum, managing his expanding network of labor camps with fewer than twenty officials.

German businesses turned to Schmelt to provide labor, and Schmelt extracted the necessary number of workers through Merin. For some positions, a prospective employer went directly to the transit camp that had been set up at Skladowa Street to make a personal selection from the pool of men and women who were imprisoned there. The use of Jewish workers was officially discouraged, in keeping with Hitler's objective to dispose of all Jews and other undesirables. However, the non-Jewish labor force was fighting the war or otherwise deployed deeper into Germany. Eager to maximize profits, the companies dutifully filled out the necessary forms to document the unavailability of any alternative workers, and then turned to Organization Schmelt for human resources. In addition to paying a daily fee per worker, they were responsible for a few pennies of food and for the cost of at least one guard per forty Jews. Schmelt's office kept meticulous records and forwarded the information to regional headquarters every two weeks.

The Jewish slave market was generating a tremendous amount of money for Schmelt. Other than his small staff, Merin was his only expense. Based on the number of laborers, he paid a token amount to Merin, who also grew rich. He allocated some of the Schmelt money for the operations of the Council and sporadically distributed token sums to the family of the laborers.

Despite the considerable paperwork and regulations, Schmelt had more requests for Jews than he could fill. Compliance was strict: if the employer failed to pay on time, fell below the meager levels of subsistence allotted for each prisoner, assigned too few guards per laborers and let too many Jews escape, or subjected the laborers to conditions that increased the mortality rate beyond an agreed-to level, Schmelt could recall the whole labor force at any time or close the factory—and then transfer the company's assets to the growing portfolio of the SS.

As Merin's promises of a brief and remunerative tour of duty for the laborers proved illusory, he had a more difficult time recruiting volunteers. To raise money and add to the labor supply, he increased the tax for exemptions, and imposed more onerous penalties on the families of those who failed to report. Evoking his own Zionist credentials, he tried to convince the leaders of the local youth groups that the labor camps could be like the working collectives, the *kibbutzim* that they hoped to establish in Palestine. It was their duty, he argued, to help their younger members find employment, their only protection from worse repression. While some Zionist leaders accepted his arguments, others opposed Merin as a Nazi tool.

Merin took a different approach with religious leaders, declaring that his policy of selective accommodation would preserve as many Jewish families as possible. Indeed, the productivity and military importance of Schmelt's camps were now well known. After the first flurry of resettlements in 1940, there had been no wide-scale deportations or mass killings in Eastern Upper Silesia. Merin took credit for all of this, but met with considerable opposition from the influential chief rabbi of Sosnowiec. It was against Jewish ethics, the rabbi informed Merin, to sacrifice some people to save the rest: let the Germans capture the Jews themselves. Merin excluded the rabbi and his followers from future public meetings and prohibited all religious gatherings.

In the meantime, Merin had quotas to fill. He authorized the Jewish police force to ambush prospects on the street, and to conduct door-to-door searches of apartment buildings.

Merin traveled frequently throughout Poland and Germany. He visited Nazi headquarters, labor camps, and other Council leaders, often in the company of Fani Czarna. At the camps, they evaluated the conditions carefully, since the Council would be held responsible for replacing people who had become too sick to work. Unproductive laborers were eliminated in routine selections by the camp officials, usually every six to eight weeks, sometimes assisted by Merin or his representatives. Those selected were told that they would be sent home; in reality, they had been condemned to death. Auschwitz was convenient to many of the labor camps. As early as September 1941, Soviet POWs were used to test the effectiveness of the gas chambers. Unproductive Jews from Schmelt camps were among the next victims.

In addition to the camps located in Germany, Schmelt set up factories and workshops within Sosnowiec and Bedzin, supervised by Germans. Many of these were businesses that had been confiscated from Jewish owners. To qualify as many people as possible, the Council created professional training programs led by skilled craftsmen. One of the largest local workshops was a Wehrmacht uniform and shoe factory close to the central square of Sosnowiec, operated by Alfred Rossner. Although this too was a Schmelt camp, workers were allowed to remain at home and received a special identification card that protected them from deportation. Rossner went beyond the minimum services required for his workers, and provided a clinic, barber, and other amenities. Word spread about the humane treatment received by Rossner's laborers. Bribes of money, gold, and diamonds were offered, "birthday presents" from prospective workers seeking the protection of the Rossner identification card.

Schmelt, Merin, and German entrepreneurs had forged a highly profitable and symbiotic partnership. The three-way alliance supported the political and economic aims of the Third Reich—except that it was tied to the lifespan of a relatively small and healthy group of Jewish workers, "the Maccabees," as these young, strong men and women were called by some of their Nazi overseers. For Merin, the alliance also lent some semblance of truth to the premise that he was saving as many people as possible at the cost of sacrificing others.

Letters were delivered to the labor camps through the regular Reich mail. Neither Merin nor Schmelt had any incentive to stop mail delivery. It was good for business and good propaganda: a letter from a loved one meant that the person was alive and working, just as Merin had promised the anxious families. Even a sputtering flow of correspondence helped to stabilize the region and to avoid unrest, which could divert military resources and interfere with the lucrative Jewish slave trade. Since the mail was moving throughout the annexed regions anyway, it was an easy accommodation.

A second mail option was Merin's official post office at Council headquarters, where letters were delivered through a community mailbag. The Reich mail system was faster, Raizel noticed, and alerted her sister: *"Probably the best is to write by mail and after two days one receives the mail, while it takes 10–12 days through the community."* Former German Chancellor Hindenburg's profile was on the postcard stamps until 1941, when Hitler began to appear exclusively.

Merin's postal arrangements were considered the most reliable in Poland; when the resistance leaders of Warsaw needed to communicate with someone in Palestine, they sent a courier to one of Merin's Council offices and mailed the letter from there.

When the mail reached a labor camp, it was processed through the central office and usually given to the Jewish Elder, who also distributed blank postcards to the workers. Additional regulations were left to the discretion of the camp commandant. He could impose additional restrictions or a second censorship review—or simply fail to distribute the mail. Keeping old letters was officially forbidden. Some camps enforced this policy by requiring prisoners to return their most recent letter before they could receive a new one. Packages of food or clothing were allowed to pass through the mail, but they were opened first and any unusual or valuable contents removed. To check what was actually received, the sender would often itemize the parcel in a separate letter, and then ask the recipient to confirm the contents, as Raizel did when she asked Sala to *"let us know if you received the blouse and the soap. Write what was in the parcel."*

Sala usually received one or more letters each week, and was allowed to send mail every two weeks. She was not forced to return her old mail. Still, it was dangerous to keep any personal possessions. The barracks were often inspected without warning, and prisoners were severely punished if they were caught with anything that was deemed to be contraband. If an inspection was looming, Dr. Leitner sometimes alerted her, but she could not always count on advance warning. She took the risk, regardless of the consequences. She would make no distinction between letters that made her laugh, and ones that made her cry: she protected them all.

It was early 1941. Soon, it would be her seventeenth birthday, the first she had ever spent away from home. She allowed herself to think about a vacation, as rumors were sweeping through the camp.

News of her possible return had also reached Raizel.

> Sosnowiec
> February 14, 1941
>
> Dear Sala,
>   Oh, how happy we are, every time we get mail from you! Every time we get close to the end of the second week we get terribly impatient, hoping to get something from you . . . What do you think about possibly coming here on vacation? Whenever Salusia hears that mail from you arrives, she jumps with joy and the children keep asking when you will come on vacation. I forgot to ask you what kind of work you are doing, in the kitchen, or in your

trade? Now about the shoes: how do they hold up, are they still in one piece?

Your girlfriends haven't seen your postcard yet. They won't come here until Saturday. How much we long for you on Friday nights. Terrible. What can we do about it? You wanted it that way and it will all be for the best.

Raizel

Some of Merin's payments from Organization Schmelt reached the family. Inflation, however, was reducing their value. Schmelt took in more than 100 Reichsmarks (RM) a month for each Jewish worker. For a few months in 1941, the Garncarz family received 13 RM through the Council. In the Jewish districts of Sosnowiec, a loaf of bread cost 5 RM.*

Sosnowiec
March 12, 1941

Dearest Sala,

We were very happy about your card, but at the same time, we are very upset because we had counted on seeing you in person. Maybe you'll have a chance to come for Passover. Keep trying to get permission to come home for the holidays.

You wanted to know whether we celebrated your birthday, but the birthday card we sent to you was returned to us. We wish you happiness always in your future endeavors and, most importantly, we hope that you will come home soon.

Sala, if only you knew how sad our dear parents are. We talk about you endlessly. Our only consolation is that you're writing, that you're well and may you always be well. Salusia keeps reminding you to come home. She wants you to know that she can already write up to eight digits.

Now, write if you need anything. We get 13 RM per month from the community office.

*Estimates of the value of the RM range from four to ten dollars.

You wrote you will hear the megillah,* no matter what, which sounds like you're making fun, but I don't know.

I'm wondering why you don't write anything about Ala. Did you quarrel? But I don't really think so. Probably you just forgot to write [about her] . . .

Raizel

Nothing escaped Raizel's notice. Her suspicions about Ala proved to be correct, as she learned by chance when someone from Geppersdorf returned home. Once again, she deployed her most elegant handwriting and language to address Ala directly. Whatever the cause, she beseeched Ala to overlook her sister's shortcomings.

Sosnowiec
March 14, 1941

Dear Miss Ala,

As I sit down to write you this letter, I am sad and upset as never before. A Miss Leiber came to see us and brought regards from my sister Sala. When we asked whether she knew anything about her relationship with you, she replied, yes, of course she did, that things used to be fine between you and my sister, but that you were no longer speaking to each other.

Good Miss Gertner, can you imagine how this hit us? No, you can't, there are no words to express how this news grieved us. We can't understand how it happened. Sala always used to write that Miss Ala was like a mother to her. This is what she wrote: Dear mother, as long as I am together with my Ala, be reassured, and don't let anybody worry about me. No mother treats her child as kindly as Ala, my Ala, treats me.

And now this out of the clear blue sky, Miss Ala! On

---

*It is a religious obligation to hear the story of Esther, which celebrates a major victory over oppression and is read aloud on the annual holiday of Purim.

behalf of my dear and caring parents, on behalf of our sister, please forgive her if she did something bad. She certainly did not do so out of vindictiveness, it's probably just all a misunderstanding, which may yet be clarified. We implore you, please forgive her, she is still young and inexperienced, she meant no harm. She wrote in her letters that she considers you a great and divine person, the personification and embodiment of all that is good and beautiful. Everything I am writing, Miss Ala, is no exaggeration and 100% the truth.

Now could she have meant to hurt you, Miss Ala? Oh no! Three times no! You just misunderstood each other. I believe that someone with my sister's disposition can be forgiven and that you can easily restore your friendship. Surely, you will also do so on account of my parents, who have been dismayed since the moment they heard the news.

Miss Ala, anyone can make a mistake in life, particularly when one is young and innocent, as is the case here. Don't be unforgiving, it would be unlike you, Miss Ala. Just think of my unhappy parents. I believe, no, I am sure, that you will not refuse my request.

Now enough. I ask you not to misunderstand me. I wanted to hear good news, and this depressed us all very much.

I am sure that my letter will be successful. Will you please, despite everything, give our regards to Sala?

I conclude with warmest regards to you, respectfully,

Raizel Garncarz.

In those few hurried moments at the Sosnowiec train station, Ala's pledge was received by Sala's mother as a covenant. Now, almost six months later, the nightmare that had enveloped the family would seem even worse if Ala had withdrawn her protection. Whatever the cause of the estrangement, it was a profound source of woe. With her characteristic directness, Raizel set out to heal the breach for the sake of her suffering parents.

She succeeded. The heat of Raizel's appeal, her intense fear that some nameless evil had isolated her sister from her important mentor, melted the temporary frost that had, in fact, arisen between the two friends. Ala brought Raizel's letter to Sala, and they read it together, Ala dismayed that she had added to the sorrow of the aged parents, and Sala confounded at how carefully and accurately Raizel read her letters. They vowed to mend the rift.

It was Bernhard Holtz who had come between the friends. Ala made no secret of her interest in men, though she also declared her determination to stay clear of serious entanglements. She had already been at the center of more than one romantic intrigue at Geppersdorf. It was therefore a great surprise to Ala's friends when she succumbed to the relentless attentions of this brilliant young university student ten years her junior. Bernhard took advantage of his place at the Bureau, where he sat next to Ala, to pursue her with a single-minded passion. Ala dismissed his courtship at first, proclaiming her intent to humor the boy, but she finally surrendered to his siege. Soon, they were using their Bureau privileges to arrange secret assignations, employing Sala to carry messages between them. They nicknamed her "Sarenka," the deer, for her ability to dart around the camp with speed and grace. This was definitely not a fit subject to share with Raizel.

Ala wrote this, presumably as a note to Bernhard or a private journal entry:

There is so much longing, a tremendous yearning for love.

A deep silent love is flowing between us. He knows, I know, we both know, that this love is hopeless.

And yet, we're carrying it in our hearts, carefully, like a precious object entrusted to us, a holy object, a wonderful treasure.

His entire being and soul quietly flows into a tremendous feeling. He is driven to me as if by a cultic force. He gives me something subtle and timid. He is young, so young. His blood is boiling . . . restless often.

We are feverish with love.
He is asleep now. I hold myself back . . .

Sala had grown impatient with her role as go-between. She was jealous of Ala's divided attention, and was more than a little shocked by Ala's indifference to social conventions, and her open relationship with Bernhard.

Camp courtships were common, not only for the elite Bureau workers. When the attention of the guards wandered at the morning roll call, friends, relatives, or aspiring lovers quickly passed notes down the line of standing prisoners, one hand over the other, until the rumpled paper found its way into the intended pocket, accompanied by a meaningful glance in the right direction. If they were lucky and were together at a food distribution, the couple might progress further with another pantomime of smiles and gestures, or perhaps a phrase or two spoken under the breath. The bravest of the men might even risk a beating by a late night visit to the women's barracks.

Sala had no lack of admirers herself: her appeal was as fresh and sincere as Ala's was mature and sophisticated. Chaim Kaufman, the earnest young shoemaker, was her most persistent suitor. He attended faithfully to her shoes, pouring all his fervor into keeping "Salusia's" feet warm and dry. She tried to respond with grateful friendship, unsure of her own feelings.

Soon, it was her turn to have notes from Chaim slipped into her hand.

Geppersdorf
March 1941

Dear child!
   Forgive me for not fulfilling your request, but I really could not. Salusia, I can share or not share your opinion, but as far as arguing about it, this is as good a time as any. Please, must there be a special reason, or a special day for confessing? Does God only listen to us on the Day of

Atonement? At a time of hardship, or moral depression and uncertainty, every person feels a need to judge and to think.

I would not want you to discuss this "matter" with my dear parents, not only because they are holy to me, but because they are innocents, not only older, simple people, but also decent and honest ones.

I regret that you had no time to consider that matter which means so much to me . . . And so our roles change, you play the hero, and I am proud of you. I look at you with different eyes, my Salusia: grown up, wise, stable, not to mention other attributes about which I will not talk now . . . right?

I understand that you are taking your first mature steps. You say in a trembling voice that we may ask; no, dear kitten, we will not ask, we will demand, and we will fight; so help us God. It is not at all true that our demands or wishes are modest, as you say. Actually, why would they have to be modest, don't we have the right for a better tomorrow, are we not equal with the whole world? Maybe it's because they humiliate us, especially you, so young and beautiful and blooming.

You say that you expect a modest future, but are you not sinning against yourself?

As you foresaw, Sala, your letter did not satisfy me, except that it was from you. No, I was not satisfied, so I hope you will correct it.

I am sending this late so you could read it in bed. Good night my dear, happy dreams, and do write. Are we agreed? Sarenka, this letter is not all that good, but it is from

Chaim Kaufman

He had been pursuing her for weeks. She had already asked her older cousin Rozia for advice. Chaim's family was from Olkusz, the same town where her cousins lived: perhaps they knew each other. Rozia responded promptly.

Olkusz
February 28, 1941

Dear Sala,

To begin with, please excuse me for not writing German very well. You write much better but, as you know, we never learned German . . .

Sala, you ask me whether I know Chaim Kaufman from Olkusz. I know him very well—but tell me, why do you want to know that? I can tell you that he is from a good family. The parents are very fine people. He is a thoroughly decent person and has a good reputation. By trade, he is a tailor, but that is all I can tell you about him.

Dear Sala, are you quite frank when you speak with him? I'll write you again to find out if you spoke to him without a chaperone.

Cousin Rozia

The very thought of a chaperone at Geppersdorf was ridiculous. Still, it was comforting that Rozia knew Chaim and his family, who owned a local bakery. Chaim was not the kind of scholarly and religious young man that her father would favor, nor would his fervent Zionism have met with much enthusiasm on Kollataja Street. But he was handsome and serious, younger and more approachable than Dr. Leitner and less of a genial clown than Hokilo.

Geppersdorf
March 1941

My dearest and beloved child,

. . . It's not worth talking about my past, which is too poor and too grey to be immortalized, a pale thing. And then quiet took over, and God only knows how long this peace would have lasted if not for you. And so, after a long quiet period I fell in love again, a love that is pure, as pure as you are. Still, I cannot accept the expression "time will tell." No, no, time will not show anything any more. I lost

74

confidence and do not trust time, I have been injured
because of Fata Morgana.*

I decided for good or bad that if you let me down (just
because you say, "time will tell"), I will finish my life in
obscurity and I shall not share my tragedy with anybody.
That is my first and last confession. Evenings, I shall drag
myself around and my only desire will be for peace and quiet.

My beautiful one, do not misunderstand my only
request. And why should I not be sincere? What would my
life's situation be, if such would even exist? You are my
everything: my future, in hard times and downfall (of
which there are many), at times when I feel capable of
anything, and also when human despair reaches a pinnacle,
a culminating point in times of doubt.

And then, when I consider everything lost, I remember
my Sala, my little enchantress, and my heart feels lighter
right away, oh how much lighter! Some kind of force takes
hold of me, quiets and soothes me. And if I am so lucky
that my "mischievous one" is good to me, then I see myself
as happy as I have never seen myself before.

And so, you must think it is enough already of my "Muse."
If I felt better, I surely would have written differently.
Unfortunately, I do not feel well. And so I interrupt, repeat
interrupt, because I am not finished. Now you know me, so
judge me, but understand me before you pass judgment.

Should I expect an answer?

                                        Chaim Kaufman

P.S. If you are still irritated, don't judge me.

His words were sweet, and he declared his intentions in a direct
and honorable way. At home, where the parameters of courtship
were clear and accepted by both parties, she might have known how

*Chaim suggests that his love has been an illusion. Fata Morgana, also known as
Morgan le Fay, was the fairy enchantress of Arthurian legend.

to respond. Here in a labor camp, a few weeks past her seventeenth birthday, she was adrift. She had hoped to benefit from the experience of her pretty cousin Rozia, who was already engaged to Leib with the blessing of her parents, but Rozia's advice was unrealistic. A chaperone! Nor could Ala advise her. Their quarrel had been patched up; since Bernhard was genuinely fond of his Sarenka, the lovers folded her tenderly between them. But Ala was a charming libertine, for whom any notion of propriety was irrelevant. She already exerted a powerful influence on Sala. Raizel would have been stupefied to see her sister accepting a cigarette from Dr. Leitner, or retrieving half-smoked butts left on the ground by guards, and smoking with Ala. Rolling cigarettes for their father at the end of the Sabbath had always been one of Sala's treasured tasks—but she had never smoked herself. Women never did.

As if sensing the pressure on her sister, Raizel was ready with a timely lesson on courtship and the standards of behavior in their community. She had exciting news to share: their beloved sister Blima was engaged. Raizel savored every moment of the drama.

Sosnowiec
March 27, 1941

Dear Sala! Mazel Tov! Mazel Tov!

It's 9:30 in the morning. I'm going out to the street. The postman is on his rounds. He comes down the street from No. 9. I go toward him. My heart tells me that he may have something for us. I resist going to the street, I have to wait, I can't be foolish. But as he comes closer to our house, he has already noticed me. What a surprise, two postcards at once. Imagine what that means to us. I took them with me to read . . . Finally, I came home, and what do you think? Mother comes toward me carrying a card, also from you, so we have three cards all together! What a great holiday it is today! We are cheered and happy when we get mail with good news from you. Even better, you are reconciled with Ala, and we wish you good luck.

But my wishes for mazel tov are not about that! Blima is engaged, actually only a pledge, but it was important enough that I couldn't hold back from writing you: I want you to dance as much as you want, be happy and content. But wait, do you think you are rid of me? Oh no! Not yet. I have to tell you everything exactly as it happened.

On Thursday afternoon, Blima hears from the matchmaker. What's going on, we ask her? The suitor has come! In the evening, Blima comes in with "Goldberg," an engaging and nice enough fellow. Nu,* the face was nothing special, just like all men.

On Friday, we asked her if this meant a pledge, but she didn't want to answer yes. Meanwhile, I don't know why, but he didn't come to visit.

On Sunday morning, the matchmaker comes again, and now the in-laws are asking to meet. Father actually goes there, taking our brother Moshe David with him. Don't be mad at me, you are probably impatient already, but you have to know everything exactly, so I must tell you. . . .

[Goldberg's father] said, I ask you for nothing more than one thing: a pledge. I like the bride, the rest is not important, not money, not furniture. I know that she is your child, and if you had more, you would offer it on your own.

Imagine, father comes home, mother goes for flour, Blima for honey cake and our brother-in-law David for a bottle, and in one hour the pledge was given by the groom.

People praise him very much. Everything will be good if only they are happy. Nu,* you are saying now, enough, right? But now we have another great joy: you and Ala have reconciled. You can't imagine how happy we were to hear that. Thank God that I wrote a letter to her and explained

*A Yiddish word, usually a half-question expressed with a shrug, as if to say, "What did you expect?"

that it wasn't your fault. Remember not to have any more misunderstanding between you.

You have to excuse me: at this moment I'm in a tumult. But it will pass. We will send you the photograph of our dear parents.

I end with the warmest greetings and kisses for you from everyone.

Raizel

The joy of Blima's engagement was short-lived. Several serious illnesses struck the family almost immediately. Raizel withheld the news, but her troubled thoughts seem to have broken her concentration. Her writing jumped from subject to subject, and her script betrayed her anxieties. For long letters, Raizel often drafted first on a separate piece of paper before mailing a clean copy. She filled her pages with a range of handwriting styles, varying from an ornate and italic calligraphy, to small, neatly formed letters, as precise and compact as a typewriter. But lately, her writing had become erratic. The more she rambled about dancing and celebrating, the more suspicious Sala became. Raizel was filling up too many pages with too few words; such profligacy of paper was unusual—and alarming. She was crossing words out. Was this a deliberate signal, a jumble of codes and innuendo, or did the messy papers suggest a disorder of another kind?

Sosnowiec
April 24, 1941

Sala!

If you would know how much we would like to send you good news. Oh! how you would enjoy it. And maybe it will really happen. How wonderful it would be if we would one day be happy. You are not against that, right?

Do you know why I write so much? Because as long as you read, we are together. Sala! Write to us a lot, a lot. If you have the opportunity, don't let it pass, always write . . .

Dear mother is making potatoes. I must remember to

eat, although for two days I haven't felt well. God forbid
that I am sick. I just need to eat more. My heart is beating
a bit too fast today, but I am already much better.

You asked if we longed for your shouting? What do you
mean? Imagine, now I sleep with dear mother. Are you
envious? I think so.

You are not yet free of me. Why do you say that you write
on the floor? Don't you have a chair? That too interests us.
Everything! Everything! Are you already tired of me? Maybe
I will remember something else. Don't laugh at me, even
though this is not so nicely written. Every second, I
remember something else, and then something else, so that
you will have more to mull over. What you probably want
is for me to irritate you. So I do it for your sake.

Salusia has new shoes . . . [my student] sends regards.

Fond regards and kisses from our dear parents. Greetings
from your sisters.

Raizel

In fact, there were grievous scenes at home, a collision of problems on too many fronts. Sala pieced together the story with help
from her friends.

Laya Dina's husband, David, had been captured in a roundup. Ever
resourceful, David had wrangled yet another reprieve and was back at
home, but they feared that he would be taken again. Most pitiful of
all, Moniek, Laya Dina's little boy, had contracted pneumonia and was
dangerously ill with a high fever. There was no money for medicine.

Moniek began to recover. Raizel was relieved, but the approach of the
Passover holiday brought fresh reminders of their family's pitiful state.

Sosnowiec
April 24, 1941

Sala,

. . . First of all, [Moniek] is out of danger. Thank God,
thank God. Oh Sala, if you could see him, how he looks . . .

but it doesn't matter. The crisis is over . . . the child lay in
bed for more than one week, with a temperature of over
104 degrees, but finally, finally. I can't give you more details.
If you knew how it upset our dear mother that I am writing
to you about the child . . . he should only now regain his
strength . . . I read your card to him, and he enjoyed it very
much. He asks only why you write so little.

Well, Sala, you wanted to know about our [Passover].
You can imagine the scene, how it was for our dear father,
who used to come home in the evening after prayers at the
synagogue. He broke out in such a painful weeping that he
was not able to say a word. So, there was complete silence
during the whole Seder.

You may wonder if it's possible that we had everything
prepared for the holiday. It's over, and we will do better
next time. For matzo, we had just enough coupons. Even if
we had more, we couldn't have eaten, because Moniek was
so very sick . . .

Raizel

David was not the only one who had been seized on the street.
Sala learned from her friends that deportations were increasing in
randomness and violence throughout Sosnowiec. Sala Rabinowicz
said that her two brothers were visiting "Mrs. Skladowa" and might
be Sala's "guest" soon, a coded message that meant that they were
being held in the transit camp at Skladowa Street and were being
sent to Geppersdorf. *"We are all dazed . . . and hardly get together,"*
her friends wrote in a group letter in early May. There were constant
references to the rampant inflation and the difficulty of finding
any form of employment. Even Bela Kohn, the most affluent of her
friends, sounded worried. She and her brother and sister were still
working with their father in the family store on the main street of
Sosnowiec, but the store had been taken over by Nazi managers.
"We have had various problems," she noted, without going into
details.

The payments from Schmelt and Merin were increasingly rare. Raizel bemoaned the absence of even these meager wages and was struggling to earn some money by tutoring students in Yiddish and Hebrew. She also alerted Sala to a new mail regulation: all letters would henceforth identify the writer and recipient as Jews by adding the middle name of Sara or Israel. Soon even the gravestones in the Jewish cemetery were required to include these middle names.

Sosnowiec
May 12, 1941

Dear Sala,

. . . Don't worry, we are healthy and we are eating. It's interesting, Sala, why the community office hasn't paid us anything for seven weeks. I don't know why. They say here that where you are, you get paid, is that true? We need the money very badly. But what can one do? I work with father a little. Blima doesn't have any work . . .

Don't wonder when you see that I sign my name as Sara. We have to now: every woman must add Sara [to her name] and every man must add Israel.

Raizel

Unbeknownst to Sala and her family, the boundaries of the war continued to shift and expand. In the spring of 1941, German forces were engaged in North Africa against British and Australian armies. The Nazis had invaded Greece and Yugoslavia. Now three million Nazi troops were looking eastward, to Russia. On June 22, Hitler attacked his former ally and his army began the drive toward Moscow, followed closely by Nazi death squads who swept up the Jewish men, women, and children along their route and executed them in mass, open-air shootings.

In Geppersdorf, the spring thaw initiated an accelerated pace of construction on the highway. More officers and guards kept arriving, which increased Sala's workload. All of her mending was still done by hand, and she could barely keep up. The long-awaited sewing machine had not yet arrived.

One morning, two guards came in and told her that she must leave the camp immediately with them. Frightened, but distracted by the novelty of riding in a car, she caught a glimpse of the town of Geppersdorf through the window. They drove along the long and charming main street, which was divided by a narrow strip of grass. The houses were mostly two-story buildings, colored in soft hues of goldenrod, pale pink, and light green. Just past the main square, they parked in front of a picturesque cottage.

A sign on the door announced the residence of "W. Pachta, Tailor." The door was opened by a heavy-set, middle-aged woman, her hair neatly coiled. She introduced herself as Mrs. Anna Pachta, and cordially welcomed the guards inside. They pointed to Sala, still standing outside the door with her basket, the regulation blue and white armband wrapped around her sleeve. She was introduced as the Jewish seamstress who would be working on the Pachtas' extra sewing machine, an arrangement struck between Mr. Wilhelm Pachta and Ackerman, the head of Geppersdorf. The guards left.

Mrs. Pachta asked her name and brought her a cup of tea and a plate of cake; Sala's eyes watered from the unexpected sweetness of the food and the simple kindness of her hostess. She looked with eagerness at the solid furnishings, the abundant decorations, and the well-appointed workshop, where brightly colored fabric samples and threads were hanging from every inch of wall space.

Soon they were joined by Elfriede, Mrs. Pachta's daughter, a pleasant-faced young woman in her early twenties, who walked with a pronounced limp. Elfriede placed Sala at one of the sewing machines. They worked side by side while Elfriede talked about her family and showed her photos of all of them, including her brother Herbert. Her father would be returning soon from a trip to the city of Breslau, Elfriede explained, and he would be so delighted to meet their new seamstress. Her brother was also away, but she offered no explanation of his whereabouts.

They finished their work and still had time before Sala had to return to the camp. Elfriede and her mother piled a plate high with fresh food, and she ate gratefully. When the guards arrived, she was sitting quietly by the front door, the uniforms folded neatly back in the basket.

Like her chance meeting with Ala at the train station, Sala's assignment to the Pachtas' cottage was a lifesaving piece of luck. Raizel began to add blessings in her letters for the Pachtas. She had no good news of her own to report.

Sosnowiec
May 17, 1941

Dear Sala,

At the moment, I am at Laya Dina's with [a friend]. Sala, you asked why we are writing so rarely. Don't be shocked, Mother was sick but, thank God, she is well again. Besides we are getting ready for the day when you will have other guests. So if you don't get mail from us, don't be worried, it's just that my head is not "with it."

Now, Sala, don't be upset that we have not sent you a parcel yet. We'll try to take care of that today. I would much rather not have told you, but we haven't had the money for packages until now. I'm just bringing this up to explain why we haven't sent you any food. Now we're sending you just some cookies. Please write us what you need most, because if we get something from the community, we will send it to you right away. But since we have no money, we have to know what you need most. We are very eager for you to get something from us.

And then we spend every minute in great anticipation of your visit over the holidays. Oh, how Mother and all of us will rejoice!

Please give our regards to the entire Pachta family and convey our thanks for how well they take care of you. Otherwise, there is nothing new, we are all well, thank God. We have only a little work, Blima has no work at all.

Moniek has recovered, thank God . . . Salusia asks why you
write her so little. Regards and kisses,

Raizel

P.S. Regards to Ala. We're waiting for you.

The Pachta family wanted to know everything about her family,
and their sympathy revived her. When Raizel wrote that Moniek, and
now their mother, had fallen seriously ill, the Pachtas mailed money
to her parents in a letter that arrived in Sosnowiec like a gift from
heaven. They followed up with a special gift for her niece Salusia.

Sosnowiec
May 21, 1941

Dear Sala!

What a surprise, how totally unexpected—and then, the
doll! I was, as usual, visiting Laya Dina and someone told
me that a young girl was at our home and brought this
package for us.

I'm going to try and give you a lot of reading to do! I
will convey everything exactly and clearly, so that you will
think you are at home.

The most important thing at the moment for you and
for all of us is that dear mother is better, she already has
gotten out of bed for the second time, a miracle for us.

[We had a visitor] who told us about you and Ala, that
she is everything for you in that strange place, and that
means so much to us. Therefore, on behalf of dear mother,
be more obedient, don't do anything to upset her, show
your appreciation, because it is very bad when one is forced
to be away from one's home, unprotected and far from all
that is familiar. So hold on to [Ala] and guard her like the
apple of your eye, because she is a treasure for you.
Remember, listen to her. Don't do anything to aggravate
her . . .

Salusia plays with her baby doll very carefully: she's

**afraid to disturb it. She asked me to thank you. And please
thank the Pachta family for sending it. Even more thanks
to them from dear mother for their conscientious supervi-
sion. May God repay them for their care of you.**

Raizel

When Mr. Pachta returned from his travels, he was just as welcoming as his wife and daughter, although more reserved. She continued to wonder about Herbert, the missing son. They never talked
about him, although once, she thought she heard them whispering
his name. As she waited for the guards in the afternoon, she sometimes studied the framed photograph of a clean-faced man who was
younger than Elfriede, somewhat stern in countenance, but with the
same fair hair and pleasing features.

She began to feel that she had been blessed with a second family,
this one proudly German and gentile and sincere in their concern for
her welfare. This was not the reunion for which she prayed, but she
was grateful.

On a warm day in June, she arrived at the Pachta home with her
usual basket of mending. The door had hardly shut behind the
guards when Elfriede announced that the weather was much too fine
to spend indoors. She and her mother had a secret plan for the day.
The Pachtas were proud of their old family and their position as the
tailors of Geppersdorf, and they wanted her to see their charming little village. Sadly, the sewing machines are broken today, Elfriede
declared, draping a uniform over the machine, and removing Sala's
blue and white armband. Let's walk into town, she said, as if it were
the most natural thing in the world.

Sala allowed herself to be swept away by Elfriede's enthusiasm.
They started at the village square. She was suitably impressed by the
old brick and stone Catholic church that stood in the middle of the
square and listened dutifully to Elfriede's proud recitation of its
six-hundred-year history. They continued along the main shopping
street. It seemed impossible that such things existed, a world of
summer gaiety and prosperity, not a cloud in the sky, not a Jew in the

street—except one. They passed a group of German soldiers. Mrs. Pachta took her by the arm and they entered a grocery store where they bought provisions for supper. When she looked back, the soldiers were gone. The grocer walked with them outside his shop, where he remained, keeping his eye on the shoemaker across the way, who stood at his door with his hands in his pockets. What would the Pachtas' neighbors have thought if they knew that their silent visitor was the daughter of Rabbi Josef Garncarz?

She returned to the camp, eager to share her adventure. But Ala had amazing news of her own. For months, they had discounted the rumors of a vacation. Raizel had been devouring these stories, hoping that her sister would be allowed to return for the Jewish New Year services in September. The rumors were true—except only for Ala.

Ala left in June. Sala Rabinowicz was the first to meet her.

> Sosnowiec
> June 18, 1941
>
> Dear Sala!
> We received your card, for which I thank you very much. You are upset that we write so little but the reason is that we can't write well in German. So our friends ask that I write this to you.
>
> We learned a lot about you from Ala, nonetheless we would rather have a personal conversation with you.
>
> Keep your eyes open and plan for tomorrow because we don't only live for today. We have a great future before us. Go down your path, the one that Ala shows you for your benefit. I believe that this one will be right. We don't have words for her, because she is such a wonderful person. It is such good fortune to be loved by someone like her. Think about and cherish all of this: good will come to you.
>
> We are sending you some clothes, and also a few homemade cookies. So please write to us soon that you have received everything in good order.
>
> Sala Rabinowicz

Bela Kohn was the next friend to fall under Ala's spell.

Sosnowiec
June 23, 1941

Dear friend,

We were so pleased to meet your dear Ala. She is even nicer than you described her. She told us everything, and it was almost as if you were with us. We all liked her and now there is no need to wonder why you like her so much.

Dear, what is new with you? When we see you, we'll probably have to spend an entire year talking, and we will tell each other everything. Nothing new here, business as usual. We're working and time goes by. Ala reprimanded us for writing to you so rarely. She is right. I hope you will forgive us. You know us—although we are too lazy to write, we are always with you in our thoughts.

Kisses and regards to dear Ala. We were taken by her very much. All of my family also sends regards.

Bela

Ala had smoothed her entry into the camp. Everything had been more bearable when they were together. It was wonderful that her friends were impressed by Ala, but no consolation to Sala, who missed her friend and lamented her new solitude. Other people had also been given permission to leave, but it never seemed to be her turn.

The Pachta family comforted her. They gave her some money to send home, the first time she had been able to do so. Raizel acknowledged the gift with gratitude and continued to be optimistic that she would see her sister again soon.

Sosnowiec
July 9, 1941

Dear Sala,

Oh, what a wonderful surprise to receive money from you for the first time! We are not only happy because you sent so much money, but because you must be gratified to have earned it with your own two hands.

But what can we do [about coming home]? Can you really not get time off for vacation? How terrible. But we keep hoping that you will come unexpectedly. This week it was rumored that you had come. Some people even said that they saw you. Perhaps they had a premonition of your arrival, may God grant us that this is true.

First, please thank the Pachta family on behalf of our dear parents, who cannot put their gratitude into words. May God give them a good life for being like parents to you.

Now you probably want to know what's happening at home, particularly the enormous inflation. The 10 RM come in very handy. . . . Otherwise, nothing new to impart. At present, David is home. We are all well, thank God, the children too. They are so much looking forward to seeing you. Maybe, maybe. Now I'm concluding with kisses and regards from our dear parents and all of us. Special greetings to Miss Ala and the Pachta family.

Raizel

It was still more frustrating when Ala came back to Geppersdorf, settled in briefly, and then announced that she was leaving again. Apparently, she had found temporary employment at home. She promised to fight for Sala's release, but this additional leave had been arranged by Ala's family, and she could do nothing for her friend.

Sala's disappointments mounted when she learned that she was about to lose her precious connection to the Pachta family. The camp was finally receiving its own sewing machine, and there would be no excuse for her to travel. Days of nourishing food, civil conversation, and the gentle, caring ways of a generous family came to an end. On the last day, they kissed her warmly and gave her photographs to remember their time together. *To dearest little Sala, in memory of Geppersdorf,* wrote Elfriede. She and her parents promised to visit, showing her the official notification they received from Ackerman thanking them for their service to the Reich.

For months afterward, the Pachtas kept their promise. They came to the camp and walked directly to her room until late summer, when Geppersdorf was enclosed in barbed wire for the first time. After that, they stopped at the front gate and asked a guard to deliver their packages of food and clothing. Sala was allowed to accept the packages and to exchange a few words with them. New guards grew suspicious of a German family's interest in a Jewish seamstress, however. One day, the Pachtas stopped coming.

Sala's friends wrote to her about catching sight of Ala a few times. Finally the day came when Ala visited Raizel and her parents. It was strange to picture Ala on Kollataja Street, still more incongruous to think of her sister and her friend talking about her, sitting side by side, and sharing a single postcard that they composed together:

> Sosnowiec
> August 16, 1941
>
> Dear Sala,
>
> Imagine, while I am writing this, I am sitting with your true friend, Ala. I can see why she is so dear to you and why she deserves our greatest respect and appreciation. Miss Ala spent quite some time with us, she herself, in person! How much we love her, and we pray that she will always have a good life! She asked us to give you warm regards and says that she already sent you a parcel. Oh, we will write you a long letter. But now it's getting late, it's just [before the Sabbath], and Miss Ala also wants to write you something, shouldn't I let her? Now, warm regards from our dear parents and all of us. Good Sabbath.
>
> Your sister, Raizel
>
> Dear Sarenka,
>
> Here I am writing again. Your sister is with me. I was at your house for an hour. Your parents were very happy. I

talked to your beloved father and mother, they are very dear.
Sarenka, please send me a certificate right away, saying that
you worked in Geppersdorf, and specify the dates. Have it
signed by the senior [overseer] and by the Jewish Elder.

Today in the community office, I read your letter. Why
don't I get mail from you?!?! Huh?

Warm regards,

Ala

Sala took Ala's request of a certificate from camp as a good sign:
perhaps it signified that she too was eligible for a vacation.

Sala had tried to prepare Ala for the grim reality of her family's
one-room apartment, and perhaps that was why Ala had delayed,
and visited first with Sala Rabinowicz and Bela Kohn.

Raizel wrote again the next day, this time without the restraint of
Ala sitting beside her.

Sosnowiec
August 17, 1941

Dear Sala!

I finally found the time to write, but now, I have more
time than usual. I quickly answered your letter so you
wouldn't complain and be nervous. I wrote a postcard,
and your loyal and dear Ala added some lines as well.

As you can see, Ala is back at home already. You're
probably curious to know why Ala came to see us. We really
didn't expect that she would show up since she was on leave
and did not have enough time, even though I asked her so
urgently. I was surprised when you wrote that we should
visit her and invite her.

In any case, all that is over. One should only remember
good things about a person. I only want to explain the
reason why it seemed that we were not paying attention to
her. I learned by chance [on Tuesday morning] that she
had come already [on Monday night]. But even when I

heard it from her mother, I didn't believe it. I thought if that's true, then they will let us know; if not, then I will not go to her. If they don't want her to see me, that's fine, then it's better not to go. And so matters stood. We have had enough disappointments . . .

Everyone knew that she had come home and asked if she had visited us, and we answered in various ways for the sake of appearances.

Then completely unexpectedly, this Friday the 15th of August between about 5 and 6 in the afternoon, I was sitting on the steps and mending dear mother's stockings, when I thought I saw the figure of Ala on the [second] floor, and before I really recognized her, I heard someone asking for the Garncarz family . . .

Oh yes! So, I was right, I had seen correctly. Naturally, I invited her into our room, and naturally, I didn't know what she thought. I figured that you would have prepared her about our apartment. It's better to have an idea about the reality so you aren't disappointed. From what I observed, Ala knew very little about what to expect from our apartment.

Okay. Now, you should know what Ala said. Well, really nothing special, only that she cannot live without you, and praised you so much that we really enjoyed it, and she eased our minds saying that you are doing well. But the thought that you are there now, without her, disturbs us. We know that such a friend as Ala is not to be found again among a thousand people.

All that you wrote about her was not a lie: we, too, finally see it . . .

She asked me if she could come with me to the post office and I consented. Then we went to her brother and she took out the package that she had prepared for you, and she showed me what she had put in, but we left late because we talked so much. That's why we stayed and wrote our postcard at her place. You are probably happy that she wrote something on it too. She wouldn't let me use my postcard, and told me to write on hers.

Because we were delayed in sending the package, we had to wait until today, Monday. Should she have sent you stale baked goods? Unimaginable! So she waited and prepared fresh. Yes, that's Ala completely. She is concerned and cares about you, as her parents do about her. About our dear parents, unfortunately, sadly, we can only sigh. She should have success in her work, she is really a good person, she should reap goodness.

And something else: when she was at our house, imagine, she had cigarettes with her and left them for our dear father, even though we said that he had some, and really, it was true. No, she said, I made the cigarettes myself for your enjoyment. Is it possible to say enough about her in words? Probably not.

Oh, now I have to stop about all this. Nu, what else is new with you, do you feel well? Continue to stay cheerful and everything will be fine. Everything with us is as it was, we are healthy and hope for good news, and are happy that you are loved by all. We talk so often about you that you must often have the hiccups!*

Stay well, you will be drunk with my letter. A thousand kisses we send you, also from our parents, Laya Dina, David, and children. Salusia kisses you very much. Special greetings for Mr. Holtz. Good night. Be well. Convey our greetings, if possible, to the Pachta family.

Raizel

She was alone, without her sisters, her friends, and now she had lost Ala and the Pachta family. The time passed with unbearable slowness.

---

* That is, "We're always bringing you up," or the equivalent of "Your ears must be burning."

Raizel kept up a steady stream of letters that predicted her sister's imminent return.

Sosnowiec
September 11, 1941

Dearest Sala,

What is there to write when you are coming home any day now? If only you could stay, then you'd still get something out of life.

We received your card today and I never saw father cry so much. When I started reading it, I couldn't believe what I was reading and I choked on my tears, father started crying terribly, mother and Blima, too, it was a terrible sight.

The holidays will be here soon and I know that you, my sister, wish to spend the time with us and you hope for a better life than you have had until now. How well you put that, Sala, and we all agree. Understand that we talk day and night of nothing but you and how much, how much we long to enclose you in our arms.

Yesterday I met Ala. We talked for a while and she said that everything will be all right and she consoled me by saying, "You will see, you will soon be together with your daughter and sister."

May you always be with us . . .

Raizel

When Sala had almost given up hope, she was visited in her little sewing room by the same SA guard who had accompanied Merin's secretary, Fani Czarna, to the camp. Now they were both veterans, two of the few people who had been at Geppersdorf for nearly a year. At his request, she was sewing some miniature dresses for his granddaughter's doll as a Christmas present, and he came occasionally to check on her progress and exchange a few friendly words.

Her name was on the list for the return to Sosnowiec. He had come to give her the good news himself. She was afraid to believe it, but soon the official notification came from the Bureau. She would be home for three days. They warned her, however, that she must return or no one else would be allowed to have a vacation.

The next day, she was on her way back to Sosnowiec.

It had been a little less than a year since she left. More than one thousand Jews had been rounded up and sent to work camps. The restrictions imposed on those who remained in Sosnowiec—their numbers swelled by refugees from other parts of Poland—continued to tighten. Every week the rations decreased and police actions became more violent. Rumors flew about worse conditions in other parts of Poland, and about Nazi camps from which no one had ever returned.

As she entered the courtyard of her apartment building, she thought of how it looked just a year ago, when they still dared to celebrate the autumn festival of *Sukkot*. To fulfill the tradition of eating outdoors, it was the custom of the neighbors to set up dining tables in the open area. The women formed a human chain, passing plates and utensils from hand to hand until the food reached the men gathered in the courtyard. Her father presided regally over his modest table, proud and distinguished in his long, snowy beard and formal coat.

Today, the courtyard was deserted. She climbed the stairs and was home.

The embraces left her weak and dizzy. She looked from face to face: her sisters seemed so tired; her father looked like a man of one hundred and twenty years. Her mother never took her eyes away from her daughter but remained silent while Sala and her sisters chattered without taking a breath.

The room was clean and held a warm memory in every corner, but little else. She had not fully understood until now: her family was still poorer at home than when she left, the food nearly as pitiful as in camp, the sense of anxiety swirling like a dank smell around the walls of the apartment. Only her niece Salusia glowed with energy and charm, almost too old for the wooden doll sent by the

Pachta family, but she had eagerly brought it to the family reunion to be properly introduced to Aunt Sala.

Despite Raizel's strong protestations, she petitioned her parents to allow her to spend one precious night with her friends. Once again, they walked as a group to the home of Sala Rabinowicz. The city seemed like one giant camp. Streets that were once familiar were now forbidden, and her friends warned her to stay close to the buildings, in case they encountered any soldiers or police. They passed other Jews, all walking quickly to reach their destination before the curfew. Instead of armbands, they now wore the yellow Star of David.

She and her friends stayed up and talked all night. They asked Sala about Geppersdorf and listened attentively, but she felt the futility of explaining life at the camp even to them, her dearest friends. Not that hunger and fear were strangers to them, but they were home, still surrounded by familiar sights and sounds. On this special night of relative freedom and renewed friendship, she could not bear to evoke the loneliness and deprivation of the camp. She preferred to hear their tales of romance and marriage, haircuts and dresses. Although they were still only seventeen, they all had boyfriends. Married men were less likely to be deported, so matchmaking had accelerated to a breakneck pace. Gucia had met her beau in the local factory where she worked. Bela was nearly engaged, and Hela would soon be a bride. The rest of them were at earlier stages of courtship but expected to be married before long.

With great fanfare, they presented her with a recent photograph of the group. She was the only one missing.

Sala did not see Ala until the last day. Ala began by telling her gently what she already suspected: her friend would not be returning to the camp at all. After shuttling back and forth between Sosnowiec and Geppersdorf, Ala had been given a new position with Moses Merin, and would be moving into her own apartment in the nearby city of Bedzin. She had worked hard to bring Sala home for this vacation, and promised Sala's parents that she would never stop working on their daughter's behalf. She even raised the possibility of informally adopting and educating Sala after the war.

They walked to a local portrait studio. Sala's hair was gently curled and pulled back from her face, and she wore Blima's old houndstooth-trimmed jacket. She laughed when Ala embellished her outfit with the same braid-trimmed hat that she had worn at the train station on the day that they left for Geppersdorf. The photographer fussed over them, and finally posed the two women in profile, her clear-eyed gaze holding Ala's until the camera released them.

She returned home from the studio, her conscience pricked at how she had indulged in a night of laughter with her friends and a visit with Ala instead of devoting all her time to her parents and sisters. She went to the drawer and retrieved her bright coral blouse, but left her journal there, locking the drawer once again. Raizel gave her some family photographs of their brother, Moshe David, and his family. The time was so brief that she had not seen him, or their oldest sister, Miriam Chaya, who lived too far away to have visited during Sala's vacation.

They talked with feigned confidence about her next visit. It will come soon, she reassured them. But without a local job or an official waiver, Sala could not refuse to return to the camp. She had heard stories about other families who were arrested if a relative failed to report for forced labor duty. And she believed what she had been told—if she stayed behind, no one else would have their vacation. How could she deny another prisoner the joy of seeing family and friends? At least she had work at Geppersdorf. One more hungry mouth would only add to her parents' problems.

The farewell this time was portentous; it was impossible to pretend that they did not fear its finality. Her sisters and mother fell back when Josef Garncarz approached her. She knew that he would utter the words she most dreaded. As if to preempt them, she rushed forward with her response, saying "Yes, I will be back! I'm here now, aren't I? I was away—but I came back. Be strong, I will return!" But he went on, in a direct and solemn way that she would always remember. "My dear child. I will never see you again." He put his hands on her head and blessed her for health, for life.

CHAPTER FOUR

Small and Grey, Old and Young, the Poor and the Rich

She was alone, standing near the window of a neighbor's apartment on Kollataja Street. Through the glass, she saw across the open courtyard and into another room of another apartment. A naked body lay on a wooden board. Four men stood, two on either side. Slowly and rhythmically, they dipped large cloths into a metal tub and washed the dead man, first his head, then his right and left side. They turned him with great care and washed his back. They did not speak but prayed silently as they worked, now drying him with fresh cloths and wrapping white linen garments around his head, torso, legs, and feet.

She woke with a start. Her second year at Geppersdorf had begun. In the darkness of the barracks, she could still see the fading vision of the *taharah,* the ritual purification of a corpse. Had she witnessed this as a child?

She had been sent back to the barracks to sleep with the rest of the women. Without Ala next to her at night, her dreams were a jumble of childhood memories and fears that persisted well into the dawn.

As her friend, Chana, anticipated, she had not recovered from the shock of being home.

Sosnowiec
September 22, 1941

My dearest Sala,

It almost feels as if you were sitting beside me still. My dear, everything passes. One always hopes for the best. How did your first day after the vacation go? Are you still under the spell of your experiences or have you come back to reality?

Chana

She was lonelier than ever. Her return to camp coincided with the holiest days in the Jewish calendar, a time for contemplation and confession.

Even Raizel permitted herself a bitter outburst.

> Sosnowiec
> September 24, 1941
>
> Dear Sala,
>   We are happy that you got back to Geppersdorf safely. May God always look after you. [It seems] that He turned away from here. We imagined a different world, but now we have come to [the holiest days of the year] and how can one have such angry thoughts? And you wrote that you have prepared yourself for the day of judgment, which is good. . . .
>   Our dear parents ask you to observe [the day of fasting for] Yom Kippur.
>
> Raizel

Her friends wrote more often now, though they still complained about the difficulty of composing in German. Her visit had given them a better understanding of how she cherished their chatter, the more idle the better. For a few minutes, she could imagine that she was together with the whole group.

Bela wrote her letters from her father's store, where several of the friends usually added their regards:

> Sosnowiec
>
> Dear Sala,
>   . . . We know how it must be for you there, especially since Ala left and you are alone . . .
>   Last Sunday, we laughed a lot—it rained every five minutes, and every time we tried to go out, it started to rain again. The rain finally stopped around seven.
>   When you read this, you will surely laugh that I am

writing about such unimportant things, but I want to write you about everything. You know very well how hard it is for me to write in German.

Chana cut her hair and it looks very good, rolled up underneath.

Well, I wrote about everything in detail, but I am sure that you will read more between the lines . . . answer me and try to write not just a postcard but a letter, so that I will have a lot to read.

The girls from the store send regards.

Bela

If there was any consolation in Ala's absence, it was the promise of receiving her letters. Ala was her teacher. When her first letter arrived, Ala's voice was as strong and lively on the page as it was in person, provoking Sala to laughter and challenging her to know her own heart.

Ala's brisk pronouncements blew through the barracks, bringing in the fresh air beyond Geppersdorf.

Bedzin
September 24, 1941

Sarenka, you giddy girl,

I know, you were disappointed, but I couldn't help myself. I know that I spent too little time with you [when you were home], but you have to understand why. To begin with, the vacation was short. Then my work, going home, even the bad weather, everything interfered this time.

But don't think badly of me, and don't lose hope. There is no reason why you shouldn't trust me. I felt your reticence quite keenly. There is, Sarenka, no excuse. You are younger and should have a little more understanding of etiquette toward your elders. We can't always say what we want to say, or all we want to say. In the camp, I protected you and surrounded you with warmth. You miss my caring, certainly, my golden precious, but Sosnowiec is different; and besides, I was in an exceptional position. I hope that you will get to know all my good sides better—those you know and those you don't know yet. Everything in its own time. The next time, Sala.

But now you have to be a good girl. Don't cry and pout. Who can and will understand me, if you act in such a foolish way? You're silent—why? Write what you think, including the most minute details. Don't be afraid, I always think of your release, just be patient.

I have remained the same Ala, even though I have so many possibilities and opportunities to become someone else. I am amazed myself: to be as attached to the camp as I am, is rare. Believe me, Sarenka, I am very sorry that you couldn't stay with me. Do you remember the hours on Saturday when you came into my bed early in the morning? We amused and puzzled [everybody]. You wrote very well about how you feel about the camp. Sarenka, are you still in such a pessimistic mood? I consider myself lucky to have so much work. In this way, day after day passes quickly . . .

Sarenka, keep trusting me, I kiss you, as always, you beautiful girl. Give regards to all women. Write me, clearly and in detail, okay? I ordered skin cream for you, I'll send it together with the photos the next time.

Yours, Alinka

Ala was working as a supervisor in one of the Bedzin workshops under Organization Schmelt. If anyone could manage to find Sala a place, it would be Ala.

Bedzin
October 16, 1941

Little, beautiful Sarenka,

Please excuse me for not writing to you in such a long time. I am so busy and have so much work. If only you knew how tired I was when I got home. Now I live on my own, my dear mom is in Sosnowiec. I don't know how many times I've been saying, "Oh dear, if only Sala were here; oh my, I miss Sarenka very much," particularly now that I live alone.

Just imagine, the two of us on our own! Sarenka! You won't recognize the room: newly painted, the furniture rearranged, clean, pleasantly warm—only, I'm all alone. I brought the [grammophone] over here last Tuesday, so I brought back my music world. Our photos, the new ones with you and me and the one with Bernhard are all over the place, even though I look so ugly in them. Everybody admires how beautiful you are. I look like a witch, really, no kidding! Your cream sits in the drawer, I didn't have a second to take care of it, but truly next week . . . Are you angry?

Your sister came to see me in Sosnowiec on Monday . . . We talked for a long time. I thought you might be offended since the vacation, but she reassured me that this was not the case. To the contrary, you supposedly said that you could not live without Ala. I am very happy, little, beautiful girl! I also like you very, very much. Do you know that? I love you and shall never forget you. Our time together in the camp—your kindness to me, all that you did for me—I have not forgotten, Sarenka. For the time being, however, things have to be as they are, but you will convince yourself that I am neither bad nor ungrateful . . .

Now, I kiss you, beautiful Sarenka, write soon.

Yours, Alinka.

Sarenka, patience! It's good that you have a job! Send me a certificate right away that you have been working there for a year.

Ala visited Raizel several times. She continued to work on Sala's release.

Bedzin
November 6, 1941

Beautiful little Sarenka,

I'm still working until late at night. The [registration for identification cards] has ended. I'll have more time now and will get everything done. Don't worry, the time when you will be working here at the shop will start soon. Believe me, when I look at the girls as they run back and forth, just as you used to, I am very upset. You have been in the camp for 13 months already. Do you remember how you leaned your little head on me on the train? Nobody can and will understand me as well as you do!

When you come . . . Oh, my God! I implore you, be obedient and well behaved. Keep clean and, as always, work hard. Yes?

. . . Today the first snow fell. Everything is white all around. I'm waiting for mail from you as well as from Bernhard . . . Before long, the three of us will be together again (all good things come in threes), God willing. Patience, courage, and don't lose hope!!!

Yours, Alinka

Ala was well aware that she continued to be a subject of conversation at Geppersdorf, despite her absence, and complained that someone was spreading a rumor that she had married: *"Damn that gossip!"*

As 1941 came to an end, Ala was nostalgic about their time together in the camp, and commiserated about Sala's voluntary conscription. There seemed to be no reunion in sight for the friends.

Bedzin
December 15, 1941

Beautiful little girl,

Now it's "December '41" again. A year ago, we were together. Do you remember the plans we made? I thought you would be released from your service, but since I had my doubts, I started my own initiatives on your behalf. I'll have no problems with you! Let me know if you have "seamstress" under the category "occupation" [in your papers]. I won't wait until Bernhard will be released, but will try for both of you.

You have no idea how angry I am that you have to suffer so much through no fault of your own. You signed up voluntarily in your sister's stead, then later I ignored you a little bit . . . but enough of past sorrow and vexation! Sarenka, just don't lose hope and don't even cry because of the delay. I'm always thinking of you. I miss you in more ways than you can imagine.

Sarenka! Are you healthy? Write me something! What can I send to you? Pa! I kiss you on your mouth.

Yours, Alinka

Germany's grip on Europe continued to tighten. France, Belgium, Denmark, Luxembourg, and the Netherlands were well into their second year of occupation. Greece and Yugoslavia were invaded in the spring of 1941. Although Hitler had to abandon his plan for a December 1941 victory banquet at the Kremlin, his armies continued the assault on Russia, with casualties mounting on both sides. Following Japan's attack on Pearl Harbor and Germany's declaration of war on the United States, American troops joined the British and Russian forces. The world war now touched five continents.

Labor camps in Poland and Germany were considered to be an essential component of Germany's war economy; and Schmelt continue to win concessions that increased the number of camps and workers he could offer to German businesses. Geppersdorf expanded yet again. Some of the first wave of administrators were assigned to new posts, including the Jewish inner circle. Kronenberg had returned to Sosnowiec, and someone else now served as the Elder. Dr. Leitner had new responsibilities at several Schmelt camps, but he continued to visit Sala at Geppersdorf and bring her cigarettes. Hokilo was transferred to a different construction site. *"I heard that you got married,"* he wrote to her, *"but I don't know whether this is true. If it is, I wish both of you good luck—and now I can just go ahead and get married, too, right??"* His jokes had apparently not gotten him in trouble when he visited her family in Sosnowiec—he was even a favorite with Raizel.

Only Bernhard Holtz and Chaim Kaufman remained with Sala at Geppersdorf. Bernhard sat at the same desk in the Bureau, more disconsolate than even she without Ala. Both of them hoped for Ala's intervention on their behalf.

Chaim continued to pursue her aggressively. Although she had tried to signal her ambivalence, it was too hard to explain during their brief and unplanned conversations during food distributions and occasional encounters at the Bureau. He too had been sent home briefly. During his vacation, he had visited her family and hinted to her parents of a future betrothal. She denied vehemently that she had made any such commitment. His talk of marriage was foolish: how could anyone fall in love in this strange place? He was humorless, possessive, jealous. Now that he had met her parents and sisters, and Ala was gone, he acted as if he had been awarded custody of her. He seemed to know when she had received mail and was always pestering her to allow him to add a few lines. Raizel seemed to be encouraging him, sending him regards and messages in her own letters. *"[Chaim] always used to add some lines,"* she noted. *"Why not now?"* The talk about their relationship had even reached her cousins in Olkusz: *"He is very much in love,"* said her cousin Rozia, who had met with Chaim during his vacation.

He kept pushing her for an answer.

Geppersdorf
[undated]

Dearest Sala,

Do not be surprised by my letter. It is autumn, dark and gloomy and raining, as I am inside my heart.

I am writing because I cannot take it any more. I waited, observed, and what's most important, I tolerated. But what of it? I tried to understand, I wanted to understand you, all in vain. Still, you don't give me any reasons for your change. So here I am again, asking why I don't deserve something better. I can't answer that; please tell me the answer. Sometimes I get the impression that you are trying to make me face some fact—if so, just tell me. (Although I suspect that you do not think about it at all.) How much has changed during our stay in the camp! There will be more changes. And yet you toy with my love? You want to lead me away from a direct path, but where are you leading me?

Please speak up. I am not dictating to you. By now, you probably know everything concerning me: I aspire to have a friend for good or bad, the kind whom no power could tear apart. In short, that's the truth. My beautiful one, even though I expect a positive answer, I ask you for a definite answer because only that will point to my life's future path. Please consider it, dearest. And please don't misunderstand me.

I send you my affectionate regards.

Chaim

What she wrote or said hardly mattered; he interpreted her responses in accordance with his own expectations. But she was no longer the uncertain teenager of 1940. Belatedly, he discovered that he was courting a stronger and more decisive young woman.

Ala had taught her well. She continued to learn on her own, a keen observer and careful listener. As one of the original Geppersdorfers, she found that she had some advantages. Those who arrived in the early days had acclimated to the camp when it was smaller. She had many friends among the small group of workers, camp guards, and officers who had arrived at the camp in the autumn of 1940. Her German was now fluent. Her skill as a seamstress had won her some respect and privileges. Her months with the Pachta family had strengthened her physically and emotionally. Perhaps all these factors would provide at least some protection against a random transport to another camp.

Because she worked directly for the Germans, people at home believed that she had extraordinary powers. *"I heard that you are able to obtain great favors,"* a friend wrote. She was asked to intervene on behalf of relatives, and sometimes for total strangers. *"Dear Sala, please be so kind as to do my brother's laundry,"* someone asked, with a sad reminder that the young man was mentally ill and illiterate. A neighbor's husband was sent to Geppersdorf and his wife begged Sala to cook for him. A friend asked her to write a letter for her brother every fourteen days. *"Ask him if he needs shoes and is his linen still in one piece?"* wrote another worried acquaintance.

She had prejudices of her own to overcome when she was asked to look out for her landlord's son, who had been sent to Geppersdorf and was struggling to remain religious within the camp. The Beglmacher family was wealthy and owned several businesses and buildings in Sosnowiec. Before the war, the landlord had traveled back and forth to America, the only person of her acquaintance who had ever crossed the Atlantic. Sala relished his tales of Chicago gangsters and Shirley Temple. But the Kollataja Street landlord had often been cruel and unforgiving when her father fell behind in paying the rent. Now the rich landlord's son and the poor rabbi's daughter ended up in the same place. She pitied the young man, thinking of Raizel. He had to be flexible, she counseled him, because the alternative was being sent away to someplace worse than Geppersdorf. When she received a precious package of unleavened bread for Passover, she gave it to him.

Whatever she could share, she did. Her cousin Abram Grunbaum was her special charge through much of 1941. He was Rozia's youngest brother, and she entreated Sala to look after the teenager, although her "baby brother" was not much younger than Sala. Rozia's expectations were high, and she did not hesitate to berate Sala for neglecting him: *"We heard that our Abram has trouble with you and that you have not been nice to him. How can you do this to him? How can you not be a cousin? . . . Sala, understand it is the first time he is away from home and he is still a child, after all, and he has no friends and you are a girl."* Rozia also voiced her complaints to Raizel, who warned Sala that her neglect would make the elderly Mrs. Grunbaum sick.

Rozia's opinion soon reversed itself. From her initial harsh criticism, Rozia grew warm in her praise of Sala's guardianship.

Olkusz
May 7, 1941

Our dear cousin Sala,

Today we received a postcard from our dear child. We all cried with joy because of the good things he said. Dear Sala, how can I express our gratitude for the kindness of your heart, as Abram has now described it to us? You cannot imagine our joy. I don't know how to thank you, dear Sala. Father asks for God to bless you with only good things. Mother says thank you and wants to kiss you and speak with you in person. My sister and I know that for the good things our cousin has done for Abram, God will repay her in the future. She will be as happy as she hopes to be. . . .

We ask ourselves why Abram has been moved to another room and I think this is also your doing, dear Sala. Our only concern, dear Sala, is that you never write us. You can't imagine how much we love you for your good heart. Hopefully, we'll soon be happy together.

Please tell my brother that we already sent him a package. Give him regards and kisses from me. My parents send their regards and kisses, and please let us know what we can send to you.

Rozia

Abram's mother died. Rozia wanted to spare him from reading the sad news in a letter and, at her request, Sala secretly met with Abram and arranged for him to recite the proper prayers for his mother.

As she had advised the landlord's son, work was their only protection. Moses Merin preached this message in his public speeches, in handbills plastered on street corners, and in newspaper articles that appeared in the few remaining Yiddish newspapers. More important than money was an identification card validated at an authorized place of employment. It was no longer sufficient for one family member to serve in a labor camp, as they had believed when the Council's first letter arrived in 1940. *"If I don't get work, I'll have to go away someplace else,"* Raizel worried.

Some of Sala's friends had already received their identification cards in the local Schmelt factories or "shops," such as the one in Bedzin where Ala worked. Bela Kohn and her siblings worked in her father's former store, under its new Nazi managers. Bela hoped that her new husband would be allowed to work with them in the store. Gucia was excited to have found steady employment in a local factory that was building cribs for government-run nurseries used by German working mothers. Her job was to whitewash the slats, nothing dangerous or heavy to lift, and the factory was clean and well managed. She worked from six in the morning until four in the afternoon. Her mother had given her permission to eat the lunch provided at the factory, even though it was not kosher; with wild inflation, and food supplies being cut every month, this was no time to be fussy, her mother said.

But Blima and Raizel had only temporary employment, as Raizel fretted in nearly every letter. They stood in long lines at the Council offices, hoping to find a steady position with one of the local factories. Without valid identification cards, they were vulnerable to the frequent roundups. Raizel used a code to alert her sister to the threat of deportation: to be caught in a "wedding" meant a summons to the dreaded Skladowa transit camp. Raizel had already been brought there once and released, and she and Blima remained at risk unless they could demonstrate proof of employment.

The victims were becoming younger: in the middle of the night, the Jewish police entered the Rabinowicz household and took away Sala Rabinowicz's younger sister Frymka, who was fourteen years old.

Her name was on their list. Frymka's father appealed to Moses Merin, reminding Merin that the Rabinowicz family had already sent two sons to Geppersdorf. Merin refused to intervene, and argued with the father that his daughter would be better off in the labor camp. Frymka went away.

Searching for alternatives, Raizel hoped that Ala's family might have enough influence to find the sisters a place in a local factory, or borrow a sewing machine for Blima. The Garncarz family had no political friends and no money for "gifts," the bribes without which there was little chance of obtaining work. Raizel and her mother decided to make a personal appeal to Ala's brother. Their trip would have been accomplished quickly before the occupation. Now, there was only one tram, attached as a separate car behind the regular tram, staffed by Jews and marked with the inscription, "Only for Jews." It was too crowded to board. To make the trip by foot, Raizel and her mother had to avoid the main streets of the city, closed to Jews.

Along a circuitous path of detours and alleys they trudged, taking hours to reach their destination.

> Sosnowiec
> November 8, 1941

Dear Sala!

Oh! what shall I write? Why haven't you received any mail from us? Why? . . . Why? . . . Why does one even write to you? If I didn't worry about causing you uneasiness, then I would be silent, because I have nothing cheerful to tell you. My dear! Weeping, oh weeping—one can do a lot of that. I would rather not tell you about the ways in which our hearts are bloodied, but I must, so that you will know why we don't write to you often.

Every day brings us new sorrow . . . If you have money, you're in, but without money, you have no help.

Yesterday, dear mother was again at Ala's brother to weep out her bitter heart. Ala hasn't come recently. Mr. Gertner

spoke very politely with dear mother, but there is no help
in sight for now. He will try to arrange a sewing machine
for Blima, but who knows if he will be successful. He did
say that he would telephone Ala in Bedzin. Our future is
dark.

Sala! Sala! What shall I write to you. On top of everything else, I wound up at the wedding. Imagine: our dear
parents don't stop weeping. The weather outside is dismal
and dark. It's snowing and raining.

Good day, good mail, good mail, good mail we await.

Raizel

Less than a week later, Raizel was relieved to report that Blima
finally found work, although their friends were attending more
"weddings."

> Sosnowiec
> November 13, 1941

Dear Sala,

You're probably wondering why you haven't received
any mail from us for several days now. But don't worry.
Remember what I said—that you shouldn't worry about
us when our minds just aren't up to it. But, thank God,
Blima is now in the shop: after great efforts and "gifts,"
we succeeded.

A second [trouble] took place in town. Imagine, I was
invited to a wedding. [One of your friends] already left to
go there, but I didn't go because I wasn't home when the
invitation came.

Raizel

At last, Blima had work. But not Raizel. She was still standing in
long employment lines every day and desperately trying to avoid
another roundup.

When the holiday of Chanukah arrived, the festival of military victory and religious freedom had acquired new symbolic resonance.

Sosnowiec

December 16, 1941

Sala,

Chanukah! The first day of Chanukah. Our dear father kindles the lights. He's singing, while crying all the time. Oh Sala, you know how he would like to see his children together, and we—our dear mother, Blima, me, and even the candles themselves—weren't exactly cheerful either.

Our dear father looks at the clock . . . yes, the time has arrived when I can write to you, and so, I'm writing. Now Sala, what's new with you, are you well, are you still working? I even didn't want to write because we all believed that you would come on vacation. Isn't it so? Or maybe you want to surprise us. How nice! Shall we not believe in that? Why? Maybe they told us the truth, that you will come home again, but when will that be?

Don't be angry that we didn't send you what you wanted. We can only send something once a month, not when we want to, and thus we're excused. Meanwhile, we hope to hear good news from you. Here, things are as usual, nothing special. We are, thank God, well. There was a big wedding here, to which I wasn't invited.

Raizel

Merin's Jewish police became a familiar sight during roundups. The rank and file wore white and blue caps, embroidered with the name of their unit; officers wore a special belt. They received a salary from the Council and were promised immunity from deportation.

At first, Merin had used his police for routine street patrols. Their role evolved, however, as it became more difficult to find laborers for Schmelt. Using lists continually updated by Merin's staff, they were dispatched to specific homes and brought people to the transit camp, using clubs and brute force if necessary. Only slightly less forbidding than the SS, they executed whatever sanctions were ordered by the Council, from confiscating ration cards and valuables, and evicting people from apartments, to taking hostages from families suspected of harboring fugitives. When the Gestapo wanted to arrest a Jew, they contacted the Council police, who brought in the alleged criminal, who might have broken the curfew, crossed a prohibited street, or stolen food. Some thirty people were executed as criminals each week. Although SS troops armed with guns were available for backup, Merin and Schmelt preferred to rely on the Jewish police. They knew the intricacies of the neighborhoods and were better than the Germans at ferreting out people in hiding.

As the chief of all the Jewish Councils of Elders in Eastern Upper Silesia, Merin was granted a special pass that allowed him to travel throughout Poland and Germany, even to Prague, to meet with his colleagues and report on his activities. He traveled to Berlin by train, but within Poland, he was driven in his private car; his chauffeur boasted that he was the only Jew to have been issued an authentic Reich driving license. In Lodz, Merin toured the hospital and consulted with his counterpart Chaim Rumkowski about ghetto management. They had much in common. Both used their Council positions for personal gain. Their egos knew no bounds: Rumkowski printed his name and image on Lodz ghetto stamps and currency, while Merin introduced a lottery, which used cards with his signature.

Until 1942, Merin could boast that conditions in Sosnowiec were far better than in Lodz. He could point with some justifiable pride to the relative safety of at least part of his community. All this was about to change.

Organization Schmelt had been living on borrowed time since its inception. Schmelt demonstrated that Jewish slavery was a boon to wartime profits and productivity. But it did nothing to advance the Nazi goal of racial purity. In fact, the unusual status of Schmelt's network of camps was an annoying obstacle to the achievement of that goal.

The organization of a high-level meeting to discuss plans for the complete annihilation of the Jews signaled the demise of the Schmelt camps. SS Lieutenant General Reinhard Heydrich, chief of the Security Police and Security Service, was in charge of implementing the Final Solution. On January 20, 1942, he convened a special meeting in an SS villa on the shore of Lake Wannsee near Berlin to coordinate the relevant government agencies.

The meeting took ninety minutes. Fifteen men, all high-ranking members of the Nazi government, pledged their cooperation. They agreed to synchronize their efforts to meet the goal of complete eradication of the Jews as efficiently as possible. Technical details were left up to Adolf Eichmann, secretary of the meeting, and head of the Department of Jewish Affairs of the Reich Security Main Office, who brought to the task his considerable experience in carrying out Hitler's anti-Semitic agenda in Germany and Austria.

It would take months to have everything in readiness for the disposal of the eleven million Jews that Hitler would control if he completed the conquest of Europe and the Soviet Union. Careful coordination and allocation of resources was particularly necessary at a time when Hitler's troops were attacking in Russia and in North Africa, and had recently launched a U-boat offensive along the East Coast of the United States. More than a half million Jews had already been murdered, mostly by Nazi execution squads sweeping through whole towns in Poland and Russia. However, mass shootings were less practical in the urban areas of western Poland. Gas chambers had already proven their superiority, and construction of the first death camps was under way. Eichmann's challenge was to deliver the Jews to their final destination.

While alternative killing protocols were being investigated, Schmelt's labor camps continued to operate at full capacity. Schmelt's allies argued vehemently against the disruption of major construction projects or assembly lines that were the primary source of essential war materials such as munitions, airplanes, tanks, radio tubes, and

poison gas. Private industry bolstered this case; the dwindling numbers of available workers made the Schmelt Jews indispensable. A
compromise was reached, and yet another reprieve was granted.
Some Jewish labor would be permitted for the use of the military.

Schmelt's office in Sosnowiec expanded. He added forty Jewish
women to the staff, who entered the building by a special rear entrance.

Raizel knew nothing of Wannsee or Schmelt, nothing of what had
been set in motion. She was enjoying the respite of a few weeks when
no wedding invitations arrived, and Blima was working. She did not
know that her fate, and that of most of the people she knew, had
been determined by distant bureaucrats.

It was a moment when she could return to one of her favorite
themes: the moral education of her sister.

> Sosnowiec
> January 1, 1942
>
> Dear Sala,
>
> Well, now we're already in '42, how time goes by!
>
> You are right, Sala, about the passing of time. It's
> amazing that you're finally realizing this—and now you
> want to know how to live your life. Truly, one must always
> accept as correct the advice of a father, a mother or a sister,
> and be obedient. As time goes by, it can never be recovered.
> But you shouldn't reproach yourself: spend the time
> happily, without worry, don't let your thoughts stray to
> anything that will be distressing.
>
> Finally, you have come to realize that only your parents
> are fully devoted to you; friends are only so on the surface.
> It's true that we don't help you at all, we can't send you any
> packages, but our thoughts, our thoughts are always with you.
>
> Raizel

After Wannsee, the pace of deportations seemed to slow down.
Merin urged his constituency to appreciate their relatively good
fortune. Just compare Sosnowiec and Bedzin to the plight of the rest

of Europe, he declared, where *"the leaders of the German and Czech Jews have lost their heads."* His Jews, the Jews of Eastern Upper Silesia, had orphanages, schools, and factories. His welfare department ran twenty-eight public kitchens, which fed about 40 percent of the total population. With a staff of thirteen Jewish doctors and twenty-six assistants, the health department operated a hospital, nineteen clinics, and ten dental clinics, and made fourteen thousand annual home visits. His Jews were allowed to write and receive mail, unlike the Jews of Lodz, who could no longer correspond abroad or even with relatives elsewhere in Poland. Nor were his Jews confined to ghettos, as they were in Warsaw, where many of the 500,000 people were homeless and begging in the streets, or in Lodz, where 164,000 people were packed into 1.5 square miles, typhus and tuberculosis were raging, and the mortality rate was appalling. Those Jews had no power, Merin asserted. Even Rumkowski was weak. Only he could talk directly with the Nazis, and only he had succeeded in reducing the number of deportations through artful negotiation and bribes.

Merin continued to solicit volunteers for Schmelt. He lectured tirelessly among the increasingly wary religious and youth leaders about the importance of satisfying the Nazi demands for labor. In these perilous times, they could not afford to protect the weak—defying a central tenet of Judaism, Maimonides' principle that the rescue of many lives does not justify the sacrifice of an individual. *"I stand in a cage before a hungry and angry tiger,"* Merin declared dramatically at a public meeting. *"I stuff his mouth with meat, the flesh of my brothers and sisters to keep in his cage lest he break loose and tear us all to bits."* To the dismay of the rabbis, Merin began to compare himself to Moses, freeing the Jews from slavery in Egypt. He confessed to an aide that he had heard an inner voice calling for him to redeem his people from bondage.

In the spring of 1942, Merin introduced a new procedure in the smaller cities around Sosnowiec. All Jews and their families were ordered to assemble in a central location for the validation of work identification cards. Accepting the importance of having a proper card, the Jews showed up on the appointed day. The unusual requirement to bring all household members raised questions, especially when most of those grey-haired people had been kept carefully hidden from watchful Nazi eyes. Nevertheless, most Jews complied, and the procedure went smoothly: cards were stamped and everyone returned home. From the small town of Olkusz, Rozia reported that her elderly father received a summons. *"Today, fliers were passed around in our town asking people to report to the Council for labor. Imagine, even Father received such an invitation."*

Old age was no protection, nor was youth. Parents of young children had been mostly spared until now, but Raizel feared that her brother, Moshe David, was in danger. Many families had more than one person who had already been deported. Sala Rabinowicz and her little sister Glika were still at home with their parents, but her sister Frymka was in a Schmelt camp at Neusalz, and her two brothers were with Sala in Geppersdorf.

Marriage could not save anyone, yet courtships went forward.

> Sosnowiec
> March 1, 1942

Dear Sala,

After such a long time of not writing, we are together in the small room and decided to write you something about us. We sit and we wonder about what you are doing, what you are thinking, maybe also about us, oh, we are not worth your thinking about, because after so much writing and asking [on your part], we don't do anything about it. But you also have to understand that it isn't the same as when you were here, we are very burdened and every day brings new torment, so that we don't have the time to write even a few words to you.

For us nothing is new, we work from morning until night, and we come home very tired, and we want to do nothing, we ask only that we get through the day and that we will all see each other and be happy—oh, that would be such joy. I believe that with God's help it will happen, only we must not lose hope, we must keep on, keep on, and still keep on. When one can be steadfast, one can get through the bad times and wait for the good times.

Now I want to write a few words about me. You surely know about my engagement. In spite of what I wrote to you, I am very happy with my dear one, too bad you don't know him. Sala [Rabinowicz] tells me now that she wrote you that I will soon be married. How much I would like you to come to my wedding . . .

Now dear Sala, I want to write a few words about Gucia, she doesn't know what to do, she has a suitor, a very handsome young man, who wants to be engaged to her and she isn't too keen.

Sala, we ask that you write something about yourself, write about everything that you do during the day from morning till evening, but write exactly about everything so that we have a sense that you are together with us and we experience what you experience.

Bela

Sala, I send you regards and kisses.

Glika

Inflation continued to rise. The cost of bread doubled. The preparations for the Passover holiday had, like Chanukah, a disturbing timeliness for the captive Jews, even if many could not afford any traditional unleavened bread.

Sosnowiec
March 28, 1942

Dear Sala,

We haven't sent you any matzo. No, I couldn't express it in words if I took half a lifetime. Dear Sala, we beg you a thousand times for forgiveness, but we're not going to have any matzo either. There is no possibility that we will get any. Maybe you're surprised that [some people] received

119

some . . . Not everyone, you understand, can afford them. The [privileged folks] can afford to buy them, but we don't belong to [that class] . . . Don't misunderstand, dear Sala, you sent us very little [money] and we know very well that you can't help us more. It is very nice of you, only one would like to receive something. Thank God that we are healthy. We've thanked God more than once [though it seems to make no difference] and that says a lot . . .

Remember, don't worry, everything is fine with us. One can't look particularly good either, [how can we]? You're asking if our dear Mom still looks as she used to. You're asking that we write often; I can do this to please you. Then I hope that I'll have only good news to report. . . . [Our brother, Moshe David] may be your guest, if not, I'll write you. Right now we're sitting together [with another family] and we talk about having Yom Kippur on Passover.*

Now I'm ending with a thousand kisses and greetings from me . . . Give kind regards to Chaim Kaufman and [cousin] Abram. [Happy holiday] especially on behalf of our dear mother, who has completely cried her eyes out and asks for forgiveness that she hasn't sent you any [food].

Remember, don't cry, don't cry, don't cry!

Raizel

The holiday came with no true Moses in sight. Chairs were empty, and plates were bare.

Sosnowiec
April 1, 1942

Dear Sala,

Just now, I'm writing from the post office. My heart is bleeding, because we didn't send you matzo for Passover. Oh God! Can you believe this? It's [the night before the

---

*That is, a day of fasting instead of feasting.

holiday], and there is no matzo, no . . . nothing. I can tell you, we're more than happy because you are not with us today. You wouldn't be as bothered anyway: nothing pulls you down as easily as it does us.

It looks like [another night of fasting] here, the candles are lit, the tablecloth is on the table. I'd much rather not write you all that much, just let me say, be happy, happy, merry and gay. Laugh as much as you can. For we do the same here at home. I even wrote you a letter, but Father, may he live long, didn't allow me to send it. I'm sure all of you there are laughing not knowing what to do and, I'm sure, you're crying too. May it be for the best, keep on laughing. Sala, remember, don't worry about us. Have a good time . . . Sala, have a good time!

Raizel

At last the holiday was over. *"We haven't sinned, did not eat bread, even though we had no matzo, but everything was kosher,"* Raizel assured her sister.

Right after Passover, Josef Garncarz became seriously ill. Raizel confided her concern in a separate letter to Chaim Kaufman, with a request: *"Please don't show this card to our Sala, she couldn't help, anyway."* Chaim did give the letter to Sala, and also shared with her a frightening postcard from his sister-in-law:

Sosnowiec
March 23, 1942

Dear Brother-in-Law,

I'm writing to you in a state of great depression. [Your brother] went away last Friday and we have no means to live on. And I have a small child. My dear Mother is very sick, may she survive all of this. I can't tell you how bad we feel, how great the pain. I am sick in bed and my dear Father is very weak. I tell you, dear Mother will not survive this. Dear brother-in-law, while I'm writing this I'm sick in bed. I'm not going to survive this. My eyes are swollen from crying. I would like to receive a letter. Dear brother-in-law, we're forced to go to the [Community] for food. No husband, no store, and no hope in life.

The letter bore no return address, but Chaim's sister-in-law lived in Sosnowiec, and the letter was postmarked from there. She wrote one more time:

Sosnowiec
April 1, 1942

Dear Brother-in-Law,

I'm writing to you in a state of great pain. All of us are sick. I haven't received any news from [your brother]. I don't even know where he went. We have nothing to eat. There's no [holiday] in this house, all we ever do is sit around and cry: it's unbearable. It's dark in every corner. My dear Mother will not survive this. You wouldn't recognize her . . .

Sala had no way of knowing her family's true situation, but now she knew that Raizel had withheld news of their father's illness, and was probably hiding other problems. Raizel, however, was unrepentant. Josef improved, she reported with relief, but he too was in the Council's sights.

Sosnowiec
April 28, 1942

Dearest Sala,

Oh, two letters at once: one asking why we don't write, and the second saying, mail received! Tears flowed, one after the other. Oh God, did you know that dear father was sick? Why should you be troubled with that? Should I have written to you about it? What would it have helped— nothing! Thank God, the worst of it is over. Dear father is now out of bed and feels much better.

Sala, you always ask if I work. Unfortunately right now, I don't know what kind of work I can get. I was just at the work office, but I think priority is given to those with a profession. I will try, after all, what do I know? One must live with faith.

Dear father is now registered for work at the employment office too, to weave straw, easy work. Calm down, calm down.

Raizel

Raizel was distracted by Josef's condition, but not so distracted that she couldn't worry about Sala's prospects. *"Oh, Sala, we received mail today from Kaufman. Are you cross with him? Why?"*

Sala had never wanted to enlighten Raizel about her ambivalence toward Chaim. His presence had comforted her family after Ala's departure. But now, Raizel's innocent reliance on him as another trusted guardian for her sister had emboldened the ever-optimistic young man. His solicitude over her father's health was presumptuously close to that of a son-in-law.

The time had come to be clear. Dreading the confrontation with Chaim, she blamed her youth and inexperience, the war, concern about her family—it was because of all of these factors that she was unwilling to make a commitment. But as she feared, Chaim was enraged. He barraged her with wild accusations and threats: *"If you have not seen the boor in me, you will now, because once I get started, it will not be pleasant for you,"* he snarled. *"Who do you think you are? What role do you want to play?"* From the high-minded poetry of his previous letters, he lapsed into adolescent insults with his final riposte: *"After all, I am not your snot nose."*

There were soon more important things for her to worry about than the overdue unraveling of a one-sided romance. The frequency of deportations from Sosnowiec had resumed, more frequent and violent than ever. *"Nobody has work for me,"* Raizel wrote. She was lucky to have been released twice from the transit camp. Some people languished there for several weeks. *"Calm down, calm down,"* she repeated in her letters, but her handwriting betrayed her terror. She alerted her

123

sister to look out for a new arrival at Geppersdorf: *"Bela's new husband will go away, maybe you will see him."* Bela was still at home, the first of their circle of friends to be married, and now expecting a baby.

Even light-hearted Hokilo was discouraged; he too had been to the transit camp several times and was fatalistic about the future. He wrote with uncharacteristic sobriety: *"In Sosnowiec, there have been many weddings, there's always a wedding . . . but with God's help, this shall one day end . . . You live such a quiet life, without knowing the first thing about this place, Skladowa."* Listing the friends and relatives who had been taken, Sala Rabinowicz excused herself for not writing to Sala very often: *"We are in a daze . . . and our thoughts are foggy too. We have nothing but worries."*

In April, Raizel was walking home from the daily lineup for work when she heard the sounds of gunfire and screaming. Suddenly, she was swept up in a crowd that was surging toward the end of her street. She had no choice but to be pushed along with them until they reached the main shopping street of Sosnowiec, and finally came to a halt at a large square. This area was usually forbidden to Jews, but today it was filled with people, Poles and Jews. She was packed in so tightly that she could hardly breathe, but she followed their upturned faces and saw what they saw: four nooses fashioned from ropes, hanging from the branches of a tree.

Hans Dreier, the tall, broad-shouldered SS chief, stood near the gallows and shouted orders. The entire square was surrounded by a cordon of Jewish police, as well as German police in helmets, armed with machine guns and hand grenades.

Four men were marched forward. Raizel gasped when she recognized Bela Kohn's father and brother among them. Dreier turned to the crowd and demanded that all eyes stay fixed on the execution.

The bodies were left hanging from the early afternoon until the evening. The Jewish police had prepared the gallows, and now they removed the bodies. Bela's father and brother had been accused of dealing in black market goods by a Nazi informant who had been working with them as a clerk. The store was closed. The employees were stripped of their work papers.

They were hanging down like chickens, Raizel told Blima when she was finally able to get home. Bela was pregnant and unemployed, her father and brother murdered; her husband deported. In Jewish homes throughout Sosnowiec, candles were lit in sorrowful memory of the dead.

> **Sosnowiec**
> **April 23, 1942**
>
> **Dear Sala,**
> **We don't know exactly what's going on. Bela Kohn is in distress because her brother died. What else can I say? Don't worry about us and calm down. I really don't have enough to say to merit a letter and no patience either.**
> **Raizel**

Organization Schmelt reached its largest size, 177 camps in Nazi-occupied Poland, Germany, and Czechoslovakia. New entrepreneurial opportunities were unlikely, so Schmelt concentrated on keeping the existing camps open. It had become more difficult for Merin to find new workers to replace those who died, as the pool of able-bodied Jews had been depleted by constant deportations to labor camps. Instead of preparing lists of potential laborers, the Council concentrated on updating its information about the elderly, those without work identification cards, and those who were dependent on social services. Anxious to satisfy Schmelt with some people, or at least to extort more money, the Council began to issue summonses to these groups, who were told to bring clothes and valuables, such as jewelry, and to report to Skladowa Street. While they waited in the transit camp, desperate family members tried to find them work. But the cost of entry into one of the local factories had risen astronomically. At the Rossner factory, which was the largest and most protective employer of Jews in Sosnowiec, the price of a position was rumored to have reached as high as ten thousand RM. The Gestapo threatened to make up any shortfall with groups that had thus far been spared—including Council members and their families. Merin introduced new tactics. The Jewish militia, supported by armed SS men, surrounded whole apartment buildings. Mothers and fathers who did not work in designated locations and had more than two children were taken away for "resettlement."

On May 12, 1942, a transport reached Auschwitz and the victims were sent straight from the railway ramp to the gas chamber in Bunker #1. In the transport were fifteen hundred men, women, and children from Sosnowiec. Eichmann's transportation plan for efficient mass murder had been activated.

A few weeks after Raizel witnessed the hanging of the Kohns, she heard the sounds of the police and the SS entering their courtyard, shouting for all residents to come outside. By the time she and the rest of the family came downstairs, the courtyard was filled with their neighbors. The wife of the landlord Beglmacher was screaming and being beaten by one of the police with his gun. Raizel and Blima stayed close to their parents, and Laya Dina and her husband shielded their two children. Just as suddenly as it began, the chaotic scene ended: responding to some order that Raizel did not hear, the SS released everyone, including Mrs. Beglmacher, and left.

A similar scene occurred at the nearby building where their older brother Moshe David lived with his wife and children—except that Moshe David was taken away by the police and brought to Skladowa. Raizel hoped that he would be sent to Geppersdorf.

> Sosnowiec
> May 14, 1942

Dear Sala,

I guess you'll be impatient to hear from me by now, but what can I do? My head keeps spinning, my head, it's just awful, but Sala, don't worry about us, we're home and Laya Dina is also home. What else should we say now? No! How lucky you are, there are many who envy you because you have work. Be happy, be glad, and thank God a thousand times every day that you still have somebody whom you can write to, given the way things are going here . . . But don't worry about that. Our brother Moshe David was sent off to work today. He should have come to your place but he'll [be sent] somewhere else. Don't worry about his wife and children, they are fine. Not to worry, everything is fine here. What's new with you? Sala, remember how lucky you are, you have no idea. Enough now, it's already late, time to sleep, one is tired after a long day.

Good night. Write more about yourself, not about us.

Raizel

Writing from a Schmelt labor camp, Moshe David wrote his first, and only, letter to Sala, hoping for information or assistance.

Ottmuth
May 27, 1942

Dear sister,

I never thought I'd be writing to you from a camp, but there is nothing one can do against fate. Now, concerning our parents, may they live long, I already asked [my wife] and Laya Dina about them, but I didn't get a reply. I am very nervous about them—perhaps you know more. Please write me immediately.

Now my dear, maybe you can use your clout with the camp administration and get permission to visit me in person. I would be so happy.

Moshe David Garncarz

"Don't complain because you don't get mail every day," Raizel warned. Her letters offered perfunctory assurances that everyone was well. She did not describe the events that were occurring at Sosnowiec, but hinted broadly: *"Probably you know from the newly arrived that business is doing well here. But don't worry, the worst is over."* The worst was not over, however. In her next letter, she inquired anxiously whether she might find work with Sala at Geppersdorf. *"If I don't get work, I'll have to go away to someplace else. You understand me now?"*

In June, the family had another close call.

Sosnowiec
June 4, 1942

Dear Sala,

You're so right, Sala, to thank God that our address is still the same. Maybe you had a premonition because we were caught in a skirmish, our dear mother, Blima, Laya Dina, David, and the children. Thank goodness, you received this mail. I was terribly nervous that you might not get [it], but then I thought, maybe it just wasn't meant for you [to hear from us]. Sala, may we be together again and enjoy talking to one another.

Raizel

Geppersdorf was also in turmoil. Work had begun to slow down, as most of the large sections of the highway had been completed. Some of the twenty-five Schmelt camps along the highway route were shut down or consolidated, and the four thousand Jews who worked there were shifted to other construction projects or redirected to the armaments industry.

Transports left every day. Sala waited anxiously to be called. From Sosnowiec, Hokilo and Ala wrote with surprise that she was still there, since so many others had already left. At Ala's suggestion, she had obtained an official note, signed by the director (with her name misspelled), documenting her time at Geppersdorf.

This is to certify that the Jewess
Sara Garncarz
has been working in this work camp since October 28, 1940,
as a seamstress.

Geppersdorf, 6/9/1942

Purst
Camp Administrator

Chaim had disappeared, but she did not know whether he had been transferred or was avoiding her. His last note delivered a release and a bitter reproof: *"I do not demand any kind of an explanation. You are free of all consequences. However, sorrow will choke you."*

A guard summoned her from the barracks and told her to report immediately to a special office within the Bureau. Although she was expecting to be transferred, this call was unusual. No one met her glance as she walked into the camp headquarters. Her confidence deserted her. She was directed to a small, bare room. A Nazi officer was standing behind a table, a large box resting next to his gun. She did not recognize him, yet he looked familiar.

Sala Garncarz, he inquired? She nodded, too nervous to speak. He pushed the box to her and she saw her name written there, next to the return address for Wilhelm and Anna Pachta. Suddenly, she recognized the man in the black uniform as the incarnation of a familiar photograph: this was the mysterious Herbert Pachta. No wonder his parents were silent about him. How frightened she would have been to know that their son wore a Nazi uniform.

Their conversation was oddly normal. He was there at the request of his parents, who had tried to deliver a package and had been told that the camp was closing down. They dispatched him to deliver a box of food, with their warm regards.

Instead of the punishment she feared, she had been treated with respect, even gentleness. Herbert Pachta nodded cordially, and she left with the package.

When her transport was finally announced a few days later, Gross Sarne was her destination. She retrieved her letters. As soon as she arrived in the barracks she found a new hiding place under a bunk.

Without Ala or the Pachta family, she was not sorry to leave Geppersdorf, but no one knew whether mail could be received at Gross Sarne. She was desperate at the potential break in communications, at a time when Raizel had abandoned any reticence about revealing her fear.

Her first letter came from Bernhard Holtz, who was now working in the office of another Schmelt camp.

> Blechhammer
> July 7, 1942
>
> Dear Miss Garncarz,
>
> Thank you very much for the lines you wrote me. So now all of you have left Geppersdorf, after all. Where has the whole lot gone to now? Is Kaufman still with you? I received mail from little Ala recently. Everything's fine with her! Unfortunately, I missed the opportunity to see her while I was in Sosnowiec on May 8 . . . Are you still working as a seamstress? What have you been hearing from home? Please drop me a couple of lines one of these days.
>
> Best regards to all Geppersdorfers,
>
> Bernhard Holtz

Although she was relieved when Raizel's letters resumed, her sister's words were far from comforting. The cards were hardly filled, and her handwriting was wild and sketchy.

> Sosnowiec
> July 10, 1942
>
> Dear Sala,
>
> Please don't worry about us. We are well, thank God, and everything is fine, with Laya Dina also. Otherwise nothing special. How is Chaim? Kisses from our dear parents and from your sisters. Warm regards to Chaim. A thousand kisses and regards from me and Laya Dina. Is everything okay with you?
>
> Raizel

At Gross Sarne, the men marched early each morning to the construction site of a bridge, rather than the highway. Although she recognized a few of the guards and officers from Geppersdorf, she was concerned about the need to prove herself all over again as a seamstress. She started off badly with the head of the camp, who ordered her to make him a motorcycle seat out of sheepskin, and delivered the assignment with a wave of his gun and a threat.

She had stayed for nearly two years in Geppersdorf. Now, in the spring of 1942, events were unfolding much more rapidly. After a few months at Gross Sarne, she was transferred by truck to a camp at Laurahutte. She avoided the arrival inspection and hid her letters. None of the surroundings seemed familiar, but some of the other prisoners whispered that they were close to Sosnowiec.

An SA guard approached her. She recognized him as the grandfather for whom she had made the dolls' clothes in Geppersdorf. He had been so eager to tell her then that she could return to Sosnowiec for her vacation, and he seemed pleased to see her now. She asked him about their proximity to her family, which he confirmed. He offered to arrange a visit: be ready at any time, he advised.

The possibility of going home energized her. She did not see him for a few days, and then suddenly, he was back again. His news was shocking: Sosnowiec is *judenrein,* he declared, using the Nazi word for a city that had been "cleansed" of Jews. He offered no more details.

Later that day, a group of Jewish men came back from the city, where they had been sent to clean up the ruins of a monstrous event. They did not know how many people had been killed, and how many remained in the city.

Interregnum:
August 12, 1942

It began with a proclamation from Merin in early August. Written in Polish and Yiddish, the printed announcement suddenly appeared everywhere, not only posted in the Council headquarters but plastered on walls and public places throughout the Jewish neighborhoods of Sosnowiec and neighboring cities.

All Jews, regardless of sex, age, or working status, must report to the sports stadium at 7 o'clock on the morning of August 12, 1942.

All Jews should wear their best clothes and carry enough food for one day.

All Jews should bring their identification and working papers, which will be checked and stamped.

All Jews will return home.

The same proclamation and procedure had already taken place in the smaller communities within Merin's domain. It happened just as Merin said: the Jews showed up, had their papers stamped, and returned home. In Sosnowiec, as in the other locations, people were particularly concerned about the requirement to bring even infants and the handicapped. However, nothing was more important than properly validated documents.

On the morning of August 11, another proclamation appeared

mysteriously on the gates and walls of the city. The August 12 assembly was a trap, it warned. Jews should stay away from the stadium and from other public gathering places. Merin was excoriated personally for corruption and collaborating with the Nazis. The statement ended with a call to arms: *"Let every person, according to his/her opportunity, find a weapon, guns, axes, knives, tailor's scissors, acid, and everything that may be useful to resistance."*

The unsigned leaflets were one of the first visible signs of a resistance movement that had been gathering strength since the beginning of the occupation, organized by leaders of Zionist youth groups. They were certain that the required presentation of working papers was a ruse. Two crudely printed issues of an underground newspaper in Polish also appeared, declaring that the Council's real objective was to capture as many Jews as possible in one place for a massive deportation.

Merin's police were quick to respond, taking down the flyers, and reiterating the dangers for anyone who did not obey the summons. Every building in the Jewish districts was assigned a Council representative to ensure that all residents left their apartments and to guard the vacant buildings.

At 7 o'clock on the morning of August 12, some fifty thousand people streamed through the streets of Sosnowiec and its neighboring cities. For this special occasion, travel restrictions were lifted and all the boulevards were reopened to Jewish pedestrians. Wearing festive clothing, hair freshly washed and combed, and carrying supplies of food and drink, the Jews of Sosnowiec entered through one small gate that led to the field, the city's largest open space. Teeming with people, from elderly Jews who had hardly left their apartments for years, to mothers and fathers wheeling babies in carriages and carrying toddlers, the field looked like a giant anthill, surrounded by a fence on all sides.

Only a few of Merin's police had been there in the morning. Once the field was filled, however, SS men entered and planted their machine guns on tripods around the perimeter.

As the sun rose and the temperature climbed, everyone waited, sweltering in their suits and dresses. In the early afternoon, a group of officials filed into the stadium. Tables were set up in the center and on each side of the field. At the center table, three men sat, one from the Gestapo, one from Organization Schmelt, and one from the Council. Hans Dreier, the Gestapo regional commissioner, presided.

The Jews were ordered to form a line. One by one, families approached the center table. Those who had working papers were told to present them for inspection. The Gestapo representative glanced at each paper, then at each family member. A wave of his finger, and the selection was over. Each person was sent to a designated section of the stadium. Group 1 comprised those with valid work permits, most of them people from the local shops who were unencumbered by elderly parents or young children. Their identification papers were stamped, and they were told to leave the field. The people selected for Group 2 did not have proper documentation but were observed to be healthy enough to work. They were sent to another section of the field for deportation to a labor camp. Those in Group 3 required additional consideration; their ability to work was compromised because of physical weakness or family circumstances, such as mothers and fathers with babies. They were told to remain on the field, because they would have to pass through the selection again. Group 4 was reserved for large families and those who could not work. They would be sent to Auschwitz.

The significance of the groups became obvious. As people from Group 3 and Group 4 began to surge in desperation toward the one exit, they were beaten back by Merin's police, armed with whips and hard rubber batons. Families found themselves unexpectedly divided at the selection table, with no last opportunity to speak or touch. As they fought for one more look and another goodbye, the SS began to fire, first into the air, then into the crowd, to restore order.

The lines crawled forward. In the evening, it began to rain, first lightly, then a steady, soaking rain, and the field grew muddy. The officials left, and the lines dispersed, the tables now empty, and darkness covered the field.

The second day began, hotter than the day before. The meager supplies of food and drink were finished. The field was in ruins, strewn with clothes, books, and suitcases. Thousands of people lay exhausted in the mud, some of them sick after drinking from the dirty puddles of water. The lines commenced again.

Raizel and Blima waited with their parents. Laya Dina and her family stood nearby, together with the wife and children of their brother, Moshe David. On the third day, Raizel and Blima approached the selection table with their parents. None of them had valid working papers. Blima, strong and beautiful, was designated for Group 2, Raizel for Group 3. Josef and Chana, and Moshe David's wife and children, were ordered to Group 4, the largest group on the field, a grieving mass of the elderly, crying babies, pregnant women, the disabled, and those too weak to speak.

Raizel began to follow her parents. She lost sight of them and began to cry. Blima heard her and ran toward her voice. She could see one guard yelling and moving toward them, but the closest guard was looking the other way. In that moment, Blima reached Raizel and pulled off her glasses. She switched jackets with her, and pulled her over to the section of the stadium for Group 2. Raizel allowed herself to be dragged away, but her wails were barely stifled by Blima's jacket.

The crowds in Group 3 and Group 4 gradually grew smaller. As the Jews were marched through the streets of Sosnowiec, some of the children were rescued by Poles. Thousands of people were taken directly from the stadium to the train station. Others were held temporarily in buildings that had been emptied on Kollataja Street, guarded by the Gestapo and the Jewish police until they too filled the cattle cars that would take them to Auschwitz.

Raizel and Blima were kept at the stadium. Blima shielded Raizel as best she could from the sight of the field, but they could not escape the screams of people insane from fear, the staccato bursts from machine guns, and the cries from dazed mothers pushing empty baby carriages.

Raizel and Blima finally left the next day. The field was slick with mud and blood and the debris left behind by the doomed souls who had gathered there. The sisters were taken to Skladowa where they met some of Sala's friends, who were also bound for labor camps. Raizel could not stop crying. "Strong, you must be strong," Blima urged her, and Raizel tried to recite her mother's last words like a prayer: "You will have your mother with you. Blima will be your mother."

Blima and Raizel were locked up in Skladowa for a few days, before being marched to the train station. They heard that they would be going to a women's camp at Neusalz. Suddenly, they caught sight of Laya Dina moving toward them. She was carrying two warm quilts. She handed one to each of them, and they had a moment to embrace.

An estimated eight thousand people were sent directly to the gas chambers of Auschwitz in the deportation that began on August 12 and ended on August 18. Among them were Josef and Chana Garncarz.

CHAPTER FIVE

Good Day, Good Mail

Raizel and Blima tumbled out of a freight train packed with hundreds of disoriented, heartbroken women.

As they walked through the gates of the Neusalz labor camp, a young woman ran toward them, yelling *"Cotton! Cotton!"* It was Sala's friend and their former neighbor, Sara Czarka, who had been there for several months. News of the catastrophe of August 12 had already reached Neusalz. Sara recognized the sisters among the new arrivals, and saw at once that Raizel appeared to be on the verge of collapse, supported by Blima. Even among these grieving women from Sosnowiec, Raizel was singular in her suffering.

Raizel would not last long at Neusalz without help. Acting quickly, as the roll call was about to begin, Sara told the sisters to volunteer for "cotton," a job that required less physical strength than operating heavy machinery or the more dangerous work of boiling and processing raw flax. They followed her instructions.

Raizel was slow to adjust to the camp, even with Blima's constant attention. She was haunted by an incident that occurred on their first day. Walking to the barracks, they passed an emaciated man pulling a wooden wagon filled with dead bodies, not an uncommon sight at Neusalz. Blima tried to hurry past him, but the man looked directly at Raizel. He signaled for them to stop, and said that he knew their brother, Moshe David. Raizel nearly fainted—she recognized him as Moshe David's brother-in-law. She wanted to ask more questions, but he seemed too sick to continue, and Blima pulled her back on the path. They never saw him again. And yet there he was, as if he had been just waiting there to greet them, Raizel kept saying.

Neusalz was one of the larger camps operated by Organization

Schmelt. About eight hundred people, mostly young, Jewish women from the Zaglembie region, were housed in fourteen wooden barracks, flimsy structures that stood in rows outside the Gruschwitz textile factory. Instead of uniforms, the women wore whatever clothes they had on at the moment of deportation, a bizarre range of outfits, from summer frocks to pajamas, some of them in slippers or barefoot, which lent a strange, surreal atmosphere to the factory floor.

The Jewish Elder of Neusalz was a charismatic former actress named Mitzi Mehler, so beautiful that she was known as "the Blonde Venus." Even the Nazis seemed to fall under Mitzi Mehler's spell, permitting her to organize entertainments for the women as well as religious observances. For the most vulnerable women, her youngest and weakest charges, she could always find an extra ration and an opportunity to rest. Mitzi Mehler made sure that Raizel and Blima slept together in the same barracks with Sara and other women from their city.

Raizel and Sala had not exchanged letters since July. It was an unbearable month filled with wild speculation and terrifying silence. Sala had no idea if anyone still remained at home, and whether she would continue to receive letters, especially now that her location kept changing.

Yet the Schmelt camps continued to send and receive mail. From Neusalz, Raizel wrote to Sala a few days after her arrival, and delivered the crushing blows: their parents, and Moshe David's wife and two children, had disappeared. Only Laya Dina and her family remained in Sosnowiec. Raizel attempted to be comforting in her despair.

> **Neusalz**
> **August 25, 1942**
>
> Dear Sala,
>
> I'm sure you're wondering about this new return address from Neusalz, but that's what happened. Blima, Sara Czarka, Frymka Rabinowicz and I are here together. Thank God,

we're not doing badly. Don't worry about us. But we're worried about you and our dear, precious, precious parents. We don't know what happened to them. May God see to it that we will have good news. Laya Dina and David apparently returned home. On the last day, on August 19, we saw Laya Dina on the way to the station, which reassured us somewhat. But we didn't see our parents. May they be well.

Sala, Sala, you are the best. We're always holding your picture in our hands and we keep talking about you. If you have more than one photo of our parents, please send it to us. Otherwise, there's nothing else to say. A thousand kisses from both of us.

Raizel

That her sisters were with two good friends, Sara Czarka and Frymka Rabinowicz, brought Sala a shred of comfort. They added their own postcripts to Raizel's letter:

Dear Sala: You'll probably be surprised to hear that I'm together with your two sisters. Don't worry about them, they are together with me in the same room and I'll look after them alright. I'll advise them, I know all about life in the camps, after all. They have very nice work, very light and clean. With me, everything is as always. Write me. Kisses, Sara Czarka

Dear Sala: I also think of you always, don't worry, they are with me. Kisses, Frymka Rabinowicz

More news came in a letter from Sala Rabinowicz. She had been allowed to return from the stadium, but her parents and younger sister Glika were sent to Auschwitz. Her appeal for fortitude was as much directed to herself as to her friend.

143

Sosnowiec
August 28, 1942

Dear Sala,

After a long silence, I'm writing you a little postcard. It is not, dear Sala, as if I had forgotten about you. But you know how things are. I hardly meet with the girls these days.

This isn't the time for apologies: that we can leave for the end. I read the last postcard you sent home. Your sisters aren't home. They are together with Frymka, and Gucia Gutman, and they all went to Neusalz. Your sister Laya Dina is home with her husband David and all the children.

Dear Sala, please don't cry! Don't cry! I do understand that it will relieve your feelings. Crying won't help you.

Regards,

Sala Rabinowicz

Laya Dina and her husband David wrote their own letter; at least for now, they were safe.

Sosnowiec
August 28, 1942

My dear sister Sala,

To begin with, I want you to know that my husband, David, and all of the children are home. It's been such a wedding: everyone has been ordered to go, small, grey, old and young, the poor and the rich. Many children saw their parents go . . . and dear Sala . . . our parents, your two sisters, Blima and Raizel, have gone to a camp together. If only I had their first postcard already! I'll write you as soon as I have it.

We are fine, everyone is well, little Salusia, too. Dear sister Sala, don't worry about our dear parents. They are not alone and you are not alone either. There are many, many people [with them]. Mr. B's wife sent away all of her children and she's on her own now. Stay well.

Laya Dina and David Krzesiwo

Yet the consistency of the three reports left no room for doubt. Her parents were lost. Many friends, their parents, and their young siblings had also disappeared, including Bela Kohn, so pregnant that she had walked to the stadium with difficulty.

Gucia Gutman was the last of Sala's friends to arrive at Neusalz, although she and her brother had been deported from Sosnowiec earlier in the summer. While she was waiting at the transit camp, a German factory supervisor bustled into the crowded room where the women were being held. "I am looking for seven women: big, beautiful, and strong!" she thundered. Gucia, five feet tall if she stretched, immediately volunteered. She and other recruits were sent to a small cotton factory. Her brother's camp was nearby. Desperate to see her brother, Gucia complained of a toothache, and asked her supervisor to send her to the men's camp, which had a Jewish dentist from Sosnowiec. She was a good worker, so the woman agreed. When she arrived at the men's camp, she explained her ruse to the dentist, who sighed, and pulled the innocent tooth. She and her brother rejoiced at the reunion so much that Gucia sacrificed a second tooth a few months later.

Gucia was transferred to Neusalz, where she heard about the deportation of August 12 and understood that her parents too had most likely been taken. The German manager of the factory gathered the women together and confirmed what they already knew: they were lucky to have escaped. He made an extraordinary offer: if any of you have sisters who were left behind, he declared, I can have them brought here to work. Frymka Rabinowicz's thoughts flew to her older sister. Was it safer for her sister to remain in Sosnowiec, or to come to the labor camp? How could she know?

In the end, Frymka decided that she could not risk bringing her sister to join her. It was a terrible decision. There would be no more letters from Sala Rabinowicz.

The Nazis recruited German women as camp guards to replace SS men who were needed at the front. At Neusalz, fifty former factory workers were offered positions. They were trained for two months at Ravensbrück, the women's concentration camp north of Berlin, and added to the security force at the camp. The Jewish women had been accustomed to Mitzi Mehler, who woke them up with her cheery salutation, "Young ladies, please wake up!" Now, they heard a German woman in SS uniform barking each morning: "Whores, get up!"

A selection was announced. A wave of horror swept through the barracks when the women learned that this inspection would include everyone, not just those who were too weak to work. Blima and Sala's friends were alarmed at Raizel's debilitated condition. They no longer believed that the sick were being sent home to recuperate, as they had been told. There was nothing left of home.

It took several days to complete the process. The women had to appear individually before a panel of SS officers. In the center of the room, a large circle had been drawn in chalk on the floor, with an X in the middle. Each girl was forced to walk naked around the complete circle, first on her legs, then on her knees. Assisted by the new SS female guards, one of the officers measured each woman's chest and thighs, examined her muscles, and checked inside her mouth and teeth. Finally, each woman's back was marked: "A," for the strongest; "B," for average; or "C," which meant transport to Auschwitz.

Raizel was mysteriously spared. She did not appear until the last day, when the inspection standards had to be relaxed if the factory was to remain fully staffed. Besides being protected by Blima and Sala's friends, Raizel had won the sympathy and respect of the religious young women at Neusalz. She was the most learned among them, a walking prayer book and an accurate Hebrew calendar.

Immediately, the women faced another threat. When the humiliating selection ended, they heard that the barracks would be inspected, and that they would all be punished if any personal belongings were found. Raizel was the last one still holding on to precious letters, journals, and photographs, and she resisted the women's pleas to give up her papers.

Someone started a small fire. Raizel turned away and allowed her manuscripts to be taken from her. Tears ran down her cheeks as her words were consigned to the flames. One day, she promised herself, she would reconstruct the poems and essays that had filled the pages of her journals.

By the fall of 1942, as camps shut down and addresses changed, mail service to and from the Schmelt camps became more erratic. Sara Czarka was assigned to clean the Neusalz office one day and came across a stack of undelivered mail for Jews thrown carelessly under a clerk's desk. She removed the letters surreptitiously, a few at a time, until she had delivered every one of the treasures to their intended recipients.

In the space of a few months, Sala had been taken from Geppersdorf to Gross Sarne and Laurahutte, then briefly back to Gross Sarne, before ending up in a camp at Brande. Her rapid movements increased the danger to the letters she had already received. Some of the transports were organized on a few minutes notice: a supervisor would enter the barracks and tell the prisoners to leave. But her luck held. At every camp, she found old friends among the prisoners, and she could pass her packet of letters to someone for temporary safekeeping. She also usually encountered a few guards and officers who remembered her as the "one clean Jew" from Geppersdorf and put her to work in the laundry and as a seamstress.

Ala always tracked her down. *"My aggravation has been boundless. I sent you a parcel with clothes and you had already left,"* Ala wrote from Bedzin, no longer a supervisor at a workshop, but now a staff member at Merin's Council. She did not allude to the August 12 deportation, although she was aware that Sala's parents had been taken.

Bedzin
September 20, 1942

My beloved child, Sarenka,

I was already very worried about you when I heard that you were transferred to another camp. I wish you all the best. If you have a chance, tell me what kind of work you're doing, how you feel, etc.

I'm working as a secretary in the Council and I am very busy. I received a card from Bernhard yesterday. He is still as competent as ever and is working a lot now.

Little Sala, I'll send you some clothes. Don't worry about your parents, everything is fine. Do you have everything you need at work? Are you still working as a seamstress? Sala, you'll also get shoes from me, just tell me how long you will stay there.

I kiss you. Happy New Year!

Ala

As if in response to Ala's last question, she heard soon after this that she would be transferred for the fifth time, this time to a place called Gross Paniow.

Unlike most of the Schmelt camps, Gross Paniow held an almost equal population of men and women. Poor sanitary conditions and contaminated food caused an outbreak of typhus in September 1942. Concerned that he would not be able to replace dead Jewish workers, the commandant imposed a quarantine period of six weeks. To preserve their strength, and also to limit contact between potentially infected Jews and SS guards, he declared a work moratorium.

In the unprecedented and relatively relaxed atmosphere of the quarantine, Sala fell in love.

Harry Haubenstock was a handsome businessman, a native of the Sudetenland region in northern Czechoslovakia that had been part of Austria for centuries. His family owned a lumber business outside of Prague. Ten years older than Sala, he met her at a ration distribution.

Soon Harry was composing little love notes, sometimes several a day, written on scraps of paper torn from a notebook. He had one ready whenever they passed each other. Occasionally, the notes were delivered by a friend, as she had for Ala and Bernhard. Harry was fluent in German and Czech, the languages of his Sudetenland home, and wrote to her in German.

Sala Garncarz, age twelve

Sala Garncarz (top)
and friends, circa 1936

Sala's father, Josef Garncarz

Sala's mother, Chana Garncarz

(Front row) Moshe David Garncarz and his wife Hendel with their two children

Jacob Goldberg and Blima Garncarz in Ulrichhammer, Sweden, 1946

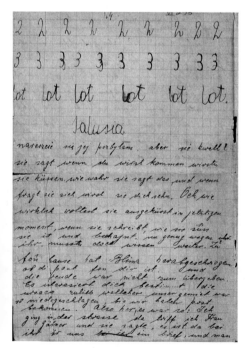

Laya Dina's daughter Salusia practices her penmanship for Sala, July 31, 1941. Raizel writes that Salusia "says that she would love to [show you] something that she learned to write. I think you will like it very much" (see p. 61 of text).

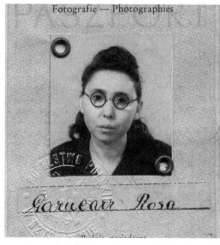

Raizel (Rosa) Garncarz, from passport issued in Sweden, 1947

Ala Gertner, 1941.
Courtesy of the U.S. Holocaust Museum

First page of
Sala's diary,
October 28,
1940, "From
the time of
departure from
Sosnowiec"

Jewish laborers working on construction of the autobahn in Geppersdorf, Germany. *Courtesy of the U.S. Holocaust Museum*

Dr. Wolf Leitner (front row, wearing white coat) and a group of Jewish men and women from the Laurahutte labor camp. Dr. Leitner is holding a doll that belonged to the granddaughter of one of the Nazi guards, who commissioned Sala to sew doll clothes for Christmas. Sala stands at far right in the top row. Photograph is signed and dated by Dr. Leitner, Laurahutte, 1942.

Nazi guards beat a Jewish labor-camp inmate. *Courtesy of the U.S. Holocaust Museum*

Jewish policemen on patrol in the Sosnowiec ghetto.
Courtesy of the Zaglembie Landsmanschaft, Melbourne, Australia

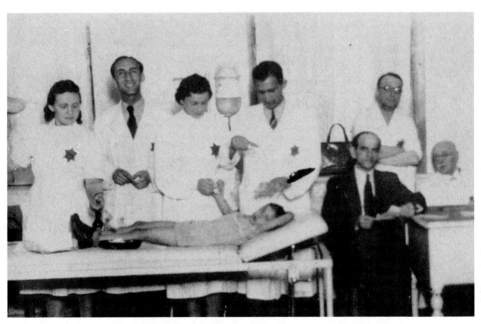

A Jewish hospital in occupied Poland.
Courtesy of the U.S. Holocaust Museum

Harry Haubenstock on a
motorcycle, prewar photograph

Sala and Harry Haubenstock in Gross
Paniow. Harry wears the "Jude" star on his
jacket. Harry inscribed the photograph
to Sala for her birthday, March 5, 1943.

Harry Haubenstock, prewar photograph   Harry Haubenstock as a child

Chaim Kaufman, prewar photograph

Elfriede Pachta, whose family befriended Sala in Geppersdorf. Photograph is signed and dated October 1942.

Ala Gertner and Sala Garncarz in Sosnowiec, September 1941. This photograph was taken while Sala was home during her three-day "vacation" to visit her family.

Prisoners were given a monthly *Eskarte* (meal ticket) in Geppersdorf. This is one of many that Sala saved.

Greetings sent from the camp at Dyhernfurth to Schatzlar. Harry Haubenstock signs first to Sala (Salusia) Garncarz, then to Wolf Leitner.

Camp sisters from
Schatzlar: Sala (left),
Gusta (center), Sala
Grunbaum (right),
Ansbach, 1945

Camp sisters
from Schatzlar: Sala (left),
Zusi Ginter (center),
unidentified (right),
Ansbach, 1945

Sala (second row,
far left) and friends
gather in Ansbach,
1945

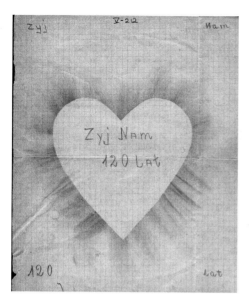

"Live for us for 120 years," birthday card for Sala from "your devoted girlfriends" in Schatzlar, March 5, 1945

Handmade birthday card for Sala from a Schatzlar friend, with Yiddish poem on the back wishing Sala "a whole life of luck," March 5, 1944

"Warm wishes for your birthday," birthday card for Sala from a Schatzlar friend, Bronia Altman, March 5, 1944

Evacuating female prisoners from Bergen-Belsen, April 28, 1945. More than 60,000 prisoners had been incarcerated in Belsen before the camp was liberated by the British Royal Artillery 63rd Anti-Tank Regiment on April 15. The barracks were burned to combat the spread of typhus. Six thousand of the sickest former prisoners, including Raizel and Blima Garncarz, were taken to Sweden for convalescence. *Courtesy of the U.S. Holocaust Museum*

Telegram from Harry Haubenstock in Cesky Tesin (Cieszyn) sent to Sala in Prague, July 26, 1945

George, the Russian officer who befriended Sala in July 1945

Sala at the Ansbach synagogue; sign announces the holiday services for September 1945

Sala and Corporal Sidney Kirschner, Ansbach, 1946

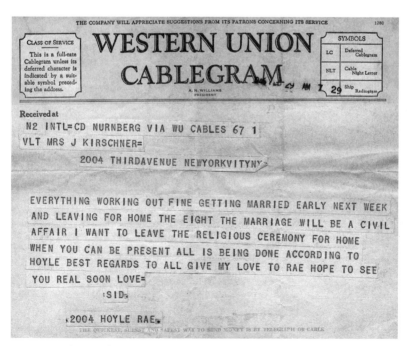

THE COMPANY WILL APPRECIATE SUGGESTIONS FROM ITS PATRONS CONCERNING ITS SERVICE

WESTERN UNION CABLEGRAM

CLASS OF SERVICE
This is a full-rate Cablegram unless its deferred character is indicated by a suitable symbol preceding the address.

A. N. WILLIAMS
PRESIDENT

SYMBOLS

LC — Deferred Cablegram

NLT — Cable Night Letter

Ship Radiogram

Received at

N2 INTL=CD NURNBERG VIA WU CABLES 67 1

VLT MRS J KIRSCHNER=

2004 THIRDAVENUE NEWYORKVITYNY=

EVERYTHING WORKING OUT FINE GETTING MARRIED EARLY NEXT WEEK
AND LEAVING FOR HOME THE EIGHT THE MARRIAGE WILL BE A CIVIL
AFFAIR I WANT TO LEAVE THE RELIGIOUS CEREMONY FOR HOME
WHEN YOU CAN BE PRESENT ALL IS BEING DONE ACCORDING TO
HOYLE BEST REGARDS TO ALL GIVE MY LOVE TO RAE HOPE TO SEE
YOU REAL SOON LOVE=

:SID:

:2004 HOYLE RAE:

THE QUICKEST, SUREST AND SAFEST WAY TO SEND MONEY IS BY TELEGRAPH OR CABLE

Telegram from Sidney Kirschner in Nurnberg (Nuremberg)
to his mother in New York, February 1946

Sala (left) with Frymka Rabinowicz and her brothers, 1946

Sala (far right), English officer, and two other war brides preparing
to leave for the United States, May 1945

Sala reading *Forward* newspaper (in Yiddish) in Central Park, New York, 1946

Sala with her two children, Joey and Ann, 1952

Sala (right) and Ann Kirschner, New York, September 9, 2001

Their romance bloomed quickly. "My gypsy," she called him, inspired by his dark eyes. "My little bride," he called her.

He was proud of her popularity, especially with the influential camp elders like Dr. Leitner, who was also at Gross Paniow. However, Harry was prone to jealousy and complained that she was capricious when other people were around. *"You always behave differently here than in your own room,"* he wrote. *"Here you always give the impression that you don't care for me."* He was older and more experienced, he reminded her. Although he hinted at his previous relationships, he declared that this love was different. Some of her friends disliked him. Still, her heart was completely engaged for the first time, and his talk of marriage was thrilling.

Gross Paniow*

My dearest little Sala,

You are an interesting person here in the camp. Everybody wants to know what you are going to do when I am sent off. Sometimes, I hardly know what to say because everybody seems to have [their own ideas]. Still, I'm glad about these questions because they show me that you are popular with everyone and that they envy me because you abide by me so loyally and courageously. I am so unspeakably happy about this, I can't really tell you.

Sometimes, I hardly know what to say because everybody seems to have their own ideas about you. Believe me, most precious little Sala, that I hardly recognize myself any longer. I have changed so much and if someone were to see me now, they would hardly believe that I should be capable of such a deep and sincere love. But I'm glad about this change because this is what my dear parents wished for me. I would be the happiest person on earth, if I had an opportunity to introduce you to my dear parents and to meet yours.

*Harry's notes from Gross Paniow and Blechhammer were undated.

My sweet girl, I'm afraid that you will be sad again because I'm writing about our dear parents, but these days I'm thinking of our loved ones every day. Salusia, sweetie, please be so good as to write me today. We will still see each other today at the food distribution.

Sala, I'm closing now and remain, with a thousand kisses,

your Harry

Harry's letters moved restlessly around the puzzle of their current situation, as if his memories or the future he imagined for them could supplant the temporary reality of the camp. His promises could not be severed from the rest of her life, however. Without permission from her parents, without knowing if they were even alive, she could only listen to this sweet chatter of love and marriage as a disembodied hope, not quite real.

Gross Paniow

My dearest Salusia!!

It's cold here, but in my heart, there's a fire burning hotter than lava and this fire burns for you alone.

Salusia, my sweetie, the [transports] are about to be put together. Maybe you could ask if it were possible for you to come along, although I don't think that girls will be able to go, what a pity.

Salusia, my precious, I'm longing for you so much. If we were free, I would make up for what we're missing here and would not leave you alone even for ten minutes.

I have a feeling of belonging to you as if we were married. But I don't need a formal wedding because one affirmative word from you is practically sacred. You said something recently that made me very happy. You said you'd give me complete freedom and would give up everything. My happiness is not because of this [offer, but] because this shows that you love me and only me.

My little bride, when will I be able to enclose you into my arms for ever? That will be the happiest moment of my life. Last night, it took an enormous effort to leave you. You were so adorable, it is a scandal how our freedom has been taken from us.

Now, my little sweet bride, a thousand kisses,

Harry "the Gypsy"

The oasis was brief. The quarantine would soon end. The rumor was that the camp would be disbanded, the prisoners dispersed to other, larger camps. Although Harry promised fidelity and eternal love, the uncertainty of their situation seemed to mock any plans for the future.

Gross Paniow

Sala,

The letter I got from you yesterday upset me very much. Unfortunately, I couldn't write any more yesterday to cheer you up. My dearest, don't worry, you know quite well that we will always belong together. Nothing can separate me from you because I love you boundlessly. Salusia, were you afraid yesterday during bunk inspection? You should have stepped forward right away and made a report. Always have a coat ready that you can throw over your shoulders quickly; you looked very cute in your pajamas.

I was on duty from 10–12; I constantly passed by your window but I couldn't come in after all. My dearest Salusia, I really didn't understand yesterday's letter. Please write in German. I promise not to correct the mistakes.

My little Salusia, I have a premonition. I believe that we will be liberated soon. Then we will make good use of our time. I'm already looking forward to that.

. . . When we are in another camp, I'm going to kiss these bad moods of yours away.

151

My sweet little bride, keep your spirits up, things will
turn out for the best. I kiss you a thousand times
Harry "Gypsy"

Her sisters were unaware of Harry's existence; it seemed to comfort
them to imagine the continued presence of Chaim, whom at least
they had met. She could not write to Raizel of love lost, or love
found. But she poured her heart out to Ala. In turn, Ala confided the
unexpected story of her romantic entanglement with a married man.

Bedzin
November 4, 1942

My sweet little Salusia! My dear!

Finally, a sign of life from you! I cannot express my joy
in words, even me, with my big mouth! Now, 12:30 at
night, I write to you with such great joy that I almost don't
know what I'm pounding out on this typewriter. And now
I have so much news from you! How happy I am that you
are finally happy. I understand you so well, maybe better
than anyone else does. I will write in German, because I
want Harry to be able to read these words. He probably
doesn't know our Polish language!

I believe you when you say that your Harry is the one
you have always wished for, and is also someone whom I
would have thought suitable for you. I wish both of you
much happiness in your warm love. My dear children, how
much I would love to be together with you! Maybe that
will happen, sometimes there are such miracles!

Salusia, I have so much to tell you about myself. It was
so wonderful for me here, so wonderful. I also had the
good fortune to befriend someone here. Two weeks ago,
however, his lawful wife arrived. What can one do! We were
robbed of our freedom and had to hide every wink and
glance between us! That has no appeal for someone like
me, who loves freedom so much.

Did you get a postcard from me addressed to the camp at Laurahutte? Today I got the first letter from you. Our girls are doing fine here, much better than in Gross Sarne, also better than in Geppersdorf with Ackerman . . .

I can't write everything that I would like to [about my love], but it was so great, so wonderful, and now everything is demolished, in one fell swoop, against both our wills. Because my feelings are not one-sided, they are reciprocated 100 percent. We are so good together! We understand each other and that brings a certain harmony, without which no love can exist. I hope that you and Harry will always find such harmony.

I heard from home about your dear parents. I asked about them, but didn't get to see anybody. How I regret that time that I didn't visit your home. But you are strong, isn't that right, my little girl? I am proud of you and will always be. And as you go on with your life, think always of me and go through life in a way that would make me content. I have utmost trust in you and therefore, I feel that I am already fond of Harry.

And now something for Harry! Well, my dear young man, allow me to address you familiarly. You are, after all, my dear Salusia's young man, so I therefore claim that right. I hope that you are worthy to be loved by my little sweet friend and that I will not be disappointed in you! I have only one wish now, to be together with you both as soon as possible! We will definitely get along with each other!

Salusia, stay well for me and happy with your dear Harry. I actually wept when I didn't find the photo you promised in the envelope. When you get a chance, you must both send me one. I have absolutely no photo of you.

Where will you both wind up now? Or are you staying there? Keep together. And always remember that love is the most beautiful light in life.

**Salusia, I will try to bring my sweet beau here. If I
should succeed, then I don't need anything else in the
world, except an end to the war. So, now you know almost
everything about me . . .**

Ala

Sala had a few photographs from home, including the individual
portraits of her mother and father that Raizel mailed to her before
August 12. Other prewar photographs were given to her as keepsakes
by friends she had met in the camps. Ala had parted reluctantly with
the photograph that was taken during their vacation from Geppersdorf. *"For my Sarenka!"* she signed on November 25, 1942, and
enclosed it in her letter.

Photographs taken within the camps were rare, but not unheard
of. Cousin Rozia had received one in 1941 from her brother in Geppersdorf, although she complained that *"it isn't sharp, and shows him
only in profile."*

Harry gave her some of his prewar photographs, one of himself as
a solemn little boy in a sailor suit, another as a dashing young man
on a motorcycle. But he wanted a photograph of him with Sala to
commemorate their romance. Someone had a camera at Gross Paniow, and agreed to take a picture. Dr. Wolf Leitner also managed to
commission a group photograph of his friends and colleagues, and
he autographed one for Sala, who stood in the upper row.

Harry and Sala met outdoors on October 28, 1942, the second
anniversary of her departure from home. The two of them stood
framed in a narrow wooden doorway. Harry posed proudly, looking
like a prosperous business executive in a proper suit and tie, except
for the yellow Jewish star pinned to the front of his jacket. Under her
short jacket, Sala wore her brother Hersh Leib's shirt to keep out the
autumn chill. She leaned against the doorway, slightly away from
Harry, and slipped her hand into her pocket, an enigmatic smile on
her face.

*   *   *

Harry swore that he would *"fight like a lion"* and urged her to *"use all your craft"* to keep them together in the upcoming transports. They arrived together at Blechhammer, a Schmelt camp where Bernhard Holtz had been in 1941. However, security was tighter here. Harry wrote less frequently, and lost his confidence about the future.

Blechhammer

My beloved Salusia,

I'm endlessly sorry—and I don't want to disappoint you—but I have lost hope that [the lagerführer] will help in any way.

My dearest, beloved Salusia, whatever happens, nothing can separate me from you, you're with me, even if there are [thousands of] kilometers between us, I will always, my sweet little bride, keep my word and be loyal. The only thing that will worry me—even though I have the greatest trust in you—is knowing that you will be alone with [people who might turn you against me].

Salusia, my beloved little bride, please write me some lines today to set my mind at ease. I am in the worst possible frame of mind. My sweetheart, all I can say over and again is that I love only you, and I will never love another.

Salusia, beloved little girl, I would have loved to kiss your tears away but one is never alone here. I bitterly reproach myself for persuading you to leave [Gross] Paniow with me. Maybe we see this all too gloomily and maybe we will still be happy together.

My dearest, for now I remain, with thousands of kisses, yours always,

Harry "the Gypsy"

His sad predictions were soon followed by an order to leave.

Sala retrieved her letters from a hole that she had dug outside the barracks. The rumor was that they were headed west. Ala wrote with concern: *"It was silly of you not to have stayed together with [Harry]."*

Was there no other way?" But she had no control over her movements: the men were leaving on one transport, the women on another.

Sosnowiec was far from *judenrein* even after the massive deportation of August 12. The elderly and nonproductive had been sent to their deaths, and many of the able-bodied young workers were deported to labor camps, but around twenty thousand Jews remained. More than two thousand people were still employed at the Rossner uniform and shoe factory. Other workshops in Sosnowiec and Bedzin were running at or near capacity, employing thousands more, and the Council continued to manage the large Jewish militia and administrative staff.

Schmelt operated with continued support from the army and from Albert Speer, the armaments minister, who intervened personally to keep the munitions factories open and major construction projects on schedule. Turned back from Moscow, and defeated at Stalingrad, the German military forces had lost the appearance of invincibility, and could not afford any disruptions. In one case, army officers fired on SS men who were trying to close down a labor camp and take away their Jewish workers. Schmelt even won permission to exchange dead bodies for live, relatively strong prisoners already on trains to Auschwitz, arousing the wrath of Rudolf Hoss, commandant of Auschwitz, for interfering with his schedule.

Organization Schmelt had additional value as propaganda. As the rest of the world slowly awoke to the deadly seriousness of the Nazi agenda against the Jews, newspaper articles about labor camps were planted to counter the reports of death camps. The subtitle of one such article in December 1942 was "a visual lesson to counter Roosevelt's tale of horror." Fritz Fiala wrote in the German language newspaper *Pariser Zeitung* that the Schmelt camps were an example of "German humanity" and were more representative of the Jewish condition than unsubstantiated rumors of nightmarish horrors in the east. Merin was quoted in the article.

More than a year after Wannsee, and despite a steady stream of complaints that reliance on Jewish labor defied the will of the Führer, there were still some fifty thousand Jews working in Germany, Poland, and Czechoslovakia for Organization Schmelt. On paper, Schmelt appeared to be complying with the official policy by closing down some of the smaller camps. But in reality, little had changed. Schmelt himself had grown rich from the lucrative slave trade, and had been promoted to SS Brigadeführer.

Still, the dream of racial purity beckoned. In the spring of 1943, Himmler finally ordered Adolf Eichmann to shut down the Schmelt camps, in coordination with a plan to annihilate the rest of the Jews. The Warsaw ghetto uprising in April had tipped the balance against Schmelt and Sosnowiec. If resistance fighters could create an unpleasant distraction in Warsaw, they might do the same in other places. Even the so-called productive ghettos such as Bialystok were to be liquidated.

Dismantling Organization Schmelt began with two decisions that were the harbinger of future woes. First, all the remaining Schmelt sites became officially classified as concentration camps. Geppersdorf, Gross Sarne, and Gross Paniow were shut down, but the other camps that Sala had passed through briefly in 1942—Laurahutte, Blechhammer, and Brande—were now attached as satellite camps to Auschwitz, or to Gross Rosen, another major concentration camp. This transition was heralded by officials, who proclaimed the new advantages to the workers with speeches and considerable fanfare at the camps.

The second decision was to force all remaining Jews from the Sosnowiec area into ghettos, as a prelude to liquidation. They were evicted from their homes and most of them moved to an outlying suburb known as Srodula; a smaller group of mostly older people were confined within the Old City quarter of Sosnowiec. The ghetto in Bedzin was known as Kamionka. Using these new return addresses, some letters were still mailed to the labor camps, moving more slowly from the ghettos through the community mailbag. Each card now bore a new Jewish Council stamp in addition to a regular postmark.

Each deportation would be the last, Merin assured his constituency. He justified his constant negotiations with the Nazis by arguing that any other path would assure the destruction of the entire community. *"As a general, I have won a great victory,"* he congratulated himself publicly after the massive roundup of August 12. *"If I have lost only 25 percent when I could have lost all, who can wish for better results?"* He ordered an extra distribution of rations for everyone, as if to lend more credence to the promise of future stability. However, conditions in the new districts of Srodula and Kamionka belied any real optimism.

All Jews were forced to leave their homes. On March 10, 1943, the ghettos were sealed. The Jewish police ruled inside, and the SS guarded the gates. As many as thirty people were crowded into each apartment; all furniture other than beds was removed and left on the ground outside the buildings. People took turns sleeping; when one left for work, another took his or her place on a mattress. Merin had long abandoned any pretense of distributing money to the families of labor camp workers. *"Regarding the payment from your work . . . I can't get it, so see if you can,"* Laya Dina wrote to Sala. She worked a twelve-hour factory shift. Her husband, David, found a position with the Council. They left the ghetto at dawn, part of a long column of people walking under police escort for several hours to reach the city, and back again at night. Salusia and Moniek were among the few remaining children in the ghetto, and were left alone for long days while their parents worked in the city. Laya Dina's prayer was laced with bitterness: *"May God grant that I don't have to write Him a postcard for sisters and parents to be able to sit together at a table and rejoice."*

The Council posted daily lists of people summoned to the transit camp at Skladowa. After each deportation, there was a general commotion as families tried to learn the fate of their loved ones as quickly as possible. Ala wrote that the roundups were constant: *"My sister from Krakow and her child aren't here any longer; unfortunately, her husband committed suicide."*

Bernhard Holtz returned to Sosnowiec in November 1942. At

Sala's request, he used his access to Council records to locate Harry and was able to forward his current address and the news that he would soon be named a Jewish Elder.

Despite declining health, Bernhard never gave up his stubborn pursuit of Ala. He was hospitalized with a serious bout of typhus. *"I would love to talk to you about Bernhard,"* Ala wrote. *"Only you can understand him. He's always the same: faithful, in love up to his ears, sincere and he's become handsome, too. I'm at the end of my rope and all because of the difference of age."*

The final phase of their complex romance unfolded in a setting that would challenge even Bernhard's capacity for love and hope.

March 12, 1943

My dear child Sarenka!

You shouldn't be surprised that I haven't written for so long. For a month, I have been working at [Merin's] headquarters in Sosnowiec, and come home so late that it's impossible to find a free moment for anything personal. Now I too am here in your hometown and work. I told my co-workers about [Geppersdorf] and of course, I also told them about you, my child! Time flies, how long has it been since [your duty] began? How are you? How do you look? I want to know everything, everything.

Little Bernhard is still in the hospital, although he's feeling better. But now there are the side effects, complications after the illness. He looks miserable, but I hope it won't be too long until he is able to start working again. His father was sent back to the camp.

So, my dear! Who knows if we will not meet somewhere! Do you want to, little one? I have to go to the hospital, since I don't know when we will come back again. Everyone lives in the Srodula [ghetto]. Do you know where that is? My mom is ill. But I can't help her. Besides, my brother has to relocate to Srodula, and my sister is already in [the Bedzin ghetto at Kamionka]. So, slowly, my family is getting smaller. I'm glad that I have a lot of work, or else I wouldn't have been able to get through all this.

Today is a wonderful day. The sun is so wonderfully warm, it's healthy weather. Is it nice where you are? What does Harry write to you? Is he already a Jewish Elder?

I have to run—stay well, I kiss you fondly.

Your Alinka

Laya Dina and David also managed to send a letter from the ghetto:

Srodula
April 11, 1943

Dear sister Sala,

To begin with, I want you to know that my thoughts are with you. You are probably desperate because I haven't written to you. Today is the first time after a long time. Better late than never. My heart is aching, beating so wildly with concern that you will think that I forgot about you because I can't always write to you, or send you something. No, I'm thinking of you alright. If I were on my own, I could write you more easily . . . I haven't had an apartment for four weeks. Finally, this week, I got an apartment. Throughout these four weeks, I was crazy, real crazy. Wherever you spend the night, you don't spend the day. At long last, I found a place to live and I can now appreciate what it means to have an apartment and a bed. Also I'm the happiest person in the world because I'm together with David . . . I had to get used to living with [him] again.

I haven't received a postcard from you. Write postscripts or whenever you can. I wish you a good holiday. May Heaven give us a happy Passover together.

Laya Dina

In the labor camp at Neusalz, Mitzi Mehler named Blima supervisor of the barracks. Her new position gave her more standing, and she helped Raizel and the other religious women to conduct a Passover seder. Blima's responsibilities also brought additional vulnerability. When Blima was late for a roll call, Mehler struck her across the face. Raizel could not forgive her, the Jewish Elder who had been so trusted, so admired for her fairness, by all the women.

At least Raizel was still able to write.

Neusalz
April 26, 1943

Dearest Sala,

I don't know what to do at all when we don't get mail from you, dearest. Tonight is Monday night, the beginning of the holiday, and the mail has been announced. Blima and I have been waiting anxiously. But no, what a great disappointment! Sala, why do you do this to us? Don't you know that your mail is our only happiness, our everything?

Oh Sala, our heart is aching! Today, [Passover] began. We are so far apart from one another, no parents, no brothers and sisters are here. We're thinking of you, Laya Dina and all our dear ones, day and night. Yes, we received mail from Laya Dina last week, they are well, thank God and at home, oh, may they be able to stay there. But nothing from our dearest parents. This is more than just a woe! We can't tear them from ourselves. May God grant that we will still see them in this life. May we be able to exchange our past experiences as soon as possible.

Please don't worry about us. Thank God, we're well and have light work. What are you doing? How's your work doing? Are you well? Why do we get so little mail from you? Are you getting mail from Laya Dina? From Ala too?

. . . Now, a thousand kisses and regards from your

sisters, missing you, and wishing you a good holiday. Oh, if only we could be together again in the future!

Please say whether Chaim is writing to you—take pity on us, we don't have anything else.

Raizel

Raizel reserved some precious space for postscripts by young writers with family in the same camp as her sister:

Dear Suzi, How have you passed the holidays? We are well: we had a seder. Fryda Lypschitz held a seder till two in the morning, only we missed our dear parents. Regards to Miss Sala Garncarz. Kisses, from Jetti . . .

Dear Mama, I'm taking this opportunity to add a few words, too. I received your postcard. Write how you passed the holidays. I did very well. We had a seder in our room till 2 in the morning.

Laya Dina mailed packages with warm quilts and food. As the mail became more and more erratic from their different locations, the four sisters tried to compensate for the uncertainty of each communication by relaying whatever news they had.

Neusalz
May 10, 1943

Dearest Sala,

Now we have your mail of April 20 in front of us and we're reading and crying. Sala, on these holidays we are so far apart from one another, everyone is dispersed over all the world. I feel so gloomy and how sweet it was at the [Passover] table with our dear old father and our dearest Mother, [who] had everything prepared for him. But today, what a shame! Not a trace from anybody! We would like to know that they are alive and well, how happy we would be.

Now Sala: over the holidays we had four days off and spent the seder evening in much the same way as you did, in great sadness, remembering the family.

Well, you want to know where we're working. Not with fine materials as you do, Sala, only with cotton, it's clean and light work. We're working regularly, from 6 to 5 in the evening with one hour lunch in between. Are you also working regularly or in shifts? How are you doing at work? . . . Well, we are very happy about the mail from dear Chaim. Where is he and where does he work? I have no news of [Blima's fiancé] dear Jacob. We received two food parcels from Laya Dina. Have you also received mail? Where does [cousin] Rozia's mail come from? Where is her sister? Are you getting mail from Ala, is she sending mail?

A thousand regards and kisses,

your sisters Raizel and Blima

Laya Dina was not receiving any letters from Sala. At the end of May, she wrote once more:

Srodula
May 22, 1943

Dearest Sala,

We're wondering why we don't get mail from you and we're very worried. Surely, you're also worried about us but, thank God, everything is fine. We're all home, the dear children are well . . . Probably you heard of the wedding. Thank God that we're still able to write you. Right now, I'm also writing to our dear sisters Raizel and Blima. Have you already received the parcel [that I sent]? Raizel and Blima replied already. Otherwise, there's nothing special. We hope for good news from you.

Regards,

Laya Dina

*   *   *

The leaders of the Jewish resistance, drawn mostly from the youth groups, recognized that the final hour was approaching. As some of the local factories began to close down, they foresaw the imminent collapse of Merin's "rescue through work" strategy, which would also eliminate the last vestiges of Merin's influence over his Nazi masters. They had been visited by Mordechai Anielwicz, one of the leaders of the Warsaw resistance movement, later a hero of the uprising, and were also in constant contact with counterparts in Czestochowa, but there were few resources to share, other than advice and information. Couriers were dispatched on weapons runs, but more often than not, they returned empty handed—if they managed to return at all.

They assembled a pathetic stockpile of arms; no more than fifteen handguns, and a few dozen grenades and homemade bombs. Hidden among their small arsenal was a typewriter and printing machine. In the absence of any serious ability to mount an armed uprising, they focused on counter-propaganda and sabotage. The Nazis were not amused when German soldiers at the front received a shipment from a Sosnowiec shoe factory with printed notes tucked inside the army boots, warning the soldiers that Germany was losing the war, and urging immediate surrender.

The underground movement had been radicalized by the August 1942 deportation. They were aware that the systematic annihilation of the Jews was under way. But their pitiful resources, and the overwhelming reality of Auschwitz only a few hours away, presented few alternatives. The destruction of the Warsaw ghetto was a sobering fact. Merin had already survived one assassination attempt and his death would bring them little other than the wages of vengeance. Messages relayed to them from Warsaw and Palestine warned of the futility of armed resistance and recommended that they join the partisans or find other means of escape. In the meantime, members of the underground moved around frequently, hiding in a network of bunkers and secret locations.

Some of them decided to join the partisans. Others were involved in a well-organized effort to obtain South American passports that was being coordinated through Switzerland and quietly financed by Merin himself as his personal emergency exit. Some Jews with "good appearances" sought Aryan identity papers to live outside the ghetto. Another escape option was to cross the mountains from Poland into Czechoslovakia and then into Hungary.

While they were finalizing their plans, Merin struck. Tipped off by an informer, a group of men and women on their way to meet the partisans were ambushed and executed by the Germans.

The remaining resistance fighters retreated to the bunkers.

Ala chose this pivotal moment to fulfill the dream that Bernhard Holtz had pursued since October 1940: she married him. They moved to the Bedzin ghetto of Kamionka. Writing on a piece of letterhead from the Bedzin Council office, she shared her delight with her friend.

> **Bedzin**
> **June 5, 1943**
>
> My dear child, Sarenka!
>
> It's been raining the whole day, a dreary cold rain. But a week ago, the 22nd of May, it was glorious weather. The sun shone strongly, it was warm and beautiful. On Sunday afternoon, I bound myself to Bernhard forever. The wedding was at the Rabbi's on the little "Srodula." Bernie looked wonderful—serious, but happy. I hope you will be as thrilled as I am when you marry your Harry.
>
> Bernhard has a job in the Council. I am glad that it finally came to this, though the time is hardly right, but you know, Sala, how much he wanted it. His most fervent wish was fulfilled.

What do you say to that? How are you? I am uneasy that you are not writing. Yesterday, together with my husband (!), I read all your letters and postcards from the camp. God grant that you will be together with us.

Stay well, my child, fond regards and kisses

Your Alinka

She signed their names as Ala and Bernhard Holtz on the back of the letter, and added: *"WE MARRIED!"*

One day in early June, while their mothers and fathers were at work, about 1,200 children of the ghetto were seized by the Gestapo. Some of the older children escaped to hiding places as they had been instructed. The parents returned from work to empty rooms.

In the days that followed, most of the factories were closed down. The workers were sent back to the ghetto.

A nurse in the ghetto hospital was the only person on duty when the Gestapo entered in the middle of the night. Anyone who could walk was sent into the streets. The nurse was given a syringe of morphine to administer to the bedridden patients. When she accidentally dropped the syringe, she was beaten. Her hands shook as she injected the morphine; following orders, she gave additional doses of aspirin to those who had not yet died.

On June 19, a woman in one of the remaining factories noticed Moses Merin through the window. He was crossing the street with Fani Czarna, flanked by Gestapo officers. The woman looked more closely. This time, it seemed to her that Merin was not walking with his usual swagger.

Merin and his closest associates were arrested and taken to Gestapo headquarters. From there, they boarded a train to Auschwitz.

No explanation for Merin's absence was given to his remaining colleagues. Ala had not been arrested with him. She continued to work at the Council. But she had been among those who had

believed in the possibility of escape through South America. She and
her sister had been corresponding directly with people in Switzerland
who were trying to secure passports. The initiative was organized by
a wealthy Jewish merchant from Bedzin who had fled to Geneva
soon after the occupation.

In the summer of 1943, even children knew about "camp" and
the looming spectre of Auschwitz.

> Kamionka
> July 15, 1943

My dear child, Sarenka,

I received your postcard, thank you. Little Bernhard
started working and has already left. I was beginning to
get nervous, but I met the black one from Seldyn [in the
ghetto] last Sunday.* She managed to put me at ease. I
just regret that you're separated from [Harry].

We're working at the Jewish Council and yet our
thoughts are always with the camp. Little Bernhard did
a lot of good things for me recently. He's a nice boy—
anyway, it's just a pity that you're not with us. Today is a
rainy day and you know how this type of weather always
makes me sentimental. Next week we'll know if we will
go to the camp. How many hours are you working in the
factory? Are you well? I'm remembering our little room
in Geppersdorf and I'm sorry that we're not together now.
Little Bernhard works with the police now.

Warm regards and kisses,

> Ala Holtz Gertner

Ala wrote one more time, to tell Sala that she was heading to
Auschwitz.

---

*Ala may be referring to Fani Czarna, Merin's associate, who was also known as "the
black one," although by some accounts Czarna was deported to Auschwitz with
Merin.

Kamionka
July 15, 1943

Dearest Sarenka,

Suddenly I'm here at the post office. The mail is going out today and how could I not write to my Sarenka? Just now, my husband, little Bernhard was here. He looks good and feels well. I'm curious about how you are, how your health is. We are well and plan to go to the camp. Today is a gorgeous day, we are in the best of spirits and have great hopes for the future . . . What's doing with Harry? Where is he? Why is he silent? [The woman from Seldyn] told me everything. We had very little time then—somebody in the Central Office must have pulled strings. Maybe I'll have another chance to talk with her.

Don't worry, girl, it'll be fine. Be brave, stay well. Warm regards from my entire family and our Bernhard.

Kisses,

Your little Ala

Sala Rabinowicz fell silent after February 16, 1943. Laya Dina wrote no more letters after May 22, 1943. She and David, their children Salusia and Moniek, were never heard from again.

Ala's last letter was postmarked on July 16, 1943.

The final liquidation began on Saturday, August 1, 1943. The timing was a surprise, because previous deportations had never started on weekends. More than six hundred SS men surrounded the ghettos in Sosnowiec and Bedzin and ordered the Jews to assemble in an open area. About 8,500 people were sent immediately to Auschwitz. Thousands more were on trains by August 9.

About four hundred people, however, had already taken to bunkers that had been dug over the course of months, the earth removed in small quantities at night to avoid attracting attention. The ceilings were too low to permit any position but lying down, but some of the bunkers could fit as many as thirty people. The last person to enter was responsible for securing the camouflage, which might be an oven, a piece of furniture, or a rug that covered the hole. Some of the bunkers were outfitted with food and water, plus mattresses, lights, radios, and a toilet pail, ready for an extended period of hiding. Some were connected by tunnels that led beyond the ghetto.

The August heat made it nearly impossible to breathe. People lay on the ground without clothes to stay cool. Some of them could hear voices outside, and understood that this attack was intended to be the end of the ghetto. To the annoyance of the Nazis, who expected to be finished quickly, the siege lasted for ten days. They were aware of the existence of the bunkers and patrolled the area with machine guns, searching from door to door and listening intently for something that would betray a hiding place. When they detected sounds or movements, they searched for the point of entry and filled it with poison gas or fired into the hole. Jews who emerged from the bunkers were shot or held for the next transport to Auschwitz.

The official end of Organization Schmelt came with the liquidation of the last Jewish ghettos in Sosnowiec and throughout the region. Schmelt himself was relieved of his duties as "Special Plenipotentiary in Charge of Jews in the Upper Silesian Region." He retired to his country home near Opole, Germany.

Himmler, who had created Organization Schmelt in 1940, had finally succeeded in dismantling it. But his determination to stop using Jewish labor had an immediate impact on Nazi resources. Jews were significant contributors to the war effort. As a result of the deportations of August 1943, two factories that were building tanks lost their total labor force overnight.

In advance of Himmler's directive, Oskar Schindler, whose factories were part of Organization Schmelt, transferred his workers from Poland to his native Czechoslovakia, where seventeen of the former Schmelt camps remained. The new site was far enough away for Schindler to continue operating with relative autonomy.

In a Czechoslovakian mountain village called Schatzlar, about one hundred Jewish women worked in another textile factory that had once been part of Organization Schmelt. They were now officially inmates of a concentration camp, but so far, little had changed.

CHAPTER SIX

The Last Birthday

Snowy mountains loomed large in the distance, a captivating landscape despite the familiar exhaustion and anxiety that accompanied the move to another camp.

Sala had been transferred to five different camps in the six months since she left Geppersdorf. Harry had failed in his attempt to keep them together. She and a group of women had been summoned one morning and ordered to leave immediately, destination unknown.

The village of Schatzlar was nestled in the Giant Mountains between Poland and Czechoslovakia. Its population of three thousand swelled in the winter when skiers began to arrive from Prague, a few hours to the south. The Czech name "Zacler" was still faintly visible at the train station beneath more recently added signs in German. Mountains circled the village and bore down on it from every direction, the lower elevations bristling with tall, pencil-thin trees topped with green.

The other labor camps had been more isolated from the surrounding towns. As Sala and the other women walked from the station through the steeply inclined streets of the village, they could look into the faces of the Czech townspeople, who saw a column of women, ill-fed and poorly dressed, most of them in wooden shoes, the yellow star sewn on their clothes. She had never crossed the mountains or seen skis before, but even the locals here used them for transportation, gliding like dancers along the snow.

Schatzlar was an unlikely site for the manufacture of essential war materials. But it was home to several textile facilities that had signed labor contracts with Schmelt, including a factory owned by the German G. A. Buhl & Sohn company. It was also in a strategic location, as Frederick the Great had discovered in 1745, when the Prussian army was investigating a route for withdrawal into Silesia. Now, nearly two hundred years later, little Schatzlar was again considered an important marker, should the Russians force the Germans to retreat into Poland.

The Buhl & Sohn textile factory was small: only about 120 women worked there. It was a relatively pleasant posting for the SS guards, who lived nearby in a private house that had been commandeered from a local Czech family. The director of the camp was married and resided with his wife and two young children in a comfortable chalet directly across the street from the factory and the barracks.

Before the first roll call at Schatzlar, Sala found a hiding place for her letters under the lowest bunk in the barracks. When she took her place in the lineup, she was told by a guard to remove her shoes, which would be returned to her later. She had carefully preserved those shoes—the same ones that she had brought from home, and that Chaim had repaired expertly in Geppersdorf—through six camps. She reluctantly surrendered them, and received a pair of clumsy wooden clogs in exchange.

She had arrived in Schatzlar with a few close friends. They were a bright and lively group of resourceful young women. Most of them had similar family backgrounds; some were from Sosnowiec. They were all veterans of the camps, but she had the dubious distinction of the longest servitude. "Share my bedroom suite," they shouted to each other as they entered the barracks, eager to reestablish the camaraderie that helped to dispel the gloom of the overcrowded wooden bunks and the unheated, drafty room.

Their bond was the envy of the camp. They shared everything, and when one of them was weak, they pooled their meager rations to support her. They kept their clothes and bodies as clean as possible, determined to avoid the additional indignity of having their heads shaved. In the middle of the night, they washed with freezing cold water, picking lice out of each other's hair and skin. They shared one brass comb that Sala had brought from home.

Eva Joskowitz was their leader, the one who united them. She was also their best food procurer: she had a source at the camp kitchen who sometimes gave her turnips, which she would peel to make a special sandwich, shared among her friends. Friedl Silberstein was another member of the group, delicate-featured and sensitive. Sala Grunbaum was the tallest: "Big Sala," they called her, to distinguish her from "Little Sala Garncarz." Zusi Ginter always had a trick or two up her sleeve, ready to do anything on a dare. Zusi had nearly been beaten for her last escapade: she had sewn herself a pair of underpants with a capacious pocket to hide stolen food. When she was summoned by the factory overseer, she started to run and potatoes started to fall out of her pants, "like a kangaroo," she laughed with her friends.

Their union went beyond the practical. They drew strength and endurance from one another, clinging to beliefs and courtesies that connected them to their prewar lives. They were shocked to discover a mother and daughter in the factory who were stealing from each other. Not us, they vowed. They kept a close watch on the orphaned young girls at the camp, some of them hardly more than children. Big Sala shared her bunk with her twelve-year-old cousin, cheerfully taking care of her "baby."

Nightly murmuring about their families filled the barracks like warm and fragrant air. They conjured up their past lives by talking about their closest relatives and friends as if they were all one family. Their homesickness, their fractured lives, the void left by the separation from mother and father, became the communal ache of the room. Their dream of the future relied on the steadfast conviction that one day, they would be reunited with their parents; one day, each of the women would be a bride and a mother.

Some of them had relatives in camps nearby. Big Sala had a younger sister in a much larger former Schmelt camp where fourteen hundred women made canvas covers for trucks. Little Sala waited for word from her sisters, hoping that Laya Dina was still in the Sosnowiec ghetto, and that Raizel would write again from camp.

The women were awakened in the barracks at 4:30 each morning. Breakfast was a cup of tepid brown liquid that resembled coffee, and a small slice of bread. Their twelve-hour shift at the factory began every morning at 5 o'clock. Zusi and Sala were assigned to the same section. They stood all day with their backs to each other, operating giant machines that processed large spools of raw flax through a trough of boiling water that refined the threads before they passed through a mechanism that coiled them on small spindles. As the spindles filled up, they had to be taken off and boxed, and another bulky spool of flax inserted into the machine. If the thread twisted or broke, it had to be manually coaxed back into place, and then restarted. The thread would eventually find its way into cloth for the German army.

Zusi's machine worked well, and her box filled up obediently with spindles of grey cotton. But Sala's machine seemed to have a mind of its own. The German factory manager would shout and accuse her of being lazy, even though it was not her fault that the threads kept breaking. Zusi tried to help her. At night, they would laugh at the manager's bad breath and how his red eyes kept staring at their legs as they ran from side to side stomping noisily in their wooden clogs, but during the day, Sala was often in trouble, struggling to keep the temperamental machine running smoothly.

Around noon, they would take a short break for lunch, usually a watery soup with potato peels, and sometimes another piece of bread. They ate with Eva, who worked at another machine in the next room. On Sundays, they might receive a pat of margarine and a tiny piece of horse meat in the soup. If one of them was lucky enough to find a chunk of potato, they shared it, slicing it thinly and layering it on the bread, which Eva heated up on a corner of her machine. As they ate, they assigned a new flavor to the sandwich. Cheese, Eva suggested? Meat? No, eggs today, Zusi corrected her, vowing that someday she would eat bread until she burst.

Every few days, raw materials arrived by train. Sala always volunteered to walk to the station, where she would unload the giant rolls of flax from the trains to the waiting trucks. It gave her an opportunity for a few minutes of contact with the outside world. She usually came back with something—a rumor from a friendly Czech train conductor, or perhaps a cigarette from the driver. Back at the camp, they unloaded the trucks and brought the flax into the factory. Inside the rolls, which had been made by prisoners in other camps, they would sometimes find pieces of paper inscribed with names or messages, to be shared that night with the other women.

One of Sala's letters reached Raizel, who now addressed letters to the camp at Schatzlar. She and Blima were still working at Neusalz, where they had received a package from Laya Dina but no letters.

A thread of mail connected the two labor camps and four sisters.

Neusalz

November 12, 1942

Dearest sister,

Is this true? We received mail from you? Oh, Sala, Sala! We are so joyous that we hardly know what to do with ourselves, and at the same time, we long for you so much. Now we found each other again. At long last! At long last! Oh, my heart is breaking! Sala! I don't know what to write first, I'm going berserk. A well of tears opened up in our eyes. You went through so much and now you're in a women's camp. But we, too, went through a lot, a lot. We are very sad that we are not together. By the look of it, that's our destiny. Keep your head up, Sala, don't despair. Maybe we will still get together in this life and then we'll have much, very much to tell each other. Oh, that's all we want, to sit together at a table with our precious, precious, most precious parents. Oh dear, when, when? And with our sister, brother and the rest of the family . . . We received a quilt, but no letter. The sender was Laya Dina. We don't understand why we didn't receive a letter from her. Are you getting mail from home? We don't, unfortunately. You are our only faithful soul. Write, whenever you can. Where is Chaim? Are you still getting mail from Ala and from Chaim? Who is together, of our mutual friends? Remember you're worth more than we are.

Now, thousands of kisses from your sisters, longing for you.

                                            Raizel and Blima

Another Neusalz prisoner added a postscript, worried about the dangerous machinery at the Schatzlar factory:

> On this occasion, I'm writing you a few lines. I'm in a room with Miss Sala's sisters. I received your mail, which I appreciate very much . . . My dear child, you mustn't lose hope and do your work. Remember your [family] and be careful with these machines, be careful with your work . . .

Sala's letters were reviewed by a young German woman who served as the camp overseer and censor. Elizabeth Bischoff was not much older than the women she supervised. She made no secret of her disatisfaction with her assignment to Schatzlar, but tried to be fair. On Christmas, she taught the women to sing carols in German and organized a performance, which she attended in her SS uniform. Bischoff also had a romantic side: in March, she called Sala to the office and gave her a letter from Harry, which she had decided to permit in consideration of Harry's beautiful writing.

Bischoff also allowed her to receive the special surprise that Harry had included for her nineteenth birthday present.

                                            Dyhernfurth
                                            March 1, 1943

My dearest Salusia,
    I've been told that mail is allowed from women's camps. I am therefore wondering, my dearest, why I haven't had any news from you yet.
    My beloved Salusia, I wish you all the very best for your birthday, beginning with a speedy reunion with your parents and my dear parents. I wish that would take place today, not tomorrow!

My dearest Salusia, I'm sending you the little photo from Gross Paniow. It is the most precious thing I own, because we were together then. How wonderful it would be if you were with me now. But every love has to be tested by suffering and separations, even though that is hardly necessary for us. You know very well that you can rely on me.

. . . My sweet little bride, I hope you still have some good opinions about men. However, please don't judge me by the usual standards, for there are no other girls for me, just one single beloved Salusia!!

My dearest, I wish you all the best for your birthday and remain yours eternally,

Harry

Harry was now a Jewish Elder at Dyhernfurth, a large chemical complex that produced poison gas, a subcamp of the Gross Rosen concentration camp that had once been part of Organization Schmelt. The photograph from their days at Gross Paniow was a treasure. Harry dated and signed the photograph on the back to "dear little Salusia on her birthday." The sight of his elegant handwriting and distinctive signature relieved and refreshed her.

Elizabeth Bischoff permitted one more letter. Harry had discovered that Sala's old friend and admirer, Dr. Wolf Leitner, worked in the Schatzlar region.

Dyhernfurth
April 7, 1943

My dearest Salusia,

I only received your cherished postcard of 2/22 yesterday. You can imagine how unhappy I've been all this time without a message from you, my sweet Salusia. I have great problems writing, but you could write more often, couldn't you?

You needn't worry about me, I hardly have any free time because I only get home at 6:30 in the evening and then

I'm on duty . . . I'm looking very well, the work here is generally light. I'm glad that you're well, only I'm worried because you have to work harder than before.

I wrote to you for your birthday, my sweet Salusia, and sent you the photo taken in Gross Paniow. You should know that I had a hard time parting with it. I would also have sent a parcel, only I didn't know whether you would get it.

Unfortunately, we didn't have the privilege of being together for your birthday. I'm very glad, dear Salusia, that you are together occasionally with Dr. Wolf, so you have at least one acquaintance from Geppersdorf near you. I extend my regards to dear Wolf.

It would seem that we have more friends who want the best for both of us than genuine friends . . . I mean that ironically, of course! People have been trying to tell me a lot about you and Wolf during the time in Geppersdorf. I told them right away that my good opinions and my respect for you, my dear Salusia, cannot be changed . . .

Dearest little Salusia, don't be angry that I'm writing you all this, but it's good to know who your friends are.

Write me what you need. I will have everything sent to you. You know that nothing is too difficult or expensive for you. My dearest little bride, I still won't give up hope that I will be able to hold you in my arms soon. I've been working feverishly on your transfer. If you were in a men's camp, I could have gotten you here at once.

Salusia, my sweet girl, go on being strong and believe in our love, and we shall be helped somehow.

I'm running out of paper, so I will close now. I could go on writing for hours on end.

I remain, kissing you a thousand times.

P.S. Many regards to everyone, particularly to your girlfriends, our dear girls from Gross Paniow!!

Harry "Gypsy"

Harry was the same as ever: passionate and eloquent—and jealous of an old friend. She rarely saw Dr. Leitner, who was constantly traveling between the many former Schmelt camps around Schatzlar. Harry's concerns about her were misplaced—as were his reassurances not to worry about him.

Now, Harry too fell silent.

Her world had steadily contracted since 1940. She had received one package since she arrived in Schatzlar: a feather blanket from Laya Dina. The thought of her sister plucking and cleaning the feathers, as their mother used to, gave her as much pleasure as the warmth of the blanket. But she had no mail from Laya Dina since then.

At least Raizel kept writing, but she did not seem to be receiving any letters back.

> Neusalz
> July 6, 1943
>
> Dear Sala,
>
> I'm trying this last one time to write you, Sala. If you're not going to reply, then that's fine also. If it's acceptable to you that your sisters must suffer so much, then we'll have to say unfortunately, so be it. What happened to your conscience? How can you remain silent after so many letters? Isn't it enough that we have no mail from our dear Laya Dina, no news from our dear parents, and now you're careless with us? We're imploring you again to write us and let us know whether you're well. How are you? Maybe you have mail from our dear Laya Dina? Are you getting mail from Ala, from Chaim? We are well and impatiently waiting for mail . . . Warm regards to Miss [Zusi] Ginter from her sisters . . .
>
> **Raizel and Blima**

As her letters went unanswered, Raizel's anger dissolved into anxiety. It was not only Sala who was silent: what about Laya Dina, Ala, even Chaim? A few weeks later, Raizel reached her again.

Neusalz
July 24, 1943

Dear Sala,

I'm writing to you in a state of impatience and anguish.
Dear Sala! Imagine how we feel about not getting any mail
from dear Laya Dina. Who knows if our dear ones are still
home? But maybe, maybe you have mail from them? Oh,
how happy we would be if this were so. We implore you,
dear: write us everything, tell us exactly how it is with you.
How is your work? Your health? We're well, thank God, and
working. We're always so happy to get mail from you. But,
Sala, why don't you write? In particular, you should write
to Laya Dina. Have you received a parcel from her? Warm
regards to Zusi from her sisters.

I'm ending with a thousand kisses and regards from your
sisters, missing you greatly.

Raizel and Blima

Months went by. Raizel did not write again. There were no more
letters, no more packages. The door had slammed shut on the outside world.

The camp friends became sisters. When the mail stopped in 1943,
they broke the frightening silence by writing to each other.

They would not stop thinking about the future. Birthdays became
the focus of their attention, celebrated with great energy and activity. Zusi's birthday had been the most elaborate so far: when she came
back from work, she saw something white on her bunk. It was a dress,
a row of buttons down the front, all meticulously stitched by hand.
Next to the dress, the friends had placed an artfully shaped piece of
bread, a "torte," they announced with great pride. Each of them had
donated a piece of bread, which they had stacked into layers.

Sometimes, only the sight of the snowcapped mountains could
restore Sala's spirits and renew her waning confidence that she might

cross them again one day. She relieved her feelings by writing a letter to Harry, even though it might never be mailed.

> Schatzlar
> [undated]
> . . . when I go to work and look at the mountains, I think of you. Come Harry, come to me, I'm so scared. Even though hundreds of kilometers are between us, nothing can separate us. You will always, always be mine. We thought it wouldn't come to this, but it has, and this is the cruelest . . . I don't even want to remember that moment, your tear-stained and drawn face—oh Harry, I ask you, tell me, when will all of this end? When, when?
> I feel better now, I will go to bed and think of you all night. Are you happy, my black gypsy? I have to get up, there's never a chance to be alone, and when I get home at night all worn out from work, I send all my thoughts to you . . . So much I would have liked to say, so much that would have made you happy. But now you are so far away. Do you still think of your sweet Salusia—or is she already gone from your mind? Do you remember that I set you free? I never wanted to tie you down. You are still entitled to do as you please, and this makes me happy. You are so far from me and perhaps now you can see my reasons more clearly.
> We will wait patiently, and leave the rest to fate.

There would be no birthday greetings from Harry in 1944. Instead, Sala's friends sent poems and cards, composed in Polish or Yiddish since no censor would see them, and delivered ceremoniously to Sala Garncarz in "the upper bunk of Room III." Some women had obtained picture postcards, traded among themselves or bartered from someone they encountered at the train station or the factory. The more artistic women drew hand-colored illustrations on blank cards.

She preserved all of her birthday cards carefully.

Schatzlar
March 5, 1944

Hallo! Hallo! Occupants of Camp #20!
Did you hear today's announcement?
Well, on March 5,
Salusia Garncarz is having her birthday
So I am joining the celebration,
To offer her my congratulations.
On your birthday, Salusia, dear,
I hasten to express my sincerest wishes.
May your desires be fulfilled speedily
So you and your Harry can live in freedom
And never know adversity again.
Let happiness shine on you,
And let evil pass you by.
Let there be hope in your heart
And don't pay attention to evil people,
Since we will not suffer here forever.
There will yet come a time
When someone will liberate us
And take us far away from the barracks.
May your next birthday
Be celebrated with your loved ones,
In joy and freedom.

Sara Weisman

The war was turning decisively against Germany. But at the same time that Hitler's armies were in retreat, the Nazis continued to ship thousands of Jews, mostly from Hungary, past the Sudetenland work camps, deeper into the Reich. Most of Hungary's large Jewish population had been spared until now. There was room for hope that they would escape the fate of their brethren—until March 1944, when the Nazis took full control of the country.

The Schatzlar barracks grew more crowded with the arrival of Hungarian women who, it was rumored, were taken off a transport on its way to Auschwitz. Some of them still wore fashionable clothes from home, and they gave the impression of looking down at the Polish women who bore the effects of having been prisoners for years. The Hungarian women were slow to adjust. Soon, their fine clothes were in ruins and their heads were shaved after a particularly vicious infestation of lice. They squabbled among themselves and there were frequent thefts. The veterans in the barracks quietly hid their possessions.

The Hungarian women were unprepared for the daily deprivations of the camp. They were so famished that they foraged through the garbage for anything resembling food, heedless of the warnings of the experienced women, who knew the dangers of eating spoiled scraps. Many of them became sick and could not work. To the general dismay of the barracks, all but a few of the Hungarians were taken away in a selection. They would be sent to Auschwitz, the destination they thought they had escaped.

Ala left on a transport to Auschwitz in early August 1943. Until then, her life would have been envied by most Polish Jews. She and Bernhard managed to evade deportation until the final liquidation of the ghetto. Now, they faced the worst prospect of all.

The trainloads of Jews who arrived at Auschwitz from the Sosnowiec region met with a particularly deadly reception: in response to the local Gestapo's warning that the transports might harbor the last remnants of ghetto resistance, many Jews were shot immediately or sent to the gas chambers without selection.

There is no record of what happened to Bernhard. Ala, however, was neither shot nor gassed. She was chosen for labor.

Ala worked first in one of the giant warehouses of Auschwitz, sorting clothes, shoes, appliances, and other valuables taken from the men, women, and children who had gone to the gas chambers; their personal belongings would be shipped back to Germany for later use. The best-known repository was nicknamed "Canada" to signify a place of abundance and untold wealth. In one of these facilities, Ala met Roza Robota, a fiery young Zionist leader who had been a resistance fighter. They became good friends.

Roza was the only member of her family not to have been gassed upon arrival, and she wasted no time in connecting with one of the underground groups at Auschwitz, some of whose leaders happened to be from her hometown of Ciechanow, Poland. She organized a group that distributed news from contraband radio broadcasts and bartered some of Canada's treasures to fund resistance activities. She also found old friends among the Sonderkommando, the notorious work squad that was assigned to the gas chambers and crematoria, their appearance distorted by the relentless heat of the ovens.

Ala was transferred to the relatively new Weichsel Union Metalworks factory, which had opened in the fall of 1943 to replace a Krupp plant that had been destroyed by Allied bombs. She was assigned to the office. Like the warehouses of Canada, the Union factory was a prized work detail in the hierarchy of Auschwitz labor; it was new and relatively quiet, the work was all indoors, and the rations were better. As many as twenty-five hundred prisoners worked there, including German civilians, filling three shifts on a twenty-four-hour-a-day schedule, producing artillery detonators and fuses.

The Union women lived in a special group of barracks. Ala slept with three other women in one of thirty-six wooden bunks. Although it had no windows and no insulation from the heat or cold, this particular barracks housed a lively group of intellectuals, teachers, and professionals. Any evening when time and energy sufficed, they gathered the younger girls together in a circle, Ala and the other women leading a spirited discussion on literature and history. The girls looked up to Ala, still charismatic and unique, even in Auschwitz. When Ala had hair, she fashioned a little ribbon from a piece of cloth. Or she slung a belt around her uniform. Sometimes, she sported a hat.

Mala Weinstein shared Ala's bunk. She was one of the youngest girls, and she worked in the inner sanctum of the Union factory, the highly restricted Gunpowder Room, or *Pulverraum,* where she and five other women pressed gunpowder into explosive devices. The Nazis preferred women for this kind of precision work. Ala was affectionate to Mala. When the young girl returned from the night shift, she sometimes found a gift from Ala, a piece of bread, or a note. Mala's bunkmates knew that she would never forget what she had seen in the first days of Auschwitz: the bodies of her three sisters loaded on a truck that took them from the gas chamber to the crematorium.

In another barracks of Union factory workers, a different group of like-minded women gathered in the evenings. Led by Zionists and resistance fighters, their discussions were political and activist. They learned the anthems of the partisans, and recited poetry of liberation, filling the barracks with songs of freedom and dreams of a future life in Palestine that seemed far more real than the horror around them. Many of the women knew nothing about the Warsaw ghetto uprising until they met Anna and Estusia Wajcblum, sisters who infused the spirit of rebellion into the barracks with stirring firsthand accounts of how the young people of Warsaw fought the Nazis. Anna worked in the Union factory, and Estusia was assigned to the Gunpowder Room. Like Roza Robota, the Wajcblum sisters knew that there was an underground at Auschwitz, and they were determined to act.

News from the outside world filtered in, overheard from the guards, who were increasingly nervous about the progress of the war, or gleaned from the reports of incoming prisoners. The spring and summer of 1944 brought Auschwitz to a new depth of hell, especially for the Sonderkommando, who witnessed the arrival and murder of more than four hundred thousand Hungarian Jews in an accelerated sequence of gassing, cremation, and burial. The relentless pace reinforced the growing fear that the Germans would kill them all before surrendering to the Allies.

In the early days of Auschwitz, the Nazis themselves had processed their victims through the death cycle, but as the volume of bodies increased, they assigned these most loathsome duties to the Sonderkommando. They were sequestered from the rest of the camp, and as an additional security precaution, the Nazis liquidated the squads at regular intervals. Some of the men cracked immediately and committed suicide; some were corrupted by the special food and privileges that went along with the job. Some sought revenge. And some dreamed of escape.

In the last months of 1944, knowing that they were approaching the end of their usefulness to the Nazis, the Sonderkommando were driven to act. According to diaries that were buried in the ground and discovered after the war, they planned an uprising that would disrupt the camp long enough for them to cut the electrified fence. In the resulting chaos, some of them might escape. But first, they needed dynamite to build bombs.

Ala Gertner was the link that connected the Wajcblum sisters and the women of the Gunpowder Room to Roza Robota and the Sonderkommando.

As many as twenty women were recruited to the conspiracy, some by Ala. Her bunkmate, Mala, joined the group, skeptical about the opportunity for escape but hoping to avenge her sisters' murder. The plan was to withhold minute quantities of the coarse black granules from the amounts that the women were given for their work. Most of the pilfering was done during the night shift, when security was less stringent.

The Nazi supervisor kept the gunpowder under lock and key. He weighed each amount carefully before distributing it. Over the course of nine months, the women gathered the precious grains. They progressed slowly, secreting a few teaspoons each day from the carefully rationed allotments, until Estusia Wajcblum boldly engineered the theft of the supervisor's key and took powder directly from the fireproof safe. The women swept their daily bounty into shreds of cloth. Estusia collected the tiny bundles and hid them in the false bottom of a tray that was otherwise filled with garbage. She passed the tray to her sister Anna, who worked during the day shift. Anna signaled to Ala when she was ready to make an exchange. They met in the washroom.

When they left the factory, Ala and her friends hid the gunpowder in their underwear or twisted it into knots of headscarves. They marched in a long column for several miles back to the camp, passing SS guards along the way. Searches were frequent and unannounced: the women tried to stay in the middle of the line so that a sudden inspection would reach them last. If the guards approached, the women simply released the powder, which fell unnoticed on the ground.

Once they were back at the camp, Ala passed the explosives to Roza Robota, who hid them in a handcart that was used by the Sonderkommando to move corpses. The last stop for the smuggled gunpowder was a makeshift bomb factory where a Russian prisoner, a former officer in the Soviet army, was secretly at work.

On the morning of October 7, 1944, the Sonderkommando blew up Crematorium IV. They had just learned that the Nazis were about to liquidate their unit, and may have rushed into action before preparations were actually complete. Using a small arsenal of stolen handguns, they attacked the SS guards and cut the electrified fence. In the brief battle that ensued, four SS guards were killed, and twelve were wounded. The eight ovens and three gas chambers of Crematorium IV were destroyed. A few hundred men escaped into the woods.

Although they had hoped to trigger a general camp uprising, the Sonderkommando were not joined by any other resistance fighters, Polish or Jewish. The SS regained control within minutes, responding with flamethrowers and machine guns. Almost all of the escaped prisoners were recaptured and shot immediately.

The aftermath of the uprising coincided with the last days of Auschwitz as a death camp. With the Russian army getting closer, and planes flying overhead every night, Heinrich Himmler decreed that the trains would stop on November 2, 1944. The giant killing machine of Auschwitz, the remaining crematoria and ovens that until recently could incinerate fifteen thousand bodies every twenty-four hours, shut down.

The investigation into the uprising, however, had just begun.

An atmosphere of secrecy pervaded the camp, as rumors proliferated and fear of reprisal intensified. Camp counterintelligence, the political arm of the SS, discovered traces of gunpowder in the wreckage of the Crematorium, although it was not clear whether the damage was caused by a bomb or by a deliberate fire that started with straw mattresses and quickly raged through the wooden buildings. Before long, the explosion was linked to the Union munitions factory. Regina Safirsztajn, the forewoman of the Gunpowder Room, was arrested, then Estusia. Acting on a tip from a Jewish woman in the Union barracks, the Nazis also seized Ala, although she had never worked in the Gunpowder Room. Regina, Estusia, and Ala were interrogated and beaten. They maintained their innocence and the Germans were unable to draw a connection between them. Rose Meth, another woman from the Gunpowder room, who was mistakenly believed to be Estusia's sister, was also arrested. The Nazis released all the women after a few days, deciding that they would learn more from careful surveillance through their network of informers.

The uprising caused a furor in Berlin. Even at this advanced stage of the war, when the German army was being defeated on every front, the Gestapo devoted considerable effort to discover the source of the explosives. While they could have killed anyone even remotely suspected of being involved in the uprising, they were determined to investigate the underlying acts of sabotage. They may also have hoped to unmask the resistance leaders.

The Nazis had good reason to fear sabotage in the munitions factories. At the Peterswaldau labor camp, the women considered it a badge of honor to tamper with the clock mechanisms that they inserted into bomb casings. Assembly line workers in a Buchenwald factory stole some of the newly manufactured guns for the underground, and effectively sabotaged many others that were shipped to the Wehrmacht. In the factory at Dora that assembled the V1 and V2 rockets, Jewish workers figured out how to damage guidance and defense systems and could take some credit for the fact that of the 10,000 rockets that were used to bomb London, only 4,200 reached their target.

Hoping to speed up the investigation into the Auschwitz uprising, the SS assigned a new spy, a handsome Czech half-Jew named Eugene Koch. His special target: Ala Gertner.

Koch was handsome, stylish, and seductive. When he tried to infiltrate the Jewish underground, the men pegged him as an informer and refused to allow him into their private meetings. But apparently Koch had greater success with Ala, meeting with her for private conversations and enticing her with food and flattery. By some accounts, Ala confided in Koch.

A few weeks after the first interrogation, Ala was arrested again, then Estusia, Regina, and Roza. They were brought to Bunker 11, an infamous site of torture so brutal that Rudolph Hoss, the camp commandant, complained that his afternoon nap was disturbed by the screams that reached his nearby villa. While the four women were being interrogated, the rest of the conspirators—Mala, Estusia's sister Anna, Rose Meth among them—collectively held their breath, tormented by the suffering of their comrades and fearing that they too would be denounced. The inquisition, and the terrible suspense, lasted four weeks.

While Roza was still being held in Bunker 11, a Jewish overseer sent a message to the men's camp, asking for a meeting with one of Roza's friends among the resistance. The men were unsure whether to respond, fearing that they would be lured into a trap. They waited. Life continued at the camp, one miserable day following another. Finally, they decided to take the risk. The Jewish overseer managed to get the Nazi guard drunk and smuggled Roza's friend into her cell. He returned with an anguished report of her appearance, black and wet with wounds, physically altered beyond recognition. He also brought back a written note in which she swore that she would never betray her comrades. Roza's final exhortation was the Hebrew motto: *Chazak V'amatz,* be strong and brave.

According to a civilian secretary to the Auschwitz "political department" who was present at the interrogations, Roza revealed that she received the gunpowder from Ala. Roza also disclosed the name of her Sonderkommando contact, but she knew that he was already dead. According to the same source, Ala admitted to her tormentors that she had received gunpowder from Regina and Estusia. All four women were more courageous than men she had seen under similar circumstances, the secretary concluded.

Seeking to dramatize the consequences of sabotage, Commandant Hoss decided to execute the women—but in one of those inexplicable Nazi perversions of logic, the man who oversaw the murder of millions of men and women was forced to wait for additional authority to legalize the killing of these particular four women. The decision was forwarded to the highest court in Berlin, which prolonged the suspense for a few more weeks. On Christmas Day 1944, the verdict arrived.

Estusia smuggled a note to a friend: "I know what is in store for me," she said, "but I go readily to the gallows. I only ask you to take care of my sister. Please don't leave her, so that I may die easier." Fearing that Anna would throw herself on the electrified fence, Estusia's friends hid Anna in the camp's infirmary to prevent her from witnessing her sister's execution.

The ground was so cold in early January that the prisoners had to kindle a fire in the snow before they could construct a platform to support the gallows. On January 5, 1945, the workers of the day shift were assembled in a large open square near the kitchen building. The front rows were reserved for the women of the Gunpowder Room. In a dramatic setting designed for maximum effect, Commandant Hoss read the sentence of death aloud "in the name of the law." The guards slapped the women if their eyes wandered. A band played a military air.

The prisoners of Auschwitz looked straight ahead as Ala Gertner and Regina Safirsztajn were marched to the gallows. One of Ala's friends described her as composed, but defiant as she stepped on the platform; a moment later, she and Regina twisted in the cold wind, like two marionettes.

Hours later, Commandant Hoss read the sentence for a second time to the assembled workers of the night shift. Roza Robota and Estusia Wacjblum were hanged a few minutes later.

The last roll call at Auschwitz would be held on January 17. The Nazis worked furiously to destroy the equipment and evidence of the extermination process and evacuated all but the sickest prisoners. About fifty-six thousand people were sent on a death march. On January 27, three weeks and one day after Ala was hanged, the Russian army would enter Auschwitz.

Across the mountains, throughout 1944, rumors circulated in Schatzlar that the war was going badly for the Germans. The women knew nothing about D-day on June 6, 1944, nothing about the Allied advances across France, but they felt the war's reverberations. Work at the textile factory began to slow down. Fewer deliveries of raw materials arrived. The overseers cut back the hours of operation. The women were often told to leave in the middle of the day. One day, the machines came to a stop.

The inactivity was frightening. Assuming that they were alive only because they were productive, Sala and her friends feared that they, too, were bound for Auschwitz.

In December, Elizabeth Bischoff called all the women together. They would leave at dawn to work at another textile factory a few miles away. It was a relief to learn that they would soon be working again.

They prepared for the winter trek as best they could, staying up all night to convert dresses into pants, and stuffing rags and paper into their clothes, but nothing could protect them from the biting wind that came off the mountains. Sala wrapped Laya Dina's feather blanket around her thin clothes like a coat, feeling it stiffen as soon as she stepped outside. By the time she returned to the barracks, Laya Dina's blanket was heavy and wet with snow. She spread it out to dry overnight and huddled with her friends for warmth in the unheated barracks.

Sala's twenty-first birthday arrived, bringing another outpouring of hope from "Family Six," as her friends sometimes called themselves after the number of their barracks.

Schatzlar
March 5, 1945

March 5th is a happy and a lucky day for us. For today we
are celebrating our dear Sala's birthday; alas, still behind
barbed wire. Oh, what a great holiday this would be if we
celebrated your birthday in freedom, together with your
loved ones. Let's not lose hope!

Let good luck shine on you just like the bright sunshine
that steals secretly through our camp windows.

Sala, sometimes, when the three of us are in the bunk,
and you are asleep, we hear you call in your sleep:
"Mommy, Daddy . . ." We do not want to wake you, for
we know that, at that moment, you are happily with them.
We talk it over: "Should we wake her or not?"

Forgive us, Sala dearest, that we sometimes disturb
your sweet dreams. Someday, we shall let you drink deeply
from the cup of happiness, with your parents and with
your Harry, when we are free. May you find lots of
happiness with him so that you are never deprived of
his care . . . And so Sala, may you always have your fill
of it.

Salusia dearest, may you live for 120 years, together with
your loved ones, and with your Harry. May you celebrate
your next birthday at home, and recall that a year ago, you
were in Schatzlar, celebrating your birthday with your girlfriends; you will remember it happily, now that you have
your freedom.

Your devoted girlfriends

One of the birthday cards was addressed to "Esteemed Miss Sala
Garncarz von Haubenstock." Its brightly colored photograph of
two pretty little children was a sad reminder that she had not
touched a child during the long years away from home. In that time,
she and her friends had grown from teenagers to young women, old
enough to be mothers. They dreamed of having children, but feared

the cumulative effect of these years of hunger and exhaustion. Most of them had not menstruated in years.

The last German offensive at the Bulge had been contained, and Patton's 3rd Army was racing to the Rhine. From the east, Stalin's army had reached Warsaw and Berlin. The Americans were about to enter Nuremberg. Auschwitz, Dachau, Bergen-Belsen, and Buchenwald had been liberated, their names indelibly linked with history's most infernal landmarks. For the women of Schatzlar, however, the end of the war was not yet in sight.

By March 1945, the trucks stopped delivering flax again. Bischoff informed the women that the second factory would be closed.

The director of the camp did not want to leave the women idle. Even now, German men were being sent to the front. Most of the factories in the region had been shut down completely, abandoning any pretense of contributing to the war effort.

The women were told that they would be digging trenches to protect German soldiers. Bischoff left the camp and was replaced by a local Czech woman named Machova. The women were not afraid of Machova, a former factory worker, her pudgy body squeezed into an ill-fitting SS uniform, her plain face shiny with pride. They were growing hopeful that the war would be over soon. But they were terrified when SS guards arrived to march them to the site of the trenches, armed and accompanied by vicious dogs.

Once again, the women left at dawn on a three-mile hike, which began in the thick woods behind the factory, then climbed steeply through the mountain forests. The women were carrying a motley assortment of digging equipment, from shovels to spoons. When they reached the site, the SS ordered them to begin digging and stood over them, guns ready, dogs straining to be set free. They had a special signal for the animals, a command that they would bray in a certain tone of voice. If any of the women stopped for a minute, the SS would release the dogs. It was dangerous to be the last woman in the line, closest to the snapping jaws. Some of the women had been badly bitten. They were weak with hunger. The ground was still hard and cold, resistant to their pathetic attempts to dig.

On the march back, they passed a camp with French prisoners of war; it was almost hidden in the thick woods. The captured soldiers stood by the barred windows and yelled to the women in a cacophony of languages, their hands cupped over their mouths to amplify their voices. The war is almost over, the men shouted, watch out for Nazis trying to kill you before the Allies arrive. Their warnings were loud enough to be heard over the sound of the shots fired by the SS guards.

CHAPTER SEVEN

120 *Years of Freedom*

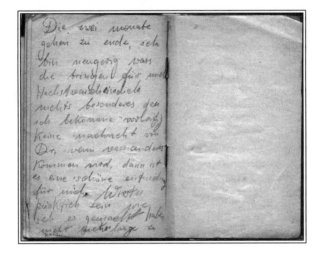

A white paper landed on the ground.

The women had been digging for weeks. The words of the French prisoners of war strengthened their resolve to endure another day of exhaustion and the terror of the dogs.

Soon another white paper fell nearby.

The guards screamed an order to keep digging. Sala looked up to see papers falling like snow from the sky. She could read them without picking them up, since the papers blanketed the ground around her. They were Allied leaflets, written in three languages, and addressed to the German soldiers, telling them that the war was over, and that they would be held responsible for their actions. The papers were signed by Stalin, Roosevelt, and Churchill.

The digging stopped early that day. The women were marched back through the woods. Relieved to be away from the dogs and the guns, the women were enveloped in a strange stillness when they entered the barracks.

In the morning, the SS guards were nowhere to be seen. The director stayed in his house. Machova disappeared. The French prisoners of war and the Allied leaflets had warned the women to be careful of last-minute efforts by the Germans to eliminate all traces of the camps. Was this moment, so close to the end, the most dangerous of all? Behind the barracks, someone left another cautionary note, apparently someone who worked for the SS men. We are watching you, it said, but the SS men are planning to bomb the barracks, so guard the doors and windows.

Alert to the possibility that the guards might throw a hand

grenade, the women organized themselves into shifts and took turns keeping watch all night, peering out at the forests around the camp. They would fight back, they vowed. Freedom was so close they could breathe it like perfume.

They passed the time by sewing flags of different colors, not knowing which army might arrive first at the camp, but prepared to welcome all liberators. Sara Weisman, the only avowed Communist among the women, sewed red patches on a shirt that she wore beneath her dress.

On the evening of May 7, the director crossed the street, carrying heavy cans of gasoline. The women watched through the window as he entered the house where he lived with his wife and children and shut the front door. They heard the sound of gunfire, then a loud explosion: the house burst into flames.

In the morning, the mountains glinted in the bright sunlight. The director's house was still smoldering. The women were alone. A few of them stripped down to their underwear and stepped into the sunshine, finding a place to sit on the patch of green outside the factory. Suddenly, Machova was there, calling to them from the front door. Ringing a bell, still wearing her SS uniform, she climbed on a chair and said, "Children, you are free."

Russian tanks drove straight to the front door of the camp. Sara Weisman was the first to welcome them with her red shirt.

Sala screamed so loudly that she lost her voice. The tears kept coming long after she could no longer speak, as the girls kissed each other over and over again. Russian soldiers spread out into the woods and captured the SS guards. They offered guns to the women and invited them to take revenge. None did. However, the French prisoners of war showed up soon afterward and accepted the guns. Machova was taken away sobbing, still wearing her uniform, although the girls protested that she had tried to be good to them.

The Russians distributed canned food, and the town baker drove up with a wagon filled with bread. Zusi was ready to fulfill her dream of eating until she burst, but Eva stopped her. We will eat the bread, she said, but nothing from a can. She was worried about the effect of unfamiliar food on empty stomachs. Sala Grunbaum was dispatched to the town to find fresh eggs and milk.

The first few days after liberation were chaos. The women slept in the barracks until Russian soldiers showed up in the middle of the night, drunk and looking for women. Czech families living close to the camp heard their screams and came to their defense. They urged the women to move to some of the nearby houses that had been abandoned by the Germans. But the women were still afraid of the Russian soldiers who swaggered around the village, wearing bras on their ears and showing off the rows of German watches that covered their arms. Gunfire could be heard occasionally. They heard that Machova was dead, executed with other SS functionaries by the Russian soldiers and the French prisoners of war.

How odd to wake up in a bed, contemplating a whole day without work, eating decent food, and wearing new clothes provided by the Czechs who had watched over them in the last days of the war. But Sala and her friends knew that their time in Schatzlar was over. They must go home. Since they had survived, surely others had also. Someone would be looking for them at home.

Sala had arranged to meet Harry in Prague if they survived, but there would be time to find him later.

Without money or identification, unsure as to how this new world worked, the women began to make plans to leave Schatzlar. It did not take long to gather their few belongings. Sala Grunbaum was reunited with her sister, who insisted that they leave all reminders of the camp behind, even letters from home, which would be covered with lice and bad memories. Besides, there were frightening rumors that the Russians would not let anyone pass over the border into Poland or Germany if they saw "Jewish papers."

Only Sala paused to make sure that her thick stack of letters, her constant companion for five years, was safe within her possession.

The friends dispersed. They would always be sisters from camp, but it was time to find their families.

201

Headed for Sosnowiec, Sala and Eva Joskowitz traveled together, walking in the general direction of Poland. Sometimes, they climbed aboard freight trains and rode on top of coal cars, which was better than finding themselves within the train and surrounded by Russian soldiers. They hardly noticed the ruined landscape around them, focused only on the goal of reaching home as quickly as possible. A few lucky days of hitchhiking brought them to the center of Katowice. They were less than an hour away from home.

They boarded a crowded tram. The sound of Polish was sweet for a moment. Then they heard the angry voice of the conductor, demanding the fare. Startled, Sala looked first at Eva, then back at the conductor, explaining that they had just been released from Nazi camps and had no money. The conductor continued to shout and called them "dirty Jews," who were not welcome on his tram or in his country.

No one came to their defense. They walked the rest of the way.

They separated when they reached Sosnowiec and arranged to meet again later. Sala walked alone through the city, and was soon back on Kollataja Street. She entered the courtyard of her building; the same janitor was at his post, and he barely lifted his head as she passed. She went upstairs to her sister's apartment first, and an unfamiliar man opened the door. She could see past him into the room, and recognized Laya Dina's furniture. Everything was familiar, everything in the same place—except no sister, brother-in-law, niece, nephew. The man at the door said that he knew nothing about the previous tenants; as their eyes met, she felt a shock of fear, and stammered that she must be in the wrong apartment. At the bottom of the stairs, she fainted.

She regained consciousness in the courtyard. She wanted to leave as quickly as possible. She had not survived the war only to fall victim to the anti-Semitism of her former neighbors. Not a single night would she spend in Sosnowiec. She left Kollataja Street without visiting her own home. If her sister's sewing machine, her mother's brass candlesticks, her father's books were still there, if her diary was still locked in the drawer where she had left it, she would never know.

She registered with the local Jewish Committee, which had set up tables near the train station. In case someone else from the family came back, it was important to leave a forwarding address. But what was her next destination? She was adrift in a world with no associations of family or culture. Detached from all landmarks, she was twenty-one years old and she was looking at a blank map.

At the registry, she wrote down Prague as her destination. If Harry had survived, he would be looking for her there.

She started again. Eva joined her, and they reversed direction, now headed back from Poland to Czechoslovakia. Looking around more carefully now, they saw evidence of the war everywhere, in the bombed-out roads, destroyed bridges, and the ruined cities. They stayed with other survivors whenever possible, although Sala always preferred to avoid spending a night at any place that looked like a barracks. At each stop, the same cycle of questions was initiated with excitement and hope: "Where have you been?" and "Who have you seen?"

A few more days of hitchhiking and an occasional train ride brought them to the city of Waldenberg, where they were delighted to find old friends. Waldenberg was in the Russian Zone, but the women were under the protection of a Russian Jewish colonel, who gave them rooms in the building where he had established his headquarters. Still recovering from the shock of Sosnowiec, she and Eva joined their friends there.

Sala was soon a favorite with the Russian colonel, George. A far cry from the brutes who had terrorized Schatzlar, George was courtly and solicitous. He took her to a concert and listened to her story. He arranged for her to travel to Prague with a convoy of Russian soldiers, escorted by an aide from his staff who was ordered to remain with her at all times.

Sala used some of the spending money she received from refugee organizations to buy a small red leather notebook, and George wrote his name and home address there. He gave her a small photograph of himself, stiff and serious in his Russian army uniform. Out of habit, she saved his scrawled notes, and his picture, the first postwar papers that she added to the collection of letters that was always with her: *"Tomorrow at 10, I will stop by and pick you up in a car. You will go to Prague."*

Just before she was scheduled to leave, a new group of survivors arrived. This time, the frenzied exchange of names and places led to a miraculous discovery: someone from Sosnowiec had seen her sisters on a list of survivors of Bergen-Belsen. The location was unfamiliar to her and there were no more details—but this momentous news lifted her spirits and renewed the hopes that had been crushed in Sosnowiec. Raizel and Blima were alive. Bergen-Belsen, however, was apparently a considerable distance away, and she had no assurance that her sisters were still there. She decided to travel first to Prague.

Climbing aboard a truck of Russian soldiers was frightening. George's aide was true to his orders, however, and guarded her throughout the trip. They dropped her off in the center of town. She was totally, bewilderingly alone in a new city. She knew no one in Prague—except, perhaps, Harry.

The scent of food drew her toward Old Town Square, where people were pouring hot soup from giant cauldrons, and offering the bowls for free to any hungry passersby. She was grateful for the hearty soup, and even more grateful for the warmth of the Czech people. She was directed to a nearby hostel, where refugees were provided with free room and board, as well as small sums of spending money. She registered for her first identification papers. She wrote Teschen (Cieszyn), Poland, as her place of birth; it was a city that had always been divided between Poland and Czechoslovakia, which might facilitate her reunion with Harry. With one simple act, she wrote Sosnowiec out of her biography.

Prague embraced her like an old friend. Finding her family proved no easier there, however. Although she signed her name on every list that she saw, it was hard to search through pages and pages of names, as she had already discovered in Sosnowiec and Waldenberg. Word of mouth was more reliable. She asked the other refugees if they had seen her parents or her sisters or brothers or Harry, and then they reciprocated with their version of the same questions. She learned that conditions in the Nazi camps had varied greatly. Those who like her had been liberated from the Sudetenland labor camps had emerged in relatively good health. She met other survivors whose experiences had been far worse. Some were emaciated and sick. Some were wrapped in grief and depression. Her five-year ordeal had been one of the longest, yet she was stronger than those who had been even briefly in a large concentration camp, or who had suffered the brutal conditions of a death march after the camps were evacuated. She learned that postwar Europe had been carved into different zones, and that the Russians were not in charge everywhere. For the first time, she understood that there were survivors all over Europe.

The shadow of Auschwitz began to take shape.

She kept looking for Harry. She met one person who knew him as one of the elders at the Dyhernfurth camp, but the man seemed evasive, wanting to know how she was related to Harry.

Finally, someone gave her an address. She sent a telegram, saying that she had arrived in Prague.

Harry's answer came quickly, also in a telegram.

I AM ALIVE. WAIT FOR LETTER. HARRY

She waited. No letter came. Instead, a stranger arrived at the hotel, and asked for her. He said that he was a relative, sent by Harry to deliver the message that she should forget him and leave Prague. The stranger would not answer any of her questions. Harry would never see her again.

She had not cried since liberation but now she sat in the hotel dining room, still holding the telegram, and the tears flowed. It was a camp sister who rescued her.

Someone shook her roughly and called her name. Zusi was standing over her. In a minute, she was enveloped in Zusi's strong hug, weeping as she told her story. "So? Screw him." Zusi's voice filled the room with a roar that drowned Sala's sobs and had the rest of the room laughing.

Zusi had returned to Poland with another friend from camp. Her father's carpentry workshop and warehouse had been turned into German offices. All of his expensive machinery was gone, her beautiful home ransacked. She found no family, and no warm welcome from her former neighbors. She stayed there for a few days, but disliked being dependent on the local Jewish Committee. Her friend convinced her to return to Schatzlar, where one of the local people offered her a job in a cheese factory. She found an apartment and settled into a routine.

It took a few weeks before Zusi realized her mistake. Stupid, stupid, she berated herself, to end up in a cheese factory without family and without friends. So she left Schatzlar for the second time.

Delighted to find Sala in Prague, Zusi proposed that they stick together. Stop crying, she demanded: there are plenty of men.

They began again. They decided to leave Prague and make their way to the English Zone, where some of the largest groups of refugees were gathering.

At the former Schmelt camp of Feldafing, it was Zusi's turn for good news. She met a friend from home, who kissed her, hung on her neck, and told her what she most longed to hear: someone from her family had been found. Her sister Itka had survived. She had been liberated in Bergen-Belsen, but was desperately ill and had been hospitalized. Together with other dangerously sick women from the camp at Neusalz, she had been sent to Sweden for medical treatment.

Sala hardly dared to ask the woman, a stranger to her, about her own sisters, who had been with Itka at Neusalz and liberated in Bergen-Belsen.

Raizel and Blima were alive, terribly ill, but alive. They too had been sent to Sweden.

"What is Sweden?" Zusi screamed. "Let's start walking!"

*　　*　　*

January 1945 had been cruelly cold. Although the German troops in Warsaw had already surrendered to the Russians, and Hitler had retreated to Berlin, Raizel and Blima were about to face the worst hardships of the war.

The evacuation of Neusalz was ordered on January 17. The women heard that they were being sent to Auschwitz, a fear that seemed confirmed a few days later when the SS summoned them for an unusually long roll call. They stood in the freezing cold while they were counted again and again. Finally, they were divided into groups and sent back to the barracks. They were told that they would leave at dawn.

Some of the women had been at the camp for nearly three years. A few wrote farewell messages on the walls of the barracks and on scraps of paper.

Raizel had been ill, but Blima made sure that she was released from the infirmary before the roll call. Now, as they waited for the first light, two sisters, daughters of a well-known rabbi, came to Raizel and asked her to pray for the entire camp. Their father had given them a certain passage of the Psalms, or *tehillim,* to recite in case of extreme danger. The Psalms were believed to have a special efficacy when recited by heart, uninterrupted by food, drink, or other speech.

Raizel led the women in prayer. One of them kept the count. They repeated the words eighty-one times, the sacred texts echoing from the walls of the barracks.

They left Neusalz on the morning of January 22. A small group of women, including the rabbi's two daughters, were sent toward Auschwitz. Over a thousand women, among them Raizel and Blima, began walking to an unknown destination, accompanied by a small contingent of SS guards. Most of them would not survive the next 90 days.

They were apparently marching toward the front, but the western route had little logic other than to prevent them from falling into the hands of the Allied liberators, who had penetrated deep into Germany. The guards themselves seemed to recognize the futility of the grim parade. The women walked in rows of five along country lanes, as the primary roads were reserved for military traffic. They covered twenty to thirty miles each day. Each woman had been given two loaves of bread, which were soon gone. Raizel wore one wooden shoe that was too tight and rags on the other foot. Itka Ginter shivered in the pajamas that she had been wearing on the morning when she was taken from home, two years before. Her shoes had been stolen. When she saw a nearby cottage that looked occupied, she and a friend ran out of the line. They begged the German woman who answered the door for food. She gave them an armful of potatoes and bread, and handed Itka a pair of shoes. They rejoined the line.

The guards no longer seemed to care about maintaining discipline. Women were dying every day, falling and remaining where they fell. The rest marched on. They crossed into Czechoslovakia. Raizel awoke one night to find that she had been sleeping in a Jewish cemetery. She stumbled around the stones, reading the Hebrew inscriptions, more fit for the grave herself than for continuing the march. But Sala was in Czechoslovakia, Blima reminded her; perhaps even close by. It began to snow, and as Raizel prayed, she found other women gathering around her.

They walked for two months, their numbers dwindling steadily. By the middle of March, they were back in Germany. They remained for one week at the concentration camp at Flossenburg, where other death marches had also converged. Disease was rampant. On March 25, those who could still walk were taken to a train station, where guards shoved them into freight cars filled with suffocating coal dust. As many as one hundred women stood in a single car, packed so tightly that Raizel could not lift her arms. Suddenly, Blima disappeared from sight. When Raizel screamed, one of the guards beat her with his gun before slamming the door shut. The sisters had scarcely been apart since the day when Blima had rescued her at the stadium.

Raizel had no idea whether the train moved for hours, or for days. When the doors were unlocked, they were brought to a room and ordered to delouse themselves with freezing water that dripped from a single faucet. Once again, her sister found her. Blima washed

Raizel's cuts and soothed her hysterics. Her mother's words came back to her: you will have your mother with you. The march began again.

After seven days, they reached the concentration camp at Bergen-Belsen, nearly 280 miles from where they began. There was no water or food. Dead bodies lay everywhere. In a frenzy to hide as much evidence as possible, the SS tightly roped the wrists of the living to the wrists of the corpses, and ordered the women to drag the bodies into open pits.

Not certain whether she was awake or asleep, Raizel slumped in a corner. Suddenly, she perceived an unusual stillness. There were empty places where she had last seen the SS guards. Blima was lying silently next to her. The walls seemed to be whispering. Something struck her, a package thrown by someone speaking in a strange tongue, though she clearly heard *Free . . . Free.* It was the British liberation of Bergen-Belsen: April 15, 1945. She tried to embrace Blima, then collapsed with the next thoughts of mother, father, sisters, brothers.

Of the one thousand women of Neusalz who began the march, fewer than one hundred were alive.

The survivors were treated at a makeshift hospital staffed by English doctors. Typhus raged so fiercely that the British liberators burned down most of the buildings to contain the epidemic. There were ten thousand bodies to be buried. When Itka Ginter's name was called, her friends reported that she was dead. "No I'm not!" she protested, before lapsing back into unconsciousness. Sara Czarka was there too, gravely ill. Raizel had typhus, and her blood counts were extremely low.

The rabbi's daughters found Raizel. On their way to certain death at Auschwitz, the train had been stopped and rerouted to another camp, where women were needed to work in the kitchen. This camp was one of the first to be liberated, and the sisters had been brought to Bergen-Belsen. When they heard that the women from Neusalz had arrived, they searched everywhere for Raizel, certain that it was her prayer that had saved their lives.

They begged the English doctor to help her, and Raizel was among the first to receive a transfusion, with blood that came from Blima. But Blima was also terribly weak, and soon she was in the bed next to Raizel after suffering a heart attack.

Bergen-Belsen was filled with dangerously ill patients. The refugee agency arranged for some six thousand of the sickest women to be taken to Sweden for medical treatment. They traveled by train to the port of Lübeck, where they were transported by ship to Sweden. Raizel was sent to a hospital and sanatorium in Karlstad for treatment of typhus and tuberculosis, some seven hundred miles away from another hospital where Blima was recovering from her heart attack. Itka and Sara were also taken to Sweden.

Raizel had a dream. She was at home, and it was Friday night. The Sabbath meal was ready and her father stood at the head of the table, regal in his long white beard and formal coat. They were about to begin when he held up his hand: "We must wait," he said. "Someone is missing. We will wait for her." Blima was safe in a Swedish hospital, so Raizel knew that her father did not mean Blima. Nor did he mean Laya Dina, who must be somewhere else, together with her children. It would have been so hard for her to survive and to protect beautiful Salusia and Moniek as well, Raizel reasoned in her dream. No, it must be her youngest sister who was missing. Her father was telling her that Sala was still alive.

Sala and Zusi set out to find their sisters. Their first destination was Bergen-Belsen, and then they would find their way to Sweden. They were joined by another camp acquaintance, Michal, who was headed in the same general direction. They crossed into the American zone and were not far from Nuremberg when they found the pretty Bavarian town of Ansbach in their path.

As they entered the town, they were struck by the absence of the devastation that they had seen everywhere else. Although the bridges outside the town had been destroyed, the streets and buildings were intact. Michal heard someone calling his name: it was Leo, a friend from the camps. Dressed in a suit and tie, Leo no longer looked like a survivor, but he greeted Michal like his long-lost brother and was hardly less excited to be introduced to the other members of their group. Ansbach will fix your fatigue, he declared, and he urged them to stay.

Leo showed them around the town with the pride of a native son. He worked for the Americans, though he was vague about his specific job. As they walked through the streets, Leo seemed to know everyone. Sala and her friends decided to rest in Ansbach for a few days before continuing their journey. Leo found them an apartment after Sala refused to consider sleeping in a refugee center on the outskirts of the city. She would never spend another night in a camp.

It was easy to fall in love with Ansbach. With eight hundred years of history to its credit, the city was charming and prosperous, small but bustling, celebrated for its music festivals and its Baroque architecture. Although it had always been the cultural and administrative center of northern Bavaria, Ansbach had none of the industrial activity that would have attracted the attention of Allied bombs. After liberation, in this beautiful city where Jews had thrived from the fifteenth century until *Kristallnacht,* a community of survivors gathered.

The historical center of Ansbach was dotted with inviting cafés. The streets rang with an international mélange of languages. The official policy of nonfraternization between soldiers and civilians that had kept the Americans restricted to the nearby Army base at Katterbach had just been lifted. There was music in every corner, fair weather, and laughter.

It was only three months after liberation. The superficial scars of the camps were fading rapidly under the soothing balm of decent food and shelter. The survivors clustered together, fused by their common experiences and language. They were young, most of them still in their early twenties. Courtships progressed with bewildering speed. Wartime romances were rekindled; if they did not lead quickly to betrothals, the couple broke up and started with someone new. Sala Grunbaum arrived in Ansbach and was soon engaged to Michal, whom she had met briefly in one of the Schmelt camps.

Zusi and a former boyfriend were reunited and soon they too were engaged. Her fiancé's brother had also survived, and Zusi immediately claimed him for her sister, Itka. She was already dreaming of a double wedding—though the second bride was still missing.

The information about the three sisters was sparse: Itka, Raizel, and Blima had been sent somewhere in Sweden, address unknown. Frustrated by the slowness of the mails, Sala and Zusi decided to resume their search in person. They made plans to leave Ansbach.

She and Zusi walked together to the bus that would take them to Bergen-Belsen. Zusi boarded first. Sala followed, one step behind Zusi, then hesitated.

A certain energy seemed to emanate from Ansbach. It was the first place that seemed to offer some balance to her long years of slavery. The thought of yet another move was oppressive, especially since she would have to live in the large refugee camp at Bergen-Belsen. She wanted to be one step closer to reunion with Raizel and Blima—but she also needed time to heal.

Once she hesitated, her decision became clear. Ansbach had become her home. They embraced, and Zusi left without her.

She moved into a different apartment under the charming old clock tower. The building was owned by Leo's girlfriend, an Ansbach native, who charged her no rent for the spare but comfortable room. Her neighbors were mostly older Germans. As far as they were concerned, the war was over, and Americans and Jews were welcome. Apparently, no one there had ever been a Nazi—or even known one. She ate most of her meals at a small restaurant just around the corner, where the owner and his family fussed over her, still too skinny, they insisted, and refused to take payment. She enjoyed solitary walks around the stimulating streets, absorbing the energy of a city coming alive with the rhythm of commerce and daily life. She was ready to start again, but had to overcome the bitterness that sometimes threatened to consume her. Her friends seemed more settled, as if they had a clearer vision of their future. She ventured beyond the survivor community and met people with different backgrounds, ignoring the gossip that she was turning away from her heritage.

She was aloof, even secretive. Although she had many admirers, she preferred to be an observer, not a participant in the swirl of courtships around her. No one knew where she lived, other than a few of her closest friends. When she went out, she refused to let anyone walk her home, returning alone to the apartment under the clock tower.

In the oldest section of Ansbach, where the streets were hardly wide enough for a single car, one building had been the scene of feverish activity for weeks. At last, a sign on the door appeared: Ansbach's two-hundred-year-old synagogue would reopen on September 7 for New Year services.

The synagogue was one of the few left standing in Germany. The locals boasted that the mayor personally intervened to save the building from the Nazi torches during *Kristallnacht* because he wanted to preserve this most outstanding example of Baroque architecture. The more practical explanation was that a blaze on the narrow street would have spread quickly through the historical center of the town. During the war, the synagogue was used by the Nazis as a warehouse and stable, its Torah and prayer books destroyed.

In June, the synagogue was cleaned and renovated by volunteers from the "Famous Fourth Infantry" of the American Army. The ornate central platform, the marble *bimah,* from which services had first been conducted in 1747, was intact, and its gleaming pink marble pillars had been restored to their original luster. Army Chaplain Morris Frank presided over a formal ceremony to consecrate the old building once again. The Torah scroll used in the processional was found in a Nazi Party office building, and was decorated with the traditional crown and ornaments borrowed from the Nuremberg Jewish community.

The synagogue was packed for the New Year service. For the European Jews, this was their first religious gathering in freedom. For the Americans and other visitors, it was a solemn encounter with the survivors, and a moment to contemplate the aftermath of the war.

213

Sala had anticipated this moment in a New Year's poem she had
written in her diary in 1942:

Yet again, we spend our most solemn holiday behind
      bars.
In the future, it will be hard to believe that we waited so
      long for our freedom.
We cannot ourselves comprehend
How they caught us in this terrible trap
To spend years away from home, in the most miserable
      conditions
Busy only with work, and contemplating the horrors
      around us.
This is the most severe blow they dealt.
However, we are quite strong. We will tell ourselves to
      endure.
After all, Jews are used to it.
Our forefathers were even more exhausted
Still, they stood watch, proud and persistent,
We will try to do the same.
Today we are judged by the Almighty
May his name be blessed forever.
Oh God! Protect us now
Because we have no one but you, our defender. You are
      everything!
Look at how weary we are, our hearts bleeding
Worrying, where are our aged parents?
How bitter is their prayer now . . .
Let it all suffice, dear God,
For you to remove our heavy burden.
Let us hope, and let us be confident,
That soon we will be one with our parents, and with our
      family.
That is the essence of our prayer.

She sat in the upstairs balcony of the beautiful old synagogue. Her parents were murdered at Auschwitz. They had seven children at the beginning of the war:* Miriam Chaya, Moshe David, Laya Dina and their six children had all been killed, although she could never know exactly where or when. Her aunts and uncles, and their children, were also dead. Blima and Raizel were alive, but gravely ill, and far away in Sweden. Hersh Leib was lost in Russia. Ala had vanished. The dream of Harry had collapsed. Only a few of her Sosnowiec friends had surfaced. She had no country. Strangers occupied her former home. She would never forget the warning of the conductor who had thrown her off the tram in Katowice. Of the 28,000 Jews of Sosnowiec, almost 24,000 were annihilated, most of them at Auschwitz. There were no graves to visit, no dates to commemorate, nothing to mark their passing.

The service ended. The congregants exchanged the traditional New Year's greetings and dispersed into the streets.

From his seat in the men's section below, an American soldier had been watching Sala. He figured that it would not be too hard for an enterprising corporal from New York City to wangle an introduction. He already knew some of the other survivors. He spoke Yiddish decently. However, he was an American. No one would tell him where the beautiful young lady lived.

Sidney Kirschner finally met Sala Garncarz a few days later. They were introduced by one of her friends. Sidney looked like the kind of studious young man her father would have liked, and she called him by his Hebrew name, *Zacharia*. He invited her for a walk, and they strolled the next day along the banks of the Rezat River, at the edge of Ansbach.

Sidney Kirschner's roots were also in Poland. He too was the youngest in his family. His parents had come from Warsaw to New York in 1918. His father had been a tailor, and then started a clothing store, which Sidney would manage with his brothers after his

*See family tree on p. 265.

discharge from the Army. Sidney had been stationed in Europe for much of the war, returning briefly to the States in 1942 when his father died. He had served as quartermaster with Eisenhower's headquarters in Reims. After flying to Paris to bring back champagne and caviar for the victory celebrations in May, he was sent to Nuremberg with the occupation forces.

In June, he and other American soldiers were sent to Dachau, which had been recently liberated. As they entered the camp, there were still bones heaped up in piles in the crematoria. The Jews who were left were the ones who had been too sick to move, hardly distinguishable from the dead.

Sidney was assigned to the 8th and 9th Air Forces in the 425th Air Depot Repair Squadron, in charge of food and supplies for the thirty-five-hundred American soldiers at the Katterbach Army Base. A few months before, the base had been a Nazi airfield. Now, American helicopters were parked in place of the Messerschmitts that had idled there. The Nuremberg stadium became the central supply depot. The giant swastikas had only recently been removed, and the stadium still smelled from the thousands of refugees who had taken shelter there in the last weeks of the war. In their place stood mountains of egg cartons, sacks of potatoes, loaves of bread, canned food, and packages of meat. Cans of gasoline were lined up in long rows. Sidney started his "ration run" just after dawn. His truck barreled down the center of the stadium, and German prisoners filled his requisitions from the lanes on either side.

Sidney's work as the supply officer brought him to Ansbach nearly every day. Riding in his jeep, accompanied by a stray dog that he had adopted, Sidney became a familiar face wherever the survivors gathered, in their apartments or at the nearby displaced persons camp. Communicating in Yiddish, he found jobs for the refugees at the base, doing laundry and tailoring. He usually arrived with an armful of canned food and coffee. Even Sala developed a taste for Spam.

Sidney was in love. After a few weeks, however, he was invited to study in England. He would be taking business courses through an Army program and living at a former boarding school in Swindon, not far from London. It was a good opportunity, he told Sala, but he promised to return. Before he left, he took one of the pages in her red leather notebook to sign a mock contract:

> **Ansbach**
> **September 30, 1945**
> **I hereby state that I, Sidney Kirschner, will return to Ansbach, be it militarily possible and within my choice, at the earliest moment.**
> **Sidney Kirschner**
> **witnessed by: Sala Garncarz**

He wrote *kosher* in Hebrew letters to signify its authenticity, and Sala signed her name below his.

After Sidney's departure, her friends let her know that they were not happy with her new beau. They would have been suspicious of anyone beyond their small circle, even though this particular American was well liked. Soldiers are not looking for wives, they muttered ominously, mistrustful of Sidney's motives. They told stories of women who fell in love, only to discover that the charming young man already had a wife back home. In Poland, Jewish families had been geographically limited and tightly bound by generations of social and religious connections. Surely this was a time to cling ever more tightly to those roots.

Sidney's family in New York was no more pleased to hear about his romance. They were immigrants too, and sympathetic to the plight of the survivors—but who was this young woman? They wanted Sidney to return home, finish college, and manage the family store.

Suddenly, Ansbach lost some of its appeal. She didn't want to be interrogated by her friends. It was a good time to visit Zusi, who was still in Bergen-Belsen. She had located her sister Itka and was waiting for a transport to join her in Sweden.

From Bergen-Belsen, Sala wrote to her sisters. She used Itka's address, hoping that the letter would eventually reach them.

> Bergen-Belsen
> October 10, 1945

My beloved sisters Blima and Raizel,

Unfortunately, fate did not decree that we should finally meet after six years. However, this does not scare me so much anymore because I have finally located you, and I hope that we will meet soon. I had already lost all hope that I would find anyone from our family. I went back home right after the war ended. Alas, our home is no more! I found nobody there, and you can imagine how I felt in my heart when I entered the main gate. It's best not to write about it . . .

I left Sosnowiec on the same day, since I could not stay there even one minute longer. We have nobody left, nobody! I have some regards from [our brother] Moshe David but nothing specific. Rozia, Sala, and Abram Grunbaum from Olkusz are [alive]. Rozia married Leib. I have no other news about anybody else and I don't expect anybody else to have survived at the hands of Hitler's bandits.

I was staying in Waldenburg, some [distance] from Sosnowiec. An acquaintance came by to tell me about a list from Bergen [Belsen] in Sosnowiec, and that your names are on it. The following day I had a chance to drive to Czechoslovakia but, unfortunately, I had to stop in Prague for three weeks.

Now I reproach myself that maybe I was too late because of that. As I entered the American sector, I found out that you had already left for Sweden. It hit me like a bolt of lightning but, at the same time, I was glad to have the assurance that you are alive. All along I doubted that you will survive the "Gehenna."*

*Yiddish word for "hell."

Having found out that you were no longer [in Bergen-Belsen], I stopped in [Ansbach] Germany, near Nuremberg. I am OK here, and I was promised all kinds of help from American acquaintances, but I would prefer to be together, finally.

I have a lot of girlfriends, good ones, with whom I spent a lot of time in camp. In fact, I did not have it so bad while I was in camp, because I had help . . . I had some mail from Laya Dina till 194[3], but then it stopped coming. I feel sorrowful; however, we need to accept our fate as others do in our situation. Now I would be very happy to receive some news from you . . .

I have the pictures of our dear father and dear mother, together with all the mail I received from home, starting from the first minute that I left for camp. All along, I watched it and guarded it like the eyes in my head, since it was my greatest treasure.

Thank God I am healthy, I look well, so you don't need to worry about me. I will send you a recent picture of me, where you can see me wearing my pullover sweater, which I still have from home.

Right now I am in Bergen [Belsen] where my friend Zusi received a letter from her sister [Itka] in Sweden, so I am writing to her sister to send my letter to you. I would like to know what plans you have; in my opinion, you should not return here if you have opportunity to emigrate . . .

Do remember that I am waiting impatiently for any news from you. Personally, I don't know what to write anymore as it is so hard to remember everything . . .

Meanwhile, I will bid you farewell. I kiss you both warmly.

Your sister Sala

Sala spent a few weeks with Zusi, her fiancé, and his brother. Zusi made sure that the brother had nothing to do with Sala, since she had already reserved him for Itka. Sala had other plans, however. Sidney was due to return from England. On the back of his mock contract in her red notebook, she wrote a journal entry:

> The two months [of our separation] are coming to an end. I'm curious what they will hold for me. Probably nothing special, as I haven't received any news from you lately. If it should turn out otherwise, then it'll be a pleasant [surprise] for me. Will you be on time, as I was? Not much longer to wait.

She returned to Ansbach. True to his word, Sidney did come back. He had enjoyed Swindon, especially the close proximity to London, where he spent every weekend. He brought Sala gifts from his trip, including a bolt of bright blue wool from Harrod's. His daily trips to Ansbach resumed.

It took nearly two months for Sala's letter to reach her sisters. Raizel responded immediately.

> Karlstad
> December 6, 1945
>
> Dearest newly found little sister,
>
> My hands are trembling. I am jumping around, going crazy: I am delirious. I don't know where to begin. So my intuition concerning you was correct, after all, and you are alive for us! My mind is frantic, confused. December 6, 1945 will be a memorable, festive day for us, for today I received a letter from you, my dearest one. I can't believe my eyes; it happened just as I was feeling abandoned and resigned. I did not doubt that you were alive, but I could not figure out how you—the one of us who knew best how to survive—remained silent. Why doesn't she let us hear from her, I thought to myself. Forgive me, Sala, for writing so incoherently. Oh God, what goes on in my mind now!
>
> My love, I read your letter ten times. My tears covered

up your words, and others had to help me read them while I tried to calm myself. It was only by sheer coincidence that we were able to learn to our great joy that you exist!

Another patient from this sanatorium arrived at the place where Itka Ginter was staying. As soon as Itka heard that I am here, she immediately sent a letter telling me that you are in Bergen-Belsen, that she has had a letter from you for two weeks, but kept it, because she did not know where to look for us. A lucky coincidence. Itka, the noble soul, rushed the good news to us immediately. May she always be blessed for this good deed.

Dearest one, I am already anxious to know when our first letter will reach you. I am happy that you are well and did not have to wander around, as we did. We suffered terribly but in spite of everything, we survived. Now that I know you are alive, I must work twice as hard to get well quickly, so that when I am healthy and strong, I will be ready to see you. Finally, after all our sufferings, after six years of horror and separation, we will be able to hug you tight, close to our heart.

Sala, I do not wish to, and will not write to you about our experiences, because no matter how much I write, it could not, would not measure up to the reality of it all. I want to talk to you, face to face, about everything. When will that be, Sala?

Right now, I am sending a request for your passage to Sweden, though I have heard that one needs to pursue the matter from Bergen-Belsen. The first transport has left already, and a second is supposed to leave soon . . . Speed it up, as much as you can. Don't delay! I am doing the same. May God help us achieve our great goal.

Do not worry about us: the worst is over. Within the next few weeks, I will leave the hospital as a "convalescent." I feel well, as does our Blima. Oh, how my mind churns and does not let me rest, as I wonder whether, God forbid, you are hungry. How can we get you over here??? And why did you leave Bergen-Belsen? Please remember to write about everything, for it will now be our only consolation.

Even when we had no news about you, I kept staring at the door as if I knew for certain that you were alive. What is there to say now? Every minute without you will be an eternity.

I used to pour out all my suffering and my bitterness in my letters to my girlfriends. I talked about you, Sala dear, time and time again. Blima has also been filled with bitterness, but also with consolation. In her last letter to me, she wrote that she dreamed about [our aunt and uncle], and their children, and that whenever she dreams about them, she gets good news. And so I hope, wrote Blima, that something new and good will happen now!

. . . To try and find you, I wrote to Czechoslovakia, to Sosnowiec, to Stockholm, and to Warsaw, hoping your name was listed somewhere. All to no avail. Then, suddenly, there was news that people were being identified from Czechoslovakia. My heart twisted that there was no trace of you. And now you have appeared again on earth's surface! Hold to it fast, fast, so you may recapture at least a bit of your lost young life . . .

If someone is destined to live, he will extricate himself from the worst situation. And so it is.

I will not write any more now, and will end by taking leave of you, dearest, and kissing you a thousand times; your sister, who longs from the depth of her heart to see you and to embrace you. We shall never again lose each other, never!

Raizel

The discovery of Sala's deliverance set off a flood of letters from Raizel. Every day reminded her of another important question that must be asked, another searing memory that must be shared.

Karlstad
December 8, 1945

Dear Sala,

. . . It is Saturday night, and there is sadness in our hearts. Thank God, three of us are alive, though each one in a different place, while at one time, in the past, just at this hour there was such joy at home. Father was attending to the Havdala,* as our dear mother was cleaning up after the Sabbath. And now, oh, —————nothing of it remains. . . . Do you remember our dearest Salusia, Laya Dina's daughter, also [Moshe David's children]? Oh God . . .

I just received a letter from Blima. She writes that she doesn't know what's happening to her, for she is afraid that this beautiful dream will end . . .

Raizel

Raizel was not strong enough to travel. She had been moved to a sanatorium, still a long trip from Blima's hospital. From there, she continued her letter-writing campaign to locate other family members. She urged Sala to join them immediately.

Rattvik
December 10, 1945

Our dear Sala,

. . . Yesterday, I left the hospital, and now I am in a home for convalescents. It's not bad here, except for the eternal separation, the three of us still scattered.

I cannot see Blima since I am not completely well, but if you came here, you would be together with her. Oh, how happy that would make me. You absolutely must go to Bergen-Belsen. Remember not to be late for the transport. I am still waiting anxiously for an answer from Stock-

*The service that ends the Sabbath.

holm, but it is most important for you to pursue it from your side.

We live from day to day, under stress, as we await your arrival . . .

Frankly Sala, I don't have much to say. Or maybe I really have too much to say. The deeper one's thoughts, the harder it is to put them into words. That is how it is with me. I would like to tell you so much, to write so much, but instead I just scribble some nonsense. Then I regret writing you so little, nothing of any significance. No, Sala, you must come here, so we can talk.

. . . In the meantime, have you found anyone from our family? As I ask, I have to sigh sadly, and answer my own question. Still, maybe someone. After all, it did happen that some frail people turned out to be more resilient than others, assuming that at the end they did not perish.

We cannot lose heart or else we cannot go on living. We must live in the present, like everyone else. We live for you, for you, and that gives us a little courage.

And so I bid you farewell with great longing.

Your sister Raizel

Raizel sensed Sala's reluctance to leave Ansbach, but could not have guessed that her sister was falling in love. *"You could ask to be sent to be with me,"* she suggested. *"You must exert pressure to accomplish it, just as a woman did who arrived here, without even being registered. She simply insisted stubbornly that she must join her dear ones, who are here."*

Sala sent Raizel a copy of the only remaining photographs of their parents, a precious reminder of home, which Raizel had mailed her during the war. There was still faint hope that they would find other living relatives.

224

Rattvik
December 11, 1945

Our dear Sala,

So the sun really did come out from behind the cloud. Is it really true? Finally, what happiness! We have a second letter from you.

Sala, as I read your words, I get goose bumps. So you went back home, to the house from which our dear parents were forced to leave. I understand why you could not stay there long.

I can see that you did wander a lot, and that you found our names on a list. Rest assured that destiny is guiding us. Do not reproach yourself that you did not find us in Bergen-Belsen; apparently that's how it had to be. My life could well have ended there because I was so very ill.

Did you get any more news about our brother Moshe David from the woman you spoke to? Maybe you could ask her to supply you with more specific news about him, since they were in camp together. We want to know even the worst news, as we are prepared for everything. I think that our brother-in-law David is also alive, if we knew where to look for him. Since the lists are of no help, we have to rely on another coincidence. I am also inquiring about our brother Hersh Leib, of whom I have found no trace. He was in Russia, in the town of D————, and worked in a gasoline refinery.*

I submitted a search for other relatives in Poland but I have received no answer. We heard that a lot of people are now in the city of Lodz. There is a list of all people there, and perhaps we will still find someone of our own.

---

*The town has not yet been identified. Mysteries would always remain about Hersh Leib, who most likely disappeared with the forced evacuation from Soviet-occupied eastern Poland.

And now dear Sala, concerning our own plans: we do not want to return to [Germany], so you have to try to come here—and then we will see what can be done. [We are] happy that you are well and that you have friends. We thank you for the photograph; this picture of our dear parents is a treasure. Oh, how much I would like to see you. I kiss you countless times, with heartfelt longing.

Raizel

Raizel was relieved to be writing again in Polish after the years of constricted expression in German. She questioned her sister closely about her life in Ansbach, reprising almost the same list that she had posed in her first letter of 1940, when Sala had first arrived at Geppersdorf: *"How do you manage, and how is your health? Do you have clothes to wear, and food to eat? Please write about yourself in greater detail."*

Raizel began to reconstruct the essays and poetry that had been destroyed in Neusalz. In her most beautiful calligraphy, she was compelled to compose again in the language of her parents.

Rattvik
December 20, 1945

Dear Sala,

I just thought, dear child, that today I should write to you in Yiddish. I am sure that you will not be angry at me for it. So often, I feel guilty. I imagine our dear father is near me and he says, Raizel, could it be that I put all my hopes in you and that you don't even write in Yiddish?

Surely, we owe this to them, to write in the language in which our parents spoke to us, the language in which we spoke to our parents. I must admit that it is harder for me because I'm thinking again in Polish. And then it comes again to my mind, how they earned [the right for us to write in Yiddish], even if we have to struggle to give them this gift? How many sleepless nights did they spend with us and how many days would they go without food when,

God forbid, something was wrong with a child? What wouldn't our dear mother do to put a child back on her feet? Nothing was too difficult for her.

It is 12 o'clock now on Friday. I see our dear mother fussing in the kitchen to prepare for Shabbat, our father getting ready to welcome a guest. Ah, that's all my imagination. I wish I had at least a picture, so that I could at least be able to kiss his high forehead and his long grey beard. When you came home the first and only time from Geppersdorf to see us, it was also on a Friday. How happy we all were, how quickly it passed by. How hopeful our dear father was to see you still alive. I read every one of your letters to him ten times. He was so sorry to put them away. You can't imagine what it meant to him, how he talked the whole day about your return home.

Beyond his words, Sala, I see our father again, his voice comes to me again. Our dear parents, they gave us their future, and it was our job to find you.

. . . My letters chase each other, one after the other, so don't be surprised if they aren't so systematically written. I need for us to be together because I feel anxious from this correspondence: writing all my feelings, our dearest, writing, writing, writing, every free moment.

Again, I hate to separate from you because when I write to you, I am with you . . .

Raizel

Sala's friends were beginning to leave Ansbach. She began to fill the pages of her small red notebook with their forwarding addresses: Palestine, France, England, America. They found relatives who sponsored their immigration, or they moved to German cities with larger communities of survivors. There was talk of starting new businesses. Marriages were announced practically every day; at last, a wedding was an occasion to celebrate, rather than a symbol of despair.

Sidney left for a brief New Year's vacation in Switzerland. When he returned, he gave Sala a watch as a gift, and told her that his final discharge from the Army would be coming through shortly. He wanted to return to New York—and he wanted Sala with him. For five years, Sala had no control over her future. Now she would be forced to choose whether to join her sisters in Sweden, pioneer with other survivors in Palestine, or emigrate to America with Sidney.

Raizel kept writing. Each delay in Sala's departure made her more impatient and suspicious. Blima had discovered the whereabouts of her fiance, Jacob Goldberg, who was the only survivor in his family. He was on his way to Bergen-Belsen, and would leave from there to Sweden. He and Blima would be married as soon as possible.

Raizel was declared well enough to travel, so she took a fifteen-hour train ride to see Blima, their first reunion since they arrived in Sweden. Both sisters had made good friends among the close community of survivors, but they wanted Sala to join them. Still unaware of Sidney's existence, Raizel allowed her voice to be harsh as she assessed her sister's infrequent letters and her stubborn unwillingness to leave Ansbach.

> Rattvik
> February 25, 1946

Sala, dear,

Your silence is of your choice. Should I be accusing you? Oh, no! I will not allow the idea to enter my mind, that you could be so inconsistent as to fail to live up to our agreement of writing regularly, every week. Is it possible that none of your mail is getting through? In that case I will agree with you that the postal services cannot be trusted . . . Words fail me and I don't know any more how to express our bitterness, loneliness, at this constant silence of yours.

Salusia, I would like for you to go to Bergen-Belsen. We have registered you for a transport to Sweden. I submitted your address, but I doubt they would look for you where

you are now. Therefore, I think that it would be best for
you to be in Bergen-Belsen. May God allow for this
longed-for moment to arrive, when we would be together
again after such a long separation . . .

Raizel

Sala and Sidney became engaged. Her future would be with him
in the United States, not in Ansbach, not with her sisters in Sweden,
and not in Palestine. Together, she and Sidney presented the facts to
her sisters, and then followed up with a second letter from Sala.

Ansbach

My beloved Sisters,

A few days ago I sent you a letter where I wrote, in great
detail, about everything that's happening in my life. It was
difficult for me to write it, but now I feel unburdened.

Your letter, Blima, and the enclosed picture arrived and
it made me very happy. A little later I broke out crying,
because I could not at all recognize you in the picture. You
seem to be so heavy, and I could never imagine seeing you
looking like that: is this altogether a healthy sign?

With God's help, I am now almost sure that I will be
able to see you sooner, and I think that you will give me a
sound thrashing for being so skinny . . . but I feel perfectly
healthy. It could be all this constant worry and the waiting
that is causing it.

Dear Blima, how much I envy all those who see you,
sit at the table with you, and partake of your cooking and
your baking. I miss you an awful lot and it almost drives
me mad. As for you, Raizel, I received your letter, written
in Yiddish; you still write beautifully and I admire your
style. As for me, I could not possibly compose anything
decent in Yiddish, no matter how hard I try, since I can't
even write three words without a mistake. All those
languages get mixed up in my head—German, Czech,

Russian and now English—so as a result, I know two words in any one.

Sidney just walked in so I will stop writing, since I want him to write to you. I don't think you will understand it because he writes in English. However, maybe someone will read it to you as I myself will not know what he wrote . . .

Stay well, strong, and keep your spirits up. I kiss you many times.

Your sister Sala

Sidney added a paragraph in English, addressing his future sisters-in-law directly for the first time.

Dear Blima and Raizel,

I'm very sorry that I can't write either Jewish or Polish—if I could, I would write a long letter—as it is, you'll have to excuse me.

Your sister Sala is the nicest and sweetest person I ever met—in fact I'm hoping to take her to America with me as my wife. Sala hopes to be able to see you before she leaves—but frankly I don't know if it will be possible. Meanwhile let's keep hoping.

Sorry I have to close now—Best wishes to you both for a very happy future—Perhaps someday we will be able to meet in person—I hope so.

Sincerely,

Sidney

Raizel responded quickly:

Rattvik
March 3, 1946

Dearest Sala,

Your letter, your letter and his—what does it all mean? A partially comprehensible puzzle, which I expect to solve when your more detailed letter arrives as you promised. We have not received it yet. We are surprised. We don't know whether we ought to congratulate you on your engagement, or whether—oh, I have no words to express our feelings. However, if what we suspect did happen, we wish you both much happiness, from the innermost depths of our being, happiness in your new life.

May you, our dearest Salusia, never, never again know suffering. May he who is now to walk with you on the road of life, give you true happiness and act as your protector.

Our joy is boundless because your happiness is also our happiness, just as your loneliness is our loneliness. I am thinking just now how our dear parents would have been delighted had they lived to lead you, the youngest child in the family, to the wedding canopy. What pleasure and joy that would have been for the entire family. Meanwhile, from afar, the only two surviving sisters whose most fervent desire is to be reunited with you and to hug you close to our heart, cannot even dream of it. Fate wants it that way, and I do not resist.

For the time being we must be satisfied just to write to each other. Who knows if that will not be our way of staying in touch forever. But, oh God, what thoughts took hold of me. I cannot even stop my tears, so let them flow and maybe they will relieve my great longing, which is turning into madness. Because, because—well, that's how it has to be! However, let's not lose hope that someday we will be with each other.

Let me tell you, Sala, about our situation here, which is difficult to describe. We are pretty well off, but will it turn out to be our lot to be separated always, and to live from day to day? It is true that our cousins will do everything possible to bring us over to them [to Palestine], but that is not feasible. Only the nearest of kin are taken into consideration, and Sweden is even [stricter] . . . Besides, we want to be with you. Blima's fiancé is trying to get to Sweden. In other words, we really don't know what to do and we are waiting for your advice.

Oh yes, about your picture: Sala dearest, you do look pale. Why do you weigh so abnormally little—112 pounds? Oh, how this hurts us. We are heavy, yes, Sala, maybe too heavy, and you. . . . We would like you to put on some weight. We are too heavy, you are too thin, be careful to at least stay healthy.

To answer your question as to our health, my lungs are almost cured. May my health continue to improve. I want to have hope that I will be well and that I will walk normally, which is difficult for me now. I hope, I hope, I hope, I hope that I will regain my strength. Blima is working and is feeling well now, but there was something wrong with her heart. We are not surprised, but it will pass. I feel that if we were together, our health would be 100 percent.

And now Salusia, as you can see, we are writing a few words in English to [Sidney]. Please explain to him that we did not compose it ourselves, so the expressions might not be too beautiful. He could write again and we shall answer him. Is he Jewish, and what kind of relationship do you have? We are terribly worried because you did not supply us with these details. We live in great expectation and we long for you—and maybe for both of you. I think that I should now end all of this foolishness of mine, and say goodbye, goodbye, and send you thousands of kisses.

Your sisters, forever longing for you.

Raizel and Blima

Raizel added one more paragraph in English:

Dear [Zacharia]!

We thank you very much for your letter. Now we hear the first time about all these things which you are writing to us. We are very happy to know that my sister found a man who is interested in her. We believe that it will be her luck. We would like very much to see her and if it is only possible, please, make your utmost and come to see us.

Don't worry that we don't understand English. You can always write to us in your own language.

Now we are ending our writing with the best wishes for you and we remain,

Sincerely yours,

Blima and Raizel

Raizel was not the only one who found it difficult to accept Sala's choice. Some of Sala's old friends feared that she was turning away from them—or from her commitment to Palestine.

Her friend Lusia wrote:

[Landsberg]
March 21, 1946

Dear Sala,

Since I have an opportunity to write to you again, let me congratulate you, first of all, and wish you all the best as I would wish myself. Salusia, I still wish to meet you in Palestine. As they say, there is no place like home. We know where our home should be, in a place where nobody has the right to throw us out or murder us. We must secure our legal Jewish existence so that we can develop, as all others do, both culturally and economically. We need to build a good and happy future for our children, one that will provide them with the awareness of a patriotic Jewish soul and not the apprehension of the Diaspora where anti-Semitism will always be taking root somewhere, as it did with the Nazis.

Salusia, I don't think you will be angry at me for these thoughts. I will not write to you about this again, as I know that destiny has decreed this. Still, man is master of his own fate so you must come with your husband to our Palestine and be happy, for the happiness of an entire nation is the greatest happiness. We must be patriots!

Please excuse this scribble, but my hand is bandaged. Send me a picture of you with [Sidney]. Salusia, be well and be happy.

Lusia

Sala discovered that an older cousin had survived. When he heard the news of Sala's engagement to an American, he assumed the responsibility of speaking in her father's place. He had stayed with the family on Kollataja Street, and he knew Sala to be an independent girl who had already been pressing against the boundaries of her family's way of life before the war. Now he must admonish her to honor the traditions of her mother and father. The destruction of their families had created a profound obligation. His words were grave, all the more so because he had lost his own young wife and child.

Sala listened. Her faith had wavered after the war. It was an agonizing struggle to reconcile the slaughter of innocents with a belief in God. To do otherwise, however, would render the sacrifice of her parents meaningless. She promised.

One major obstacle still stood between Sala and America. Sidney's mother wanted to postpone the marriage until her son was home. He had refused, declaring that he would reenlist and stay in Ansbach if his mother was not prepared to welcome his bride to New York.

The time was growing short: Sidney was scheduled to be discharged. It was critical for them to marry before he returned to New York, so that she could immigrate as the war bride of an American soldier.

Sala presented her own case to her future mother-in-law, writing with some difficulty in Yiddish.

Ansbach
[undated]

To the mother of Sidney,
    Before I took the pen in my hand, I turned it over a few

times and I came to the conclusion that I have to do it, it's my obligation. I'm hoping that I'll be properly understood. Ah! If I could only find the proper words . . . it's very difficult for me. But I have to do it so that my conscience will be clean and I will never feel guilty. The time is short.

Sidney will return home soon where he's been impatiently awaited. He longs to be home. He and I want the same thing, but it is something I won't and can't accept, something I will not make a decision about before we get the blessings and the acceptance of Sidney's mother. This is not a child's game and it is not something you can buy, or something that you can change with time. No! It is a life's problem, a life's question.

Unfortunately, I was not given the happiness of being able to ask my dearest mother for her blessing. The future dealt me heavy blows when it took the holiest and the best from me, to be able to say the word "mother" or to write and ask whether it is right for me to be married.

So we acknowledge that this is our obligation, to be waiting and waiting. For what? For the permission of Sidney's mother. We are not getting an answer. Why? I can answer this question myself. It is possible that my parents would handle this the same way: we don't really know each other. A child is everything to a mother, especially the youngest child. Like Sidney, I am also the youngest child. We want the best for them, to see everything nicer, bigger, better. And if we don't know where they are going, or with whom they go, so far away, we don't have faith. We are not sure. I can understand and tolerate this, but we have now reached the final minute.

About me, there's nothing much to write, a plain Jewish girl from a kosher home and that's all. I think it's enough. I'm putting my future in this letter. If a positive answer comes, the way we are hoping, then we remain happy. If not, then it's difficult but I'll have to say like a Jew says, always, everything is for the best. Whichever way the answer should be, please write and don't pay attention to my words, only answer what your heart and feelings are.

Please forgive that I'm writing in Yiddish and not perfect Yiddish—but you do forget how to write and I don't know English at all.

Sala

Sidney's mother gave her consent.
He responded with a telegram to New York:

EVERYTHING WORKING OUT FINE GETTING MARRIED EARLY NEXT WEEK AND LEAVING FOR HOME THE EIGHTH THE MARRIAGE WILL BE A CIVIL AFFAIR I WANT TO LEAVE THE RELIGIOUS CEREMONY FOR HOME WHEN YOU CAN BE PRESENT ALL IS BEING DONE ACCORDING TO HOYLE* BEST REGARDS TO ALL HOPE TO SEE YOU REAL SOON LOVE SID

On Sala's twenty-second birthday, she married Sidney Kirschner at the Ansbach town hall. Sala's friends signed the registry as witnesses.

After the wedding, Michal hosted a crowded party in his apartment. They drank toast after toast to the new couple, and Michal climbed on the table to deliver a stern and tipsy message to Sidney that they demanded only the best for their Sala, and expected to hear wonderful, joyous news of their future life in America.

Sidney boarded a train the next day, carrying a box of leftover wedding cake to enjoy on the long ride to Le Havre, where he boarded a boat to New York.

Once back in the States, Sidney filed the necessary immigration papers. It was a complex and frustrating procedure, and he was

---

*"According to Hoyle" meant "by the rules." Edmond Hoyle was an English author of books that codified the rules for card games.

told by the Red Cross that it would take years before Sala arrived. So he wrote directly to the general of the 8th Armed Forces. Within weeks, he was able to write to her with good news.

New York
April 23, 1946

Dearest Sala,

How happy I am, because today I received mail from you. And what a letter!!! [The news] from the army in Frankfurt was the best of all. Now it can't take that much longer. My God, enough time has gone by that I haven't been able to be together with my Sala, my Sala, who is my whole life. I'm counting every day, every minute until you come to me.

The little cutting [I am enclosing] is from a paper here in New York and it says that the longest it will take for you to come here is the end of [June]. Maybe you can come much sooner. I need you very much.

Don't be afraid to go onto the ship, Sala. From my own journeys I can tell you that I didn't get sick, the journey was very nice. Only my heart was aching, because I knew that I left you back in Ansbach . . . How many times I nearly cried just to be together with you, but I got over it thinking that you'll come soon . . . I'm missing you very much. Now I know what real love means. Every minute that we're not together is too much.

The first day of my return was very nice. All my brothers and my sister with her child were there. The first thing they said was, "Mazel Tov"—and asked for photos of you right away. Everybody, everybody says how beautiful you are. I already told them that a long time ago in one of my letters. I don't need anything now, only you. Since you're there, Sala, I'm very happy. I'm working in the store as I used to. Mama keeps talking of the time when you will be here. We will have a wedding soon—a big wedding, as it ought to be. We will talk more about you when you get here. And your sister, maybe we can take her over to America. Only come, my dear Sala, there are so many things for us to do, come to me soon. Amen.

My mother is very happy that you received the parcel. Was everything okay? Is everything okay??? . . . As you have told me not to, I won't send you any more parcels—but I'll send one to your sister, if only you'll let me know what to send.

Are you well, precious Sala? I hope that everything is in order. My Mother and Grandmother send best and warmest regards. Give my regards to everyone in Ansbach. Yours, forever,

Sidney

Sala was eager to leave Ansbach. The survivors had continued to disperse, and those who remained seemed to be jealous of her improved prospects as the wife of an American. She no longer felt fully integrated into the once tightly knit community. Nor was she comfortable in the English-speaking world of Sidney's Army friends. Leo, who had once smoothed her entry into Ansbach, had disappeared. His mysterious work for the Americans had never been fully explained. There was talk of black market activities and even some arrests.

When her papers were finally in order, Sala traveled by train to Paris, where she stayed in her first real hotel and wrote to Sidney. It would never be mailed, but she now added a picture postcard of the Eiffel Tower to her precious papers. From Paris she went to Le Havre, where she waited for the rest of the passengers, who were arriving from other locations in Germany, France, and Poland.

Just a little over a year after liberation, she and hundreds of other war brides were headed for New York aboard the USS *George Goethals*. In place of the armband that once identified her as a Jew, she wore an American flag on her sleeve. Despite the bouts of seasickness that she had feared, she made good friends, and enjoyed the music of an Army band.

She arrived on May 30. It was unseasonably hot, and she was sweltering in a blue dress that she had sewn from the heavy wool that Sidney had brought from London.

People began to disembark. The names of the war brides who would be going through special immigration procedures were called. But not her name. An hour passed. Everyone else left the boat.

A representative of the Jewish agency approached her. Speaking in Yiddish, the short little man told her not to worry, and assured her that he would help her to find her husband. She refused his assistance. She had no intention of getting off the boat. She knew no one in New York. If her husband did not claim her, she would cross the Atlantic again. From there, she would go straight to Palestine.

Vexed and sweaty, she held on tightly to the railing of the boat and to her small suitcase.

And then her name was called.

One week later, she was married again, this time by a rabbi, on June 8, 1946. She was wearing a borrowed wedding gown, taken off a bride the week before by Sidney's ever practical mother. She had no family, no friends at her wedding.

She settled in New York. Somewhere in the three-room East Harlem apartment that she and Sidney shared with his mother, Sala hid the box of letters. She said nothing about them or about her life during the war, for nearly fifty years.

The Other Side of Silence

"She's here again," my mother says, with a mock groan.

She is always happy to see me. Perhaps I only imagine an imperceptible chill when my alter ego enters the room, that part of me that is always poised to pounce when an innocuous chat between mother and daughter takes a turn into the land of Sosnowiec and the labor camps.

We have shown each other different faces, as if the letters reflected features that were hidden or obscured, magnifying some and minimizing others. In my mirror, I see Sala, restless and romantic, sparkling with life, protean and decisive. I used to think we were so different, my mother and I. But now I'm not so sure.

Our project has blurred the distinctions between parent and child. As I became her biographer and memoirist, I learned more about her than even she could remember. "Ask Annie" became her playful deferral to inquiries from other people, as if I could perform some sublime act of ventriloquism.

Wary of Nietzsche's caution that "when you look too long into the abyss, the abyss also looks into you," I wondered about the cumulative effect of this immersion on me. I checked myself periodically for cracks in my psyche, like a cautious search for deer ticks after a hike in the woods. But in the end, I was merely a visitor to her world. I was not the one who experienced five years of hunger, fear, and vio-

241

lence. I was, as Auschwitz survivor Jean Améry has written, "a blind man speaking of color."

A more lasting concern was the probity of subjecting my mother, once the most silent of survivors, to my scrutiny. Having once accepted her restrictions, now I found myself amplifying her pain. As I solved mysteries, I proffered brutal facts in place of what had sometimes been her hazier, inconclusive version. I filled in gaps with mordant details that were unknown to her—and could have stayed that way. In the house of memory, which used to belong to her alone, she invited a visitor who proceeded to move in and take over, filling every corner with numbers and names and dates, and poking a harsh bright light into every dark corner.

Still, she has allowed me to continue.

There is nothing left, she warns, but I always find another detail, another anecdote. Or even another object: she just remembered to show me the handmade brass comb that she took from home and shared with her friends in Schatzlar. When I ask her about the clothes she wore in camp, she remembers that she wore Hersh Leib's shirt on the day she was photographed with Harry. Then she leaves the room, returning a few minutes later with that shirt and with the handmade coral blouse that she sewed in Sosnowiec sometime before 1940. On another visit, she produces the small red leather notebook that she used after the war and we spend hours looking through it. There is the handwritten address of George, the Russian colonel who sent her to Prague, and my father's contract promising to return to Ansbach. I tease her that there must be yet another box of letters stashed somewhere.

Never one to procrastinate, she is determined to finish what she started when she gave me the letters, not only "because of what Annie started with this whole adventure of hers," but because her gift deepened our understanding and appreciation of her life's work. With detachment and amazement, she too marvels at the young Sala who saved the letters: "It is a miracle to me. How did it happen? I can't figure it all out, how I got them, how lucky I was."

Together, we try to solve the remaining puzzles.

*   *   *

It is hard to imagine two more different women than Raizel and Ala, with their diametrically opposed views of women's roles, sexuality, and religion. Yet they were both mentors to my mother. She started out closer to Raizel, hardly knowing any other way. But her curiosity and forced independence threw her into Ala's orbit. When both women were taken from her, Sala found her own balance, her roots deeply entwined with Raizel's, but also nourished by Ala's different energy: savvy, individualistic, modern.

What drew Ala Gertner to my mother's side in that first encounter at the train station? Sala's youth, her pure good looks, the obvious distress of her mother . . . perhaps it was the scent of good luck that clung to my mother like perfume. Whatever the motivation, Ala's spontaneous act of generosity at the train station rubbed a deep and sustaining color into the grim world of the labor camps.

Ala lived by a code that blended the pragmatic with the idealistic, neither saint nor sinner, but a human being caught between miserable, unthinkable alternatives. She used all her resources, all her intelligence and connections to help her survive. I knew her well, I thought, until July 15, 1943, the date of her last letter to my mother. And I learned enough about her life at Auschwitz to believe that she might have withstood even the death camp. With liberation so tantalizingly close, why did she risk everything?

The more I learned, the more confused I became. So much was still unknown about Ala's role, and about the uprising and the investigation. Even eyewitness reports published soon after liberation were rife with inconsistencies and inaccuracies. The contradictions have been compounded over time as memories became more fragile, even for these most searing events.

If you happened to be in the reading room of the New York Public Library on November 15, 1992, you might have seen a woman suddenly bang her fist on the table and throw down a book, exclaiming "No, it can't be!"

That was me. I was reading for the first time that Ala had broken under torture and implicated some of the other women involved in the uprising. Sitting that day at the wooden tables of the library, I felt lightheaded and cold, somehow diminished. I wanted a heroine; instead, I was discovering a real woman. I allowed myself to feel disillusioned, as if Ala's legacy had been ambushed. My distress was echoed in my mother's voice when I told her that Ala may have betrayed her friends. "They would never have honored her," she protested. She had been present when a monument was dedicated to the four women in Jerusalem. Now it was my mother who was subdued, lost momentarily in her memories.

But the Nazis failed: Ala's heroism was all the greater for her humanity. If she broke under torture, her confession took nothing away from her decisive, defiant acts of resistance. I found her courage even more striking when I reflected on her life before Auschwitz. Unlike some of the other conspirators, who were veterans of the Warsaw uprising, Ala had no previous involvement with any resistance groups. To the contrary: Ala worked for Moses Merin, who cooperated with the Gestapo in the ruthless suppression of the underground. She may have been working for him as early as 1940, when she went to the labor camp at Geppersdorf.

Her actions suggest a profound evolution. Something happened that forced her into action, she who had remained private, pragmatic, and self-protective until then. But if she had found ways to navigate the horrors of Auschwitz, what was her motivation to join the resistance movement? Is the answer as simple as her determination to defy the Nazi oppressors and to strike a blow for freedom?

My mother and I discuss what Primo Levi called the Grey Zone, that morally ambiguous space where survival is all that matters, where words such as *hero, villain, martyr, resistance, betrayal, honor,* and *liberation* are neutered by the exigencies of the concentration camp. I wonder aloud why Ala would have entangled her own chances for survival with a larger set of moral imperatives. Was she driven by despair? Revenge? Love? Hope?

Now it is my mother's turn to pound her fist on the table. Sitting in her kitchen, my mother cuts through my cynicism and doubt: "Ala had the chance to act. And because of her privileges in Auschwitz, she was physically strong enough to seize that opportunity. She wanted to take that chance, she wanted to do something that would be remembered." Suddenly, it is young Sala at the table, powerful and defiant, reliving the moment when she threw a Nazi armband on the ground before the SS officer. "I didn't care about him. Yes, I cared about living, but I had to let go of my fear, to take control in some way."

The only certainty is that Ala lost her life at Auschwitz. She left no family behind and might have vanished without a trace, except that she left her mark on history, on my mother, and on me.

"I live in a world of my own thoughts, where my plans and dreams float about," Ala Gertner wrote, as if gently deflecting my longing to understand her. *"I hope that you will get to know all my good sides better—those you know and those you don't know yet. Everything in its own time."*

Harry, I discovered, had a girl in more than one camp. Perhaps he was most attached to Sala; after all, he could not have given anyone else his baby pictures. I like to think that he was serially monogamous—and to acknowledge his unusual circumstances. After all, no one knew who would survive.

Then again, Harry did not try very hard to wait.

After Harry and Sala were separated into different transports, he was sent to Dyhernfurth. His work as an overseer of a poison gas factory was dangerous and the conditions, particularly for the men, were brutal. Harry was friendly with one of the Jewish Elders, and when the elder fell out of favor and was sent to Auschwitz, Harry replaced him. I contacted women from Dyhernfurth who remembered Harry very well and described him as lively, personable, and "as handsome as Apollo." They recalled his close relationship with a married woman who used her job at the camp kitchen to cook for him. A jealous type, she watched him carefully, because other women were circling around him. He spoke German like a native, they noted.

Harry was remembered less fondly by men, who said that he had a bad name among the survivors, and they characterized him as a womanizer.

The one who finally married Harry was a young and pretty woman from his hometown. Their families knew each other before the war, prominent members of a small community of affluent and assimilated Czech Jews.

The camp at Dyhernfurth was evacuated in January 1945. About one thousand prisoners were forced to march for miles in frigid weather, sleeping at night in open fields. They were crammed into cattle cars that brought them to the concentration camp at Flossenburg, where typhus and spotted fever were raging. (Raizel and Blima were also taken to Flossenburg on the death march from Neusalz.) By April, the last remaining, half-dead prisoners were near Dachau when they were overtaken by American soldiers and liberated. Somewhere along this miserable route, Harry vowed that if he and the young woman at his side were to survive, he would marry her.

He was thirty-two, she was eighteen—about Sala's age. Both lost their entire families in Auschwitz. They married right after the war. Two daughters were born.

I never knew about Harry until Sala gave me the letters. On the other side of the Atlantic, Harry never told his family about Sala. With the help of a researcher in Israel and a friend in Germany, I finally succeeded in tracking down his daughters.

We met in the beautiful city of Cologne. I was a stranger from the United States who had their father's baby pictures and love letters to a woman who was not their mother. The Harry I knew was frozen in 1942, but suddenly here he was in the family photo album: Harry with babies, middle-aged Harry in a bathing suit, aging Harry wearing glasses, a bit heavier but still suave in a tailored suit, his hair combed back, and that same knowing expression on his handsome face. The pictures of Harry in color startled me, in contrast to the black-and-white photographs that I knew so well.

His daughters told me about his difficult life after the war, how he had reclaimed the family businesses only to lose everything all over again when Communists confiscated privately owned companies in 1948. He was hired by a local bakery, and arrived at work every morning by three o'clock. His wife was intellectual, intense, and nervous, full of regrets for their lost affluence, for having married too young, for having returned to Czechoslovakia after the war. She suffered from serious bouts of depression. Her dreams were thwarted at every turn. The family tried to immigrate to Australia but could not obtain visas. The government initiated trials against former Stalinists, many of whom were Jewish, and anti-Semitism came back into vogue. Free speech was dangerous. Harry locked the doors before he allowed the family to discuss anything political, afraid of spies and retaliation by the government.

Harry hated the Communists, but there was no hope of escape during the long years of the Cold War, when Czechoslovakia was a satellite country of the Soviet Union. Finally, the Prague Spring of 1968 relaxed some of the immigration restrictions. Even then, the family's plans were spoiled. Harry suffered a stroke, and he and his wife were forced to remain behind when their daughters left for Germany. Harry slowly regained the power of speech, first in Czech, then in German. He and his wife followed their daughters to Germany a few years later. Since Harry was unable to work, his wife supported the family. Her depressions worsened. He had two heart attacks after they settled in Germany.

Harry's daughters said that he was a wonderful father and grandfather, thoughtful and caring. He only told them funny stories about the war, never anything serious. He loved nothing better than playing with his children, never lost his optimism or his charm—or his cultured, Austrian-inflected German.

I liked Harry's daughters immediately. In a peculiar way, we felt like sisters, Sala's American girl and Harry's German daughters. We talked about the mysterious influences of our parents' secrets, about growing up Jewish in Communist Czechoslovakia, in Germany, and in the United States, about Harry's avowed atheism, and Sala's renewed faith.

We did not dwell on Harry's wartime experiences, and I did not ask any questions about Harry's role at Dyhernfurth. Like my mother, I wanted to believe the best of Harry. I had already discovered that allegations of mistreatment by Jewish Elders or supervisors *(kapos)* were not uncommon after the war—and were often unfair, though difficult to disprove. Any position of authority assumed by a prisoner in a Nazi camp could have engendered fear and hatred among co-prisoners. These "promotions" were usually involuntary, and refusal to serve could have resulted in immediate execution. "You could treat one hundred people well, but if you did something to the hundred and first, they spat at you and called you a *kapo,*" the widow of a former Jewish Elder told me, still bitter at the insults hurled at her husband after the war.

I was on surer ground with the revelation that Harry was a charming rascal, a temporizing suitor. It was hard not to read his letters ironically: *"You are my first real love, and you will always remain that."* Without knowing why he refused to see my mother in Prague, I had imagined a bundle of extraordinary reasons. Instead, I encountered Harry, the irresistible rogue who was faithless not once, but several times, until peace caught up with him. Or perhaps this time, he found true love.

Harry died in Germany. Sadly, his wife committed suicide not long afterward.

As one survivor said, "After Harry, who could live?"

Harry's inconstancy caused no permanent damage. My mother was soon on her way to Ansbach.

Sidney Kirschner fell in love as quickly as if he too had been a survivor. As I constructed the timeline of my parents' courtship, discounting the time when he studied in England and traveled in Switzerland, I realized that Sidney proposed after they had known each other for barely four weeks. He never wavered, despite the obstacles posed by his mother and the complexities of marrying a war bride.

The vast majority of survivors chose a partner who shared the same experience and language. Sidney and Sala blended their worlds. I knew how hard my mother worked to assume her new identity as an American wife and mother, but I never appreciated the total confidence that my father placed in her, or the way that he finessed the differences between them. My mother's friends became his friends. His family became her family. As they continue to navigate the ups and downs of a marriage that is now more than sixty years old, he still declares that he married "the nicest and sweetest woman in the world."

When I was growing up, our family rarely traveled. Between tight family budgets and my father's long hours at the store, I recall just one long car trip to Detroit, where we visited one of my mother's camp sisters from Schatzlar, and stopped on the way home to see Niagara Falls. We spent our summers with my father's family at nearby Rockaway Beach.

Our first and only family trip to Europe came belatedly in 1994, a few years after my mother gave me the letters. It started with my plan to retrace her steps throughout the war. I had planned to travel alone, but when my brothers, Joey and David, offered to join me, I was delighted by the novel prospect of traveling together. My mother's choice to give me the letters had always seemed perfectly logical to my brothers, since I was the closest thing to a family scholar. Too bad that our parents could not come with us, we said. My mother had broken her silence, but we could not ask her to go back in person, to tread the very streets of her nightmares.

Unexpectedly, she reacted to our plans with exaggerated annoyance: "You're all going to go, and nobody invited me?" We stared at her, caught like children who had been trying to sneak away. Soon, she and my father were as excited as we were.

It was to be the most unusual of family vacations. Old enough to have children and mortgages of our own, my brothers and I would be leaving our spouses and jobs behind, sharing rooms, meals, and experiences with our parents as if we were children again. "Are you going to visit family?" someone asked me the day before I left. "No one is alive," I replied. "We are visiting ghosts."

We planned to travel for two weeks to visit the seven camps, as well as Auschwitz, Sosnowiec, Prague, and Ansbach. My brothers became the storytellers, Joey capturing the journey through his evocative photographs, David through video. They both kept diaries. "This is not a trip, but a mission," Joey declared on the first night. My father added his running commentary on the war, as he had experienced it as an American soldier, which gave us a broader historical context for my mother's travails. At last, someone else was asking the questions.

In the town formerly known as Geppersdorf, we walked around the village square and found the old brick and stone Catholic church where my mother once went sightseeing in disguise. There was no trace of Anna, Wilhelm, or Elfriede, and we could not find their home. Herbert Pachta, the SS officer, was reported to have died in action. Our Polish guide stopped a man on the street and asked him if he could direct us to the former camp barracks. He pointed with his cane to an empty field in the distance. Surprisingly, there was no sign of the modern highway I had expected to find. As we drove along the narrow local streets, my mother stared out the window. She held a tape recorder but kept her voice low: "I walked here, I worked here. Here I got hurt, here I cried, here I dreamed . . . it is all too much to fathom. I am a little bit bewildered."

Suddenly, we crossed an overpass. The scene roared to life. Below us was the four-lane highway built by Jewish forced laborers, the once iconic *Reichsautobahn,* now the prosaic E22. Right below us, cars were racing along at seventy miles per hour.

We found the site of all seven camps. Except for Schatzlar, she had always been remarkably close to home. "I thought I was deep deep deep into Germany," my mother marveled, when we drove into Laurahutte, barely thirty miles from her home.

In Schatzlar, we met the elderly town historian, whose son-in-law happened to live in the former home of the camp director, nearly destroyed on the eve of liberation. He and a friend walked us around the former Buhl & Sohne factory, now locked and vacant, and then into the woods, where we found the location of the French prisoner-of-war camp marked with a plaque. "It is as though they had been waiting for us," David says. The town historian said that we were the first family who had ever returned.

On the day we went to Sosnowiec, my mother stopped speaking. As the first city signs appeared, I had to remind myself to breathe. Would she get out of the car?

Sosnowiec nearly doubled in size after the war and became a regional industrial center, complete with corporate headquarters and universities. The city bustled with activity along the main commercial streets, but it was drab and nondescript, with none of the historic character of Krakow, or the energy of Warsaw.

Nothing remained of Jewish life in Sosnowiec. The casual visitor would never imagine that the city had once been home to twenty-eight thousand Jews. The streets were filled with young people, whose parents and grandparents might remember one or two Jews other than the man most mentioned in local brochures, native son and composer Wladyslaw Szpilman, "The Pianist" in Roman Polanski's film.

The train station where Sala and Ala first met was easy to find. We walked to the square where Bela Kohn's father and brother were hanged. We could not find the location of the school that Sala and Raizel attended. The street where Organization Schmelt headquarters once stood was now a pleasant park with tennis courts. Schmelt himself apparently committed suicide on May 17, 1945, in Schreiberhau, Kreis Hirschberg, Silesia. There was nothing to mark the reign of Moses Merin, who was presumably gassed at Auschwitz after his abduction on June 19, 1943.

My mother directed us to her home.

Kollataja Street was a short walk from the train station. Lined on both sides with three-story apartment houses, the narrow street was shabby and dark. The sliver of dun-colored sky was almost obscured by an intricate web of power lines that crisscrossed the street. The stone façade of nearly every building on the block was broken.

From the moment we entered the cobblestoned courtyard of

Number Six, I fell into a kind of trance. I followed my mother's eyes as she looked up at her apartment, just visible below the roof. We entered the building silently. She pointed to the cracked mosaic of the foyer floor, and nodded in recognition at the sight of the old wooden mailboxes. We climbed the worn steps in single file, my mother caught between Joey and me. On the top step, she saw the door to her apartment and stopped. She cowered on the landing for a few long minutes, shaking with emotion and tears. "Don't break down now," I pleaded with her, as she covered her eyes with both hands. "They'll be afraid to let us in if they see you crying." The door was opened by a bent, elderly man, and two younger men were visible through the open door. They seemed friendly, and after a brief exchange in Polish with our guide, they motioned us in.

I struggled to look past the confusion of rickety furniture and bottles and electric wiring and piles of clothes to see what my mother must be seeing. In this one room, Sala had lived and slept and worked with five other family members until her brother left for Russia and she went to Geppersdorf. Eight adults now stood in the low-ceilinged room, and it was crowded. We had seen a sink in the outside hallway, but no bathroom. The outhouse in the courtyard still served the needs of the entire building. The only natural light came through the small, high window, the one through which young Sala climbed to the peaked roof. She pointed across the courtyard to Laya Dina's apartment. I thought of Salusia, the vibrant child I saw through Raizel's eyes, remembering how she could only write the alphabet in 1940, but could compose her own little letter to Aunt Sala in 1942: *"I prayed to God that I should see you as soon as possible and that you should bring me a doll."*

Everything was spotless then, my mother reminded herself as if we were not there. Her eyes were glassy. The cigarette smoke, the clutter and grime, seemed to cast a bad reflection on her mother's housekeeping. Joey stood next to her, as if his physical presence would help to hold her together.

"This is the worst experience in my life," she said quietly, speaking into a tape recorder after we left. "I'm glad that I am here," she continued. "But now it is a closed chapter. I never want to come back again. All I see is the family I left here, and I have come back to a terrible, terrible, dirty little room that is hardly fit for anyone to live in. And yet here I grew up and loved every single thing in it. I don't see 'things.' I just see my people. I see them in every corner."

Later that afternoon, my brothers and I listened to her recorded voice. She came back, she said, because "Annie had to see it." I cried, ready to end the trip right there. But Joey made me listen to the rest of the recording: "I am coming back as a whole person," she said, and I could hear her voice filling with confidence and satisfaction. "I am so much more now than I was when I left."

I imagined Raizel in that room, writing. She would have hardly noticed her surroundings as she stuck to her task. "I'll be the one to write to you," she had once said, and she kept that promise for seven years, until her boat steamed into the harbor of New York City on November 25, 1947.

The Great Hall of Ellis Island was nearly empty by the time she met her brother-in-law for the first time. It had taken some time for Sidney Kirschner to complete the government bond that guaranteed that Raizel would be financially self-supporting. Raizel greeted Sidney in English but conversed more comfortably with him in Yiddish as they made their way up to his mother's apartment in East Harlem.

They were waiting for her at the door, Sala and her baby son, Joseph. The sisters had not seen each other for six years. There was a little more weight on Raizel's small frame, but she looked nearly the same. Sala, however, was dramatically different from the girl of seventeen last seen by Raizel during Sala's three-day vacation in 1941. Although Sala had sent wedding pictures to her sisters in Sweden, nothing prepared Raizel for the reality of seeing her younger sister in the United States, now twenty-three and a wife, mother, and daughter-in-law. A mother! And already so American!

Sala wanted Raizel's entry into New York to go more smoothly than her own. She had been miserable, nodding and smiling to strangers, shrinking from booming voices that she could not understand, nearly fainting from the heat in her European wool clothes. Even her wedding was a bad memory. She missed her family so. And she sobbed with humiliation and anger when people handed her envelopes with money, as if she was a poor little orphan. Josef and Chana Garncarz had burned paper in the stove to dispel the appearance of needing charity. Now, despite Sidney's assurances that she would have everything in New York, she believed that his family was acting out of pity. Finally, someone explained the custom of giving money to the bride and groom.

Raizel wept most over Sala's baby, too emotional at first to do anything but look at Joey, his bright blue eyes and ready smile. Raizel had once feared that she and Blima were the only survivors. Now here was a nephew, named in memory of their father. It was a miracle, she repeated.

As Raizel held the baby, Sala peppered her with questions about Blima. Raizel had written about Blima's marriage, about her heart condition, but Sala demanded more details. Blima and her husband were still in Sweden. Although Sidney had sponsored their immigration, they were waiting for the necessary paperwork. Sala was worried about her sister's health, convinced that Blima would recover faster in the United States.

The three-room apartment on East 110th Street and Third Avenue belonged to Sidney's mother, who welcomed Raizel and made her as comfortable as possible on the living room couch. Sidney worked across the street at Kirby Clothes, the family store, and attended college at night to complete his degree. For a few weeks, Raizel stayed in Manhattan, but her plan was to move to Brooklyn and begin a new life as a teacher.

Raizel's immigration had been sponsored by the American *Bais Yaakov* organization, an offshoot of the schools started in Poland by Sarah Schenirer. Some of Sala and Raizel's former teachers had survived and were now helping other women from Sosnowiec who wanted to teach in the United States. Raizel was eager to find a congenial Jewish community and resume her religious life, which had been stymied in Sweden, and was nearly impossible in the crowded diversity of East Harlem, where Saturday was just another day to work and play. Raizel found friends and roommates among the other young aspiring teachers, and moved to Brooklyn.

Raizel soon completed her training. An affectionate but exacting first-grade teacher, she deployed her intuitive skills and love of children to great advantage in the classroom. Her life revolved around her school and synagogue. Always good at languages, Raizel acquired English easily, but relied on Yiddish, the language spoken in the living rooms and stores of her Brooklyn neighborhood.

A close friend served as a matchmaker and recommended an interesting young rabbi from Frankfurt, who had just arrived in New York after a wartime saga that took him from Germany to Poland, Lithuania, Japan, and then Shanghai, where he had spent five years with his yeshiva teachers and friends, unable to leave. When Raizel first saw Ezriel Lange, he was dancing, and the ecstasy on his face presaged a talent for happiness. Raizel had been in Brooklyn for nearly two years and she was ready for marriage.

"But his height, he is far from *'lange,'*" she could not help observing to her friend. "And Raizel, what about you?" retorted the woman, looking tiny Raizel up and down.

Raizel and Ezriel were married in Brooklyn one month later. Sidney and Sala paid for the wedding and a down payment for a brownstone. The youngest guest at the wedding was Joey, a well-behaved toddler in a suit from his father's store.

Blima and Jacob finally arrived from Sweden in 1949. The years that followed were a period of almost perfect joy for Sala. She had a home of her own, a brand-new apartment in Queens. The three sisters were reunited, and she had a new baby daughter to share with them. The baby girl was given the Hebrew name of Chana, after their mother. Bending tradition, Sala adopted the baby's English name from Queen Elizabeth II, whose new princess was named Anne.

The birth of the next generation brought a profound joy to the surviving women, who feared that they would be unable to bear children, whispering among themselves of poisoned rations and years without menstruation. My mother had a special bond with Joey, who was born less than two years after she was liberated. I have an old photograph that captures their closeness: my beautiful, vivacious mother lying on a blanket spread out on the grass, five-year-old Joey stretched out next to her, both of them propped up on their elbows, their dark heads angled close to each other, sharing some private joke. You could miss me easily in this picture, a pale small thing off in the corner, my baby neck hardly strong enough to lift my head above my shoulders.

Blima's heart condition did not improve. She was unable to enjoy her new life in the United States for long. Blima had saved Raizel from the slaughter of August 12 and had taken care of her sister in the labor camp, on the death march, through typhus and tuberculosis and recuperation in Sweden. Now, Raizel could not return the favor, nor could any doctor help her sister. Ezriel did not allow Raizel to attend Blima's funeral, although Sala was there. Blima had been a mother to her younger sisters, and it was too hard to lose a mother twice. Sala withdrew into herself. Joey was six years old, and knew that something bad had happened to his mother. Her smile was gone, and she wore the same black dress every day. I was hardly old enough to speak, but I was afraid of this sad and silent mother. When the period of official mourning ended, my mother took me by the hand and we walked to a small room where our apartment building held the garbage. She helped me to push her black dress down the incinerator chute as a sign that she was back with us again.

I called Raizel "Aunt Rose." My father's family used to provoke my mother by telling her that I was just like my aunt: bookish, myopic, buck-toothed, small-boned. Yet I found it hard to be close to Aunt Rose. We shared a love of learning, but what I studied in my public school was foreign to her. I loved reading English novels, playing Chopin on the piano, listening to the Beatles, and going to the movies. My brothers fared slightly better with her, since they received a more extensive religious education. The cousins who might have bridged the gap never arrived: Aunt Rose could not have children. Of Chana and Josef's eleven children, only my mother extended their legacy to the next generation. Aunt Rose and Uncle Ezriel were beloved in their classrooms and in their neighborhood, and adopted a succession of young students who loved them like parents. When these young men had children of their own, they honored Raizel and Ezriel as their grandparents.

Only two years apart, Raizel seemed much older than my mother. Sometimes, she found the differences between our families too hard to accept. Once—only once—my mother wore pants to visit Aunt Rose and Uncle Ezriel. Aunt Rose was angry; she had been embarrassed in front of all her friends. "I thought Rose was going to faint," my mother recalled. Uncle Ezriel stepped in. He was the one who calmed my aunt down, softened her rough edges, her tendency to judge. He was rigid about nothing except the need for tolerance and humility, and said, "She's your sister, take her the way she is."

As I grew older, the distance between us increased. I never doubted Aunt Rose's love for me, but too often, I bristled at what I imagined to be her disapproval of my way of life, so secular, contemporary, and alien. Her religious code seemed uncompromising and judgmental. We saw each other rarely, separated by boundaries more complex than the few miles between my home in Manhattan and hers in Brooklyn. When my son was born, we brought Aunt Rose and Uncle Ezriel to attend the circumcision, which my parents had helped me to arrange in consultation with a proper rabbi. My mother fretted over the food and utensils, making sure everything met the highest kosher standards, and displaying the caterer's name to prove their credentials. Despite all that was going on that day, I remember our chagrin when Aunt Rose went past the lavish spread of food and took an orange on a paper plate. In her world, compromise was generally not a good thing.

We talked mostly by phone, sparring lightly, respectfully. "How are the children?" she would begin. She never lost her surprise that I worked and hired others to share the responsibility of raising my three children. "And tell me, what do you do now?" she would ask.

I could never manage to explain my career choices to her, feeling the words freeze in my mouth every time. Aunt Rose's postwar life in Brooklyn was scarcely different from my grandparents' in Poland. She did not have a television and had never touched a computer, and she rarely left her immediate neighborhood except for doctor visits and summer trips to a bungalow colony in the Catskill Mountains. I didn't try very hard to explain myself to her. The truth was that we perplexed each other, neither one of us willing to leap to the other's side. "All the best," she would say at the end of each call.

I thought it might be easier for me to understand Raizel through her letters. I interviewed her many times, feeling somewhat like a selfish intruder. She never said that. But I did have to work hard to get her attention. I thought she would be excited to see the mountain of letters she wrote so long ago. She was not. Although her memory of events, especially the cataclysm of August 12, 1942, was extremely sharp, it was old news, and her suffering was no more important than anyone else's. She was just a drop of history, one unimportant individual. To complain was to question God. We are like children, too simple to understand divine intentions.

We talked about my mother's decision to take her place at the labor camp. It still seemed logical to Raizel from the distance of decades. *"I was problematic, very problematic,"* Aunt Rose told me. *"I didn't trust myself in anything. I had no confidence. I complained that I was not pretty. I was not this, I was not that . . . Sala was beautiful. Not that being beautiful would protect her. But I felt sure that she would not get lost."*

Raizel hardly remembered Ala and did not recall Ala's first visit to their apartment. So perhaps it was coincidence that soon after meeting Ala in 1941, Raizel searched inward for more insight and tenderness for her sister: *"Sitting here writing, I shed many tears, it's been such a long time already and I remember so, so many things: How we often had arguments, but all of that is forgotten already, how much I want to see you, how much, how much. May God hear me, I can't describe it in words."*

My questions about Kollataja Street and the poverty of their family earned me her sharpest looks of disapproval. She never considered herself poor. How could she, when their childhood was so rich in other ways? "I had one dress for school and another dress for Sabbath. We were not starving—what else did I need?" she demanded. Her material needs after the war always remained simple, in accordance with her limited means, but even there, her standards were high. She cared about her furniture and her apartment, and she had a few pieces of jewelry that she treasured. She was fastidious about her clothes and would not wear anything that was not perfectly tailored. She admired my mother's style and her ability to make anything look chic and fresh, but her own clothes were well worn and always somber. I came under close scrutiny when I visited Aunt Rose in Brooklyn, so I usually wore the same outfit, with slight variations for the season: a loose-fitting skirt, right down to the ankles, and a blouse buttoned at the neck and wrists, nothing sheer, nothing too bright, and skip the lipstick. She noticed everything. If a hem was crooked, or a button was missing, she was sure to notice—and comment.

Aunt Rose sought perfection in everything and everyone around her—and in herself as well. *Rebbetzen* Lange, the rabbi's wife, was so faithful in her religious practice that one of her adopted sons nicknamed her *Rebbe-tzain:* "ten times a Rabbi." Things must be done in a certain way, whether the activity was praying or teaching or cleaning. Any deviation, however minor, was to be avoided. As her hands swelled and her fingers became painfully twisted with arthritis, she would not allow anyone else to scrub her metal pots, although she could hardly hold the steel wool in her clenched fist.

Her yearning for perfection made it nearly impossible for her to make a decision. There was always more information to be gleaned, more thought to be given to any issue, large or small. Yet when Uncle Ezriel died, she acted immediately to arrange for his burial in Jerusalem. He had wanted to spend his last years there, and she had resisted. "I am not going to hold him back now," she declared, although her choice meant that she would never be able to visit his grave. Her own health was too weak.

Brooding on her past and on her future, she wrote to my mother after liberation:

> **I was no angel. I keep thinking about it all the time and it bothers me. What can be done? One thing you should know, Sala, is that the acknowledgment of one's guilt can mitigate it, but only if one starts to reform oneself. Let us forgive each other everything, and together ask forgiveness for the sins we committed against our dear parents.**
>
> **All alone, all alone, in peace and quiet, and filled with our own thoughts, we must be satisfied by self-reproach . . . and rectification through good deeds.**

POSTSCRIPT

I dressed in a long skirt and blouse, as if we were going to see Aunt Rose in Brooklyn, instead of visiting her grave on a bright Jerusalem morning in the year 2005. The September sun was merciless, and I was already sweating. In this ancient cemetery on the Mount of Olives, my parents and I were searching for Raizel and Ezriel. With the help of the driver who brought us to the cemetery, I found the correct entrance and then followed the instructions we received from their adopted son: enter the archway, count four steps up, turn left, and walk down thirteen rows. But we were already lost. Two gravediggers were working a few yards away, stopping frequently to mop their brow, and to watch our progress. The graves were inscribed in Hebrew, and I traced each name with difficulty, not even sure if I was seeking Rose, or Raizel. There were no clear paths, and I walked across the uneven rows, trying to avoid stepping on graves. The wind blew the low-lying thorns and they snapped at my skirt, then at my bare legs, with unexpected fury, and I felt a prickly pain as my skin broke. I wrenched my skirt free with some violence, looking around at once for my mother, who would be sure to notice the little stains of blood.

The cemetery was built into the rise of the mountain. My mother and father were above me, wandering along separate levels, walking slowly to study the name on each grave. The sun was confusing me. I went back to the entrance and started again, counting the steps and rows out loud this time. Suddenly, the driver shouted: he found them.

Raizel and Ezriel lay next to each other. The white gravestones were horizontal, and each was covered with a fine layer of brown dust. My father took off his hat and brushed the sand away. My mother touched her lips to the inscription, bending so low that she seemed to fold into the stone. She sobbed. I heard her repeat Joey's name over and over. The sun was so hot that I feared that she would collapse.

I continued to extract memories from my mother like dark jewels. I persisted even after Joey was diagnosed with a brain tumor, even when the overwhelming reality of my brother's final illness reduced these more ancient sufferings to thin wisps of history. She had allowed me to become the storyteller, but only she could tell her sister that she had lost her son. Joey lived to see his first grandchild, Michelle, but not his second.

Her name is Hannah Rose.

SALA'S LABOR CAMPS

Wartime Location	Dates	Current Location
Geppersdorf, Germany	10/28/40–6/42	Rzedziwojowice, Poland
Gross Sarne, Germany	Summer 1942	Sarny Wielkie, Poland
Brande, Germany	Summer 1942	Prady, Poland
Laurahutte, Poland	Summer 1942	Siemianowice Slaskie, Poland
Gross Paniow, Poland	Fall 1942	Paniowy, Poland
Blechhammer, Poland	Fall 1942	Blachownia Slaskie, Poland
Schatzlar, Czechoslovakia	12/42–5/8/45	Zacler, Czech Republic

SALA'S FAMILY

Sala's Immediate Family
Josef Garncarz and Chana Feldman Garncarz; killed
Their children:

1. Miriam Chaya   married, two children, family of four killed
2. Moshe David   married to Hendel, two children, family of four killed
3. Laya Dina   married David Krzesiwo, two children (Moniek and Salusia), family of four killed
4. Hersh Leib   went to Russia in 1939; presumably killed
5. Avram Yitzhak   died before the war
6. Chaim Pincus   killed in the Polish army
7. Feigele   died before the war
8. Yankov Aaron   died before the war
9. Blima   survived; married Jakob Goldberg; no children; died in 1953
10. Raizel   survived; married Ezriel Lange; no children; died in 2002
11. Sala   survived; married Sidney Kirschner; three children, eight grandchildren, two great-grandchildren

The Family of Sala's Mother, Chana Feldman (partial listing)
Asher Alter Feldman (Sala's uncle) was married to Tobele. Both were killed.
Their children:

1. Yakob Hainoeh   married, children, entire family killed
2. Blima Yockevet   married, children, entire family killed
3. Esther   married, children, entire family killed
4. Miriam   married, children, entire family killed
5. Aaron Yosef   married, children, entire family killed

6. Leah Dina   left Poland for Palestine in 1936; married Yechiel Ophir; one child, three grandchildren, 11 great-grandchildren; died in 2002

7. Moshe Leib   survived; wife and child killed; no children

8. David   killed

9. Shlomo   killed

10. Melech   killed

11. Mendel Wolf   killed

The Family of Sala's Father, Josef Garncarz (partial listing)
Abram Simcha Garncarz (Sala's uncle) was married to Rachel; both died before the war.
Their children:

1. Moshe Chaim   married Matel Sczydlov; left Poland for Trieste in 1924, then Palestine in 1943; six children and 19 great-grandchildren; died in 1979

2. Raizel Lea   married Yaacov Fischel; killed with three of her children; two other children survived and moved to Palestine; five grandchildren and 14 great-grandchildren

SOURCE NOTES

General

From 1940 to 1946, Sala collected 352 letters, documents, and photographs. This narrative was developed by weaving together the evidence of the letters with my interviews with my mother and with many other survivors. Acknowledging the vagaries of memory, I have attempted to corroborate the oral testimonies whenever possible with other sources, including archives and published research.

Historians Michael Berenbaum, Douglas Greenberg, Bella Gutterman, Peter Hayes, and Mark Roseman have graciously reviewed and commented on the work in manuscript. A special note of gratitude to Deborah Dwork for her generosity as a scholar and friend.

The original letters are written mostly in Polish or German. The spelling, grammar, and handwriting reveal the uncertain expression of writers under duress; most of them acquired a working knowledge of German hastily after the occupation. They were mindful of the fact that their letters would be read by a censor. To add to the complexities, they occasionally sprinkled Yiddish, Polish, and Hebrew words, family abbreviations, and codes throughout the correspondence. These challenges were met superbly by a team of translators, especially Regina Gelb (Polish), who also served as consultant and friend during the long gestation of this book, and Renata Stein (German).

I have edited and shortened the texts that are included here—a total of eighty letters out of the complete collection. The original letters are preserved as the Sala Garncarz Kirschner Collection at the Dorot Jewish Division of the New York Public Library, and can be found online through www.nypl.org and www.letters-tosala.org.

Prewar Life in Sosnowiec, Poland, and During the Occupation

The description of life in Sosnowiec is based on my interviews with my mother and with Raizel Garncarz Lange, as well as invaluable discussions with Rose Grunbaum Futter, Sala Grunbaum Singer, Sarah Czarka Helfand, Gucia Gutman Ferleger, and Frymka Rabinowicz Zavontz.

Additional details about life in Sosnowiec before and during the occupation were drawn from *Eyewitness Accounts of the Impoverishment, Enslavement, Murder of 100,000 Jewish Citizens of Zaglembia,* translated by Pawel Brunon Dorman, English language verifier Amalie Mary Robinson. This unpublished collection includes ninety-two depositions taken immediately after the war. The original Polish documents are in the archives of the Jewish Historical Institute in Warsaw. My thanks to Jeffrey Cymbler for bringing this extraordinary resource, and other important bibliographic citations, to my attention.

See also the *Encyclopaedia of Jewish Communities, Poland,* vol. 7, Lublin Kielce districts, translation of *Pinkas Hakehillot Polin: entsiklopedyah shel ha-yishuvim ha-Yehudiyim le-min hivasdam ve-'ad le-ahar Sho'at Milhemet ha-'olam ha- sheniyah.* It was edited by Abraham Wein and co-edited by Bracha Freundlich and Wila Orbach. Authors are Daniel Blatman, Rachel Grossbaum-Pasternak, Abraham Kleban, Shmuel Levin, Wila Orbach, and Abraham Wein. Published in Hebrew by Yad Vashem, Jerusalem 1999. Lance Ackerfeld and Osnat Ramaty have translated parts of this book as *The Book of Sosnowiec and the Surrounding Region in Zaglebie* by Jewish Gen Inc. and the Yizkor Book project at www.jewishgen.org/yizkor/pinkas_poland/po17_00327.html. Also see Jacob Robinson and Philip Friedman, *Guide to Jewish History under Nazi Impact* (New York: Yad Vashem, 1973); Hadasa Priwes's article, "Under the Soldiers' Boots," translated by M. Hampel at www.jewishgen.org/yizkor/Zaglembia/zag534.html; and Jerzy Tomaszewski (ed.), "Jerzy Tomaszewski in Najnowsze dzieje Zydow w Pdsce (Warsaw, 1993).

Nazi Labor Camps and Organization Schmelt

The description of life in the Schmelt camps is based on my interviews with my mother and Raizel, as well as interviews with Hokilo Dattner, Zusi Ginter Bloch, Itka Ginter Bloch, Sala Grunbaum Poznanski, Rose Grunbaum Danziger, Tyla Estreicher Beerie, Sarah Czarka Helfand, and Gucia Gutman Ferleger.

No comprehensive study of the Schmelt camps has yet been published in English. "Sala's World" by Deborah Dwork and Robert Jan van Pelt provides an excellent overview of the Schmelt labor camps; see *Letters to Sala* (New York: New York Public Library, 2006). My own first glimmers of understanding the context of

Sala's story came from Professor Alfred Konieczny's entry on Schmelt in the *Encyclopedia of the Holocaust* (Tel Aviv, 1990); "The 'Schmelt Organisation' in Silesia," in Marcin Wozinksi and Janusz Spyra, eds., *Jews in Silesia* (Krakow: Ksiegarnia Akademicka, 2001), 173–79; and "Jewish Slave Labor Camp in Jeleniow, 1943–1944," Wroclaw, Poland, 1999.

See also Avihu Ronen's "Everyday Life in Schmelt Organizations's Forced Labor Camps," in *Dapim Le'Heker Tekufat Ha'Shoah* (Haifa: Haifa University, 1993), vol. 11, pp. 17–41. Professor Ronen has graciously summarized for me some of his relevant research, most of which is not yet published in English.

The history of the *Reichsautobahn* is discussed by Erhard Schutz and Eckhard Gruber in *Mythos Reichsautobahn: Bau und inszenierung der "Strassen des Fuhrer" 1933–1941* (Berlin: Christopher Links, 1996), quoted by Deborah Dwork and Robert Jan van Pelt in "Sala's World," in *Letters to Sala* by Ann Kirschner (New York: New York Public Library, 2006). Avner Feldman describes Geppersdorf in "In the Ghetto and Camps," Zaglembie Memorial Book, vol. 30, edited by Y. Rappaport, translated by Lance Ackerfeld, edited by Judy Montel (Yawa Bletter); English translation can be found online at http://www.jewishgen.org/yizkor/Zaglembia/zag549.html.

Important discussions of the Nazi use of Jewish labor are found in Peter Hayes's *Industry and Ideology: I. G. Farben in the Nazi Era* (Cambridge, England: Cambridge University Press, 2000); Raul Hilberg, *The Destruction of the European Jews* (New York: Quadrangle Books, 1971); Konrad Kwiet, "Forced Labor of German Jews in Nazi Germany," *Leo Baeck Institute Yearbook XXXVI* (1991). See also Christopher R. Browning, *Nazi Policy, Jewish Workers, German Killers* (New York: Cambridge University Press, 2000); Browning, *Nazi Germany's Initial Attempt to Exploit Jewish Labor in the General Government: The Early Work Camps 1940–41* (Berlin: Edition Entrich, 1994); and Browning, *The Origins of the Final Solution: The Evolution of Nazi Jewish Policy, September 1939–March 1942* (Jerusalem: Yad Vashem, 2004).

Other sources include Helmut Krausnich et al., *Anatomy of the SS State* (New York: Walker & Co., 1968); and Benjamin Ferencz, *Less Than Slaves: Jewish Forced Labor and the Quest for Compensation* (1979; rept. Bloomington: Indiana University Press, 2002).

A list of the Schmelt camps, with their dates of operation and the German businesses that utilized them, is found within the "Catalogue of Camps and Prisons in Germany and German-Occupied Territories, September 1, 1939–May 8, 1945," prepared by International Tracing Service Records Branch, Documents Intelligence Section, Arolson, July 1949, reprinted as *Das Nationalsozialistische lagersystem* (CCP) (Frankfurt, 1990).

A helpful reference to the markings on the letters and postcards is Sam Simon's *Handbook of the Mail in the Concentration-Camps, 1933–1945: A Postal History* (New York: Port Printed Products Corp., 1973).

Source Notes

Moses Merin and the Jewish Council

Moses Merin (also known as Moshe, Moniek, or Marek Meryn) appears as a character in Konrad Charmatz, *Nightmares: Memoirs of the Years of Horror Under Nazi Rule in Europe, 1939–1945,* translated by Miriam Dashkin Beckerman (Syracuse: Syracuse University Press); and as Moniek Matroz in Ka-Tzetnik 135633's *Sunrise Over Hell,* (London: Corgi, 1978). (See an excerpted version, "The Congregation-Council," at http://www.jewishgen.org/yizkor/Zaglembia/zag003E.html#page5.)

Merin's trusted secretary, Fani Czarna, is sometimes called Fania or Fanny Czarna or Felicia Schwartz, or "the black one."

Merin and his administration are discussed extensively in Isaiah Trunk's definitive *Judenrat: The Jewish Councils in Eastern Europe under Nazi Occupation* (Lincoln: University of Nebraska Press, 1972). See also Philip Friedman's "The Messianic Complex of a Nazi Collaborator in a Ghetto: Moses Merin of Sosnowiec," in *Roads to Extinction: Essays on the Holocaust* (New York and Philadelphia: Jewish Publication Society, 1980); and his "Two 'Saviors' Who Failed: Moses Merin of Sosnowiec and Jacob Gens of Vilna," in *Commentary,* 1958. For additional details, see "The Judenrat in Zaglembie (Under the Leadership of Moshe Meryn)" in the Zaglembie Yizkor Book, the Yizkor Book Project.

There is a provocative analysis of Merin and his policies in Avihu Ronen's "Wer zum Leben, wer zum Tod," edited by D. Kiesel et al., in *Institutionen, Politik und Identitat der Judische Selbstwerwaltung im Getto Von Zaglembie (Institutions, Politics, and Identity of the Jewish "Self-Government" in the Ghetto: A Case Study of Zaglembie)* (Frankfurt and New York: Campus Verlag, 1992), excerpted at http://www.avihuronen.com/english/articles/eng-judenrat.html.

For the story of the South American passports, see Ruth Zariz, "Attempts at Rescue and Revolt: Attitudes of Members of the Dror Youth Movement in Bedzin to Foreign Passports as Means of Rescue," *Yad Vashem Studies,* vol. 20, Jerusalem Yad Vashem Martyrs' and Heroes' Remembrance Authority, 1976. Remarkably, Jeffrey Cymbler has acquired an original envelope handwritten by Ala Gertner, with her sister's name and return address, written to Herr Szwarcbaum in Lausanne, Switzerland. It was mailed in February 1943 but not received in Lausanne until November, at which point the Bedzin and Sosnowiec ghettos had already been liquidated and Ala was in Auschwitz.

August 12, 1942

These events were described to me by Raizel and by Rose Grunbaum Danziger, both of whom were present at the Sosnowiec assembly point at the stadium. There are additional descriptions of the deportation in *Eyewitness Accounts of the Impoverishment, Enslavement, Murder of 100,000 Jewish Citizens of Zaglembia* (see

270

above). The comparison of the stadium field to an anthill is found in the testimony of Gena Lewkowicz, p. 79.

Depending on the source, the number of Jews captured in the deportation ranges from 30,000 to 70,000. The Sosnowiec stadium was probably one of several assembly points, with the others taking place at nearby Bedzin and Dabrowa Górnicza. Reports on the number of Jews sent to Auschwitz that week range from 4,000 to 30,000.

Avihu Ronen describes the massive deportation in "The Day of Disillusion: the Great Deportation from Zaglembie on 12.8.1942," in *Massuah*, no. 17 (April 1989), pp. 102–47; an abstract is available at http://www.avihuronen.com/english/abstracts/abs-punkt.html. For other accounts see Natan Eliasz Szternfinkiel et al., "The Annihilation of Sosnowiec Jews," publication of the Main Jewish Historical Commission in Poland, no. 25, Katowice, 1946.

Ala Gertner and the Auschwitz Uprising

These events were described to me by Israel Gutman, Mala Weinstein, and Rose Meth. I am deeply grateful to them, to Lidia Vago for her advice and encouragement, and to Anna Heilman, sister of Estusia Wacjblum, for her willingness to read and comment on my account. The monument to the four heroines of the uprising is in the garden of Yad Vashem in Jerusalem.

The most comprehensive reference on the Auschwitz uprising is Lore Shelley's indispensable *The Union Kommando in Auschwitz: The Auschwitz Munition Factory Through the Eyes of Its Former Slave Laborers* (Lanham, Md.: University Press of America, 1996). Considerable inconsistencies remain over such details as the number of people involved, their roles, and the timeline of the smuggling effort. While most published accounts use January 6, 1945, as the date of the Auschwitz hanging, I have chosen to follow the date that Anna Heilman cites in *Never Far Away*. There are also differences of opinion as to the relationship between the Sonderkommando plot and other Jewish resistance plans. Erich Kulka, an historian and Auschwitz survivor, threw up his hands at the complexities—factual and psychological—of creating the definitive account of the uprising. His conclusion was that the uprising was far less important to the Nazis than the underlying concern about sabotage. In his view, the four women were scapegoats who bore the brunt of Nazi fury over sabotage that was being practiced on a much larger scale.

For a sampling of the relevant scholarly research, see also Reuben Ainsztein, *Jewish Resistance in Nazi-Occupied Eastern Europe* (New York: Barnes & Noble, 1974); Nathan Cohen, "Diaries of the Sonderkommandos in Auschwitz: Coping with Fate and Reality," *Yad Vashem Studies*, vol. 20, 1990; Jozef Garlinski, *Fighting Auschwitz: The Resistance Movement in the Concentration Camp* (London: Julian Friedmann, 1975); Tzipora Hager Halivni, *Preparing for Revolt in*

Auschwitz-Birkenau: Heroes and Martyrs (Jerusalem: World Congress of Jewish Studies, 1989); and Halivni, "The Birkenau Revolt; Poles Prevent a Timely Insurrection," *Jewish Social Studies,* vol. 41, no. 2, 1979; Anna Heilman, *Never Far Away* (Calgary, Alta.: University of Calgary Press, 2001); Primo Levi, *Survival in Auschwitz* (New York: 1961); Ber Mark, *The Scrolls of Auschwitz* (Tel Aviv: Am Oved, 1985); Filip Müller, *Eyewitness Auschwitz* (New York: Stein & Day, 1979); Micheline Ratzerdorfer, "They Did Resist: Jewish Women's Resistance in Auschwitz," *Amit Women,* vol. 61, no. 4, 1989; Yuri Suhl, *They Fought Back: The Story of the Jewish Resistance in Nazi Europe* (New York: Crown, 1967); Tzvetan Todorov, *Facing the Extreme: Moral Life in the Concentration Camps,* translated by Arthur Denner and Abigail Polk (New York: Henry Holt, 1996).

Schatzlar, Neusalz, and Dyhernfurth

Details about the factories and daily life in the camps were the result of interviews with Raizel, Itka Ginter Bloch, Sarah Czarka Helfand, and Frymka Rabinowicz Zavontz (Neusalz); Sala Grunbaum Poznanski, Dasha Rittenberg, Tyla Estreicher Beerie, and Gucia Gutman Ferleger (Schatzlar). The 1993–1994 interviews about Dyhernfurth were conducted in Israel by Ruth Winter.

The route of the Neusalz death march is traced in Martin Gilbert's *Atlas of the Holocaust* (New York: William Morrow, 1993). See also the in-depth account in Bernard Robinson and Amalie Mary Reichmann-Robinson, "Some Consequences of the Schmelt Organization as Experienced by Affected Individuals," available at http://www.shtetlinks.jewishgen.org/Zaglembie/Zag001.html; and Fela Kurzfeld's description in *Testimonials of Survival,* ninety-six personal interviews from members of Kibbutz Lohamei Hagetot, vol. 4, pp. 1693–1708.

The description of the Dyhernfurth death march is based on a case that was filed by the U.S. District Court for the Eastern District of Missouri in the U.S. Court of Appeals for the Eighth Circuit against Adam Friedrich, an SS guard from Dyhernfurth. See the summary at http://caselaw.findlaw.com/data2/circs/8th/041728P.pdf. The case also cites the Nuremberg Trial, 6 FRD, 69, 1008 (1946) quoting the June 21, 1945, report of the War Crimes Branch of the Judge Advocate's Section of the 3rd U.S. Army.

Additional Sources and Inspirations

Appelfeld, Aharon. *Beyond Despair.* New York: Fromm International, 1994.
Bauer, Yehuda. *Rethinking the Holocaust.* New Haven, Conn.: Yale University Press, 2001.
Berenbaum, Michael, ed. *A Mosaic of Victims: Non-Jews Persecuted and Murdered by the Nazis.* New York: New York University Press, 1990.

Berger, Joseph. *Displaced Persons: Growing Up American After the Holocaust.* New York: Scribner, 2001.

Borowski, Tadeusz. *This Way for the Gas, Ladies and Gentlemen.* New York: Penguin, 1976.

Bourguignon, Erika. "Memory in an Amnesic World: Holocaust, Exile, and the Return of the Suppressed." *Anthropological Quarterly,* vol. 78, no. 1, 2005, pp. 63–88.

Bromwich, David. "The Uses of Biography." *Yale Review,* vol. 73, no. 2, 1984.

Czernichow, Adam. *The Warsaw Diary.* New York: Stein & Day, 1979.

Dawidowicz, Lucy S. *The War Against the Jews 1933–1945.* New York: Holt, Rinehart & Winston, 1975.

Des Pres, Terrence. *The Survivor: An Anatomy of Life in the Death Camps.* New York: Oxford University Press, 1976.

Dobroszycki, Lucjan, ed. *The Chronicle of the Lodz Ghetto, 1941–1944.* New Haven, Conn.: Yale University Press, 1984.

Dobroszycki, Lucjan, and Barbara Kirshenblatt-Gimblett. *Image Before My Eyes: A Photographic History of Jewish Life in Poland, 1864–1939.* New York: Schocken, 1977.

Donat, Alexander. *The Holocaust Kingdom: A Memoir.* New York: Holt, Rinehart & Winston, 1965.

Dwork, Deborah, and Robert Jan van Pelt. *Auschwitz: 1270 to the Present.* New York: W. W. Norton, 1996.

———.*Holocaust: A History.* New York: W. W. Norton, 2002.

Edelheit, Hershel, and Abraham J. Edelheit. *A World in Turmoil: An Integrated Chronology of the Holocaust and World War II.* New York: Greenwood Press, 1991.

Eliach, Yaffa. *Hasidic Tales of the Holocaust.* New York: Random House, 1982.

Eliot, George. *Middlemarch.* rpt Boston: Houghton Mifflin, 1956.

Epstein, Helen. *Children of the Holocaust.* New York: Penguin, 1988.

Farmer, Paul. "The Banality of Agency: Bridging Personal Narrative and Political Economy." *Anthropological Quarterly,* vol. 78, no. 1, 2005, pp. 125–35.

Feig, Konnilyn G. *Hitler's Death Camps: The Sanity of Madness.* New York: Holmes & Meier, 1979.

Gage, Nicholas. *Eleni.* New York: Ballantine, 1996.

Geehr, Richard S., ed. *Letters from the Doomed: Concentration Camp Correspondence 1940–1945.* Lanham, Md.: University Press of America, 1992.

Gilbert, Martin. *The Holocaust: A Record of the Destruction of Jewish Life in Europe.* New York: Hill & Wang, 1979.

Gutman, Israel. *Resistance: The Warsaw Ghetto Uprising.* Boston and New York: Mariner Books, 1994.

Hartman, Geoffrey. *The Longest Shadow: In the Aftermath of the Holocaust.* New York: Palgrave Macmillan, 2002.

————, ed. *Holocaust Remembrance: The Shapes of Memory.* Oxford: Blackwell, 1994.

Heller, Celia. *On the Edge of Destruction: Jews of Poland Between the Two World Wars.* New York: Columbia University Press, 1977.

Helmreich, William B. *Against All Odds: Holocaust Survivors and the Successful Lives They Made in America.* New York: Simon & Schuster, 1992.

Hoffman, Eva. *Lost in Translation: A Life in a New Language.* New York: Dutton, 1989.

Krakowski, Shmuel, and Israel Gutman, eds., *Encyclopaedia of the Holocaust.* New York: Macmillan, 1990.

Krausnick, Helmut, et al. *Anatomy of the SS State.* New York: Walker & Co., 1968.

Kugelmass, Jack, and Jonathan Boyarin, eds. *From a Ruined Garden: The Memorial Books of Polish Jewry.* New York: Schocken, 1983.

Langer, Lawrence L. *Holocaust Testimonies: The Ruins of Memory.* New Haven, Conn.: Yale University Press, 1991.

————. *Versions of Survival: The Holocaust and the Human Spirit.* Albany: SUNY Press, 1982.

Lifton, Robert. *Death in Life: Survivors of Hiroshima.* New York: Random House, 1967.

Lipstadt, Deborah. *Denying the Holocaust.* New York: Free Press, 1993.

Myerhoff, Barbara. *Number Our Days.* New York: Simon & Schuster, 1978.

————. *Remembered Lives: The Work of Ritual, Storytelling, and Growing Older.* Ann Arbor: University of Michigan Press, 1992.

Novak, Philip. *The World's Wisdom.* San Francisco: HarperCollins, 1995.

Richmond, Theo. *Konin.* New York: Random House, 1995.

Rittner, Carol, and John K. Roth, eds. *Different Voices: Women and the Holocaust.* New York: Paragon House, 1993.

Rosenfeld, Alvin H. *A Double Dying: Reflections on Holocaust Literature.* Bloomington: Indiana University Press, 1980.

Roseman, Mark. *A Past in Hiding.* New York: Picador, 2000.

————. *The Wannsee Conference and the Final Solution.* New York: Picador, 2003.

Rousset, David. *The Other Kingdom.* Translated by Ramon Guthrie. New York: Reynal & Hitchcock, 1947.

Rylko-Bauer, Barbara. "Lessons about Humanity and Survival from My Mother and from the Holocaust." *Anthropological Quarterly,* vol. 78, no. 1, 2005, pp. 11–41.

Spiegelman, Art. *Maus I: My Father Bleeds History.* New York: Pantheon, 1986.

————. *Maus II: And Here My Troubles Began.* New York: Pantheon, 1991.

Stanislawski, Michael. *Autobiographical Jews: Essays in Jewish Self-Fashioning.* Seattle: University of Washington Press, 2004.

Vishniac, Roman. *A Vanished World.* New York: Farrar, Straus & Giroux, 1983.

Weiss, Aharon, ed. *The Holocaust Martyrs' and Heroes' Remembrance, Yad Vashem Studies,* Jerusalem: Yad Vashem, 1990.

Wiesel, Elie. *Night.* New York: Bantam, 1989.

Yahil, Leni. *The Holocaust: The Fate of European Jewry.* New York: Oxford University Press, 1990.

Yerushalmi, Yosef Hayim. *Zakhor: Jewish History and Jewish Memory.* Seattle: University of Washington Press, 1982.

Young, James E. *Writing and Rewriting the Holocaust.* Bloomington: Indiana University Press, 1990.

———. *The Texture of Memory: Holocaust Memorials and Meaning.* New Haven, Conn.: Yale University Press, 1993.

Zariz, Ruth. *A Surplus of Memory: Chronicle of the Warsaw Ghetto Uprising.* Berkeley: University of California Press, 1993.

ACKNOWLEDGMENTS

My mother's gift unfolded over the course of fifteen years. Friends became advisers, and advisers became friends.

I am grateful to the survivors who entrusted their memories to me. These men and women are giants among us. I have done my best to portray them with accuracy, affection, and respect. May they live to 120 years.

My father, Sidney Kirschner, has not exactly received equal time here, yet that inequity has never compromised his pride in my work or his generous good humor. My world was constructed around his love of my mother and our family, his boundless curiosity, and his connoisseur's appreciation for beauty in nature, music, and art.

I am lucky in love. Harold Weinberg is a man of many talents. My beloved husband cheerfully steps into whatever may be the latest role that has emerged in the course of our long and happy marriage. From the sublime responsibilities of a soul mate and father to more mundane duties of copyeditor, accountant, and alarm clock, he fulfills them all with the brilliance, dedication, and compassion that also distinguish him as a neurologist. He has my heart and my soul, forever.

Elisabeth, Caroline, and Peter are the critics who strike the deepest fear in their mother's heart. Their idealism inspires me. They ask hard questions about justice and motivation and responsibility, and I hope I will not disappoint them. They already know that their *bubbe* sets the bar for integrity and courage.

I am lucky in friendship. When Lorraine Shanley and I met as graduate students, I could not have known how profoundly I would benefit from decades of conversations and thousands of Scrabble games. Her knowledge of books and publishing, and her excellent judgment, guided me through every step of writing this book. As we peer into the rearview mirror of our intersecting lives, and look ahead to the future, she will always be my best friend.

As a writer, I have traveled in the company of a wonderful confederation of confidantes and experts. Jane Stine's insights are scattered throughout these pages. She helped me to find my backbone as a writer and gave me a title. Her supernatural powers of articulation are exceeded only by her *joie de vivre*. Flip Brophy is my agent, adviser, and friend. Who knew that one role could flow so easily into another? Bruce Nichols brought his editorial wisdom and sharp pencil to the manuscript; I am grateful to him and to Martha Levin, publisher of the Free Press, for their confidence in this project and their commitment to quality in the making of this book.

The Sala Garncarz Kirschner Collection now lives at the Dorot Jewish Division of the New York Public Library. I have learned much from Paul LeClerc and David Ferreiro, guardians of history and my esteemed colleagues.

Sala's Gift stands at the intersection of public and private history. Readers of this book will determine sustainability beyond our family. But that does not take the next generation off the hook. I hope these letters will also remain beloved as my mother's legacy to my brothers, Joey and David, and to her grandchildren, Jennie, Jeremy, Elisabeth, Caroline, Peter, Gabby, Rachel, and Yael.

If we are blessed with a peaceful world, Sala's great-grandchildren may even be reading these letters in the twenty-second century: Michelle, Hannah Rose, and Joseph.

Tell the story, then, in your own way.

INDEX

Index

Index

ABOUT THE AUTHOR

Ann Kirschner began her career as a lecturer in Victorian literature at Princeton University, where she earned a Ph.D. in English. Her subsequent career as an entrepreneur in media and technology included the creation of Internet businesses for the National Football League and Columbia University. A frequent contributor to conferences and publications on higher education and interactive media, Ann Kirschner is University Dean for the Honors College of The City University of New York. She lives in New York with her husband, Harold Weinberg, and her children, Elisabeth, Caroline, and Peter.